EUROPEAN FOREIGN AND SECURITY POLICY:
STATES, POWER, INSTITUTIONS, AND AMERICAN HEGEMONY

The European Union's (EU) Common Foreign and Security Policy (CFSP) stipulates that all member states must unanimously ratify policy proposals through their representatives on the EU Council. Intergovernmentalism, or the need for equal agreement from all member nations, is used by many political scientists and policy analysts to study how the EU achieves its CFSP. However, in *European Foreign and Security Policy*, Catherine Gegout modifies this theory, arguing instead for analyses based on what she terms 'constrained intergovernmentalism.'

Gegout's theory of constrained intergovernmentalism allows for member states, in particular France, Germany, and the United Kingdom, to bargain with one another and to make rational decisions but also takes into account the constraints imposed by the United States, the European Commission, and the precedents set by past decisions. Three in-depth case studies of CFSP decision-making support her argument, as she examines the EU position on China's human rights record, EU sanctions against Serbia, and EU relations with NATO.

(European Union Studies)

CATHERINE GEGOUT is an assistant professor in the School of Politics and International Relations at the University of Nottingham.

European Union Studies

European Union Studies features the latest research on topics in European integration in the widest sense, including Europe's role as a regional and international actor. This interdisciplinary series publishes the research of Canadian and international scholars and aims at attracting scholars working in various disciplines such as economics, history, law, political science, and sociology. The series is made possible in part by a generous grant from the European Commission.

The first series of its kind in Canada, and one of only a few in North America, *European Union Studies* is unique in looking at the EU 'from the outside,' making sense not only of European integration but also of the role of the European Union as an international actor.

GENERAL EDITORS:

Jeffrey Kopstein
Professor of Political Science
Director, Centre for European, Russian, and Eurasian Studies
University of Toronto

Amy Verdun
Professor of Political Science
Director, Jean Monnet Centre of Excellence
University of Victoria

CATHERINE GEGOUT

European Foreign and Security Policy

States, Power, Institutions, and American Hegemony

UNIVERSITY OF TORONTO PRESS
Toronto Buffalo London

ISBN 978-1-4426-4094-8 (cloth)
ISBN 978-1-4426-1034-7 (paper)

Printed on acid-free, 100% post-consumer recycled paper with vegetable-based inks.

Library and Archives Canada Cataloguing in Publication

Gegout, Catherine, 1973–
European foreign and security policy : states, power, institutions and American hegemony / Catherine Gegout.

(European Union studies)
Includes bibliographical references and index.
ISBN 978-1-4426-4094-8 (bound). – ISBN 978-1-4426-1034-7 (pbk.)

1. European Union countries – Foreign relations.   2. National security – European Union countries.   3. European Union countries – Military policy.
I. Title.   II. Series: European Union studies (Toronto, Ont.)

KJE5105.G43 2010   342.24′0412   C2010-900377-2

University of Toronto Press acknowledges the financial assistance to its publishing program of the Canada Council for the Arts and the Ontario Arts Council.

 Canada Council   Conseil des Arts    ONTARIO ARTS COUNCIL
for the Arts   du Canada   CONSEIL DES ARTS DE L'ONTARIO

University of Toronto Press acknowledges the financial support for its publishing activities of the Government of Canada through the Book Publishing Industry Development Program (BPIDP).

For my parents, and Nathalie

La politique étrangère ne sera plus la juxtaposition d'antagonismes qui s'af-frontent, mais la conciliation amiable et préventive de divergences qui existent, qui s'avouent et se discutent sans s'exacerber.

[Foreign policy will no longer be the juxtaposition of conflicting an-tagonisms, but rather the friendly, preventive reconciliation of real differences, recognized as such, and discussed in ways that don't make them worse.]

Robert Schuman, Pour l'Europe

Contents

PART THREE: THE UNEXPECTED ACTORS IN THE CFSP SYSTEM

List of Tables and Figures

Tables

Figures

Acknowledgments

The preparation of this book was financed by the French Foreign Affairs Ministry (research conducted at the European University Institute, Florence); the Fulbright program at the University of Pittsburgh; the European Union (with a post-doctoral Marie Curie Fellowship at the London School of Economics and Political Science); and the University of Nottingham Research Leave Fund (research at the University of Cambridge).

The text is the result of numerous challenging, exciting, and fruitful discussions with academics, colleagues, practitioners, students, friends, and family. I am grateful to Christopher Hill, who has been a constant support and inspiration in my efforts to understand the ins and outs of European foreign policy, and to Mark Pollack for his detailed comments on the theoretical part of the book, as well as his encouragement throughout the project. Extensive and constructive comments were made by Thomas Risse, and very useful criticisms by Jan Zielonka and William Wallace. Karen Smith was an efficient, helpful, and attentive mentor during my time at LSE. I am grateful for the incisive comments on my work from Andreas Bieler, Frédéric Charillon, Adam Morton, Matthew Rendall, and Philippe Schmitter.

I would also like to thank all the following scholars who took time to share their valuable expertise with me: Richard Aldrich, David Allen, Ester Barbé, Federica Bicchi, Fraser Cameron, Sir Brian Crowe, Maria Green Cowles, Chad Damro, Renaud Dorandeu, Geoffrey Edwards, Catherine Goetze, Ayla Gol, Eva Gross, Adrienne Héritier, Jean-Paul Jacqué, the late Dominique Jacquin-Berdal, Knud Erik Jorgensen, Michael Koehler, Margot Light, Lauren McLaren, Jan Meyer-Sahling, Christoph O. Meyer, Ken Morita, Costanza Musu, Simon Nuttall, Oke Odudu, Jorge de Oliveira e Sousa, Franck Petiteville,

Claire Piana, Vanessa Pupavac, Wyn Rees, Eric Remacle, Andrea Ribeiro-Hoffmann, Volker Rittberger, Alberta Sbragia, Frank Schimmelfennig, Michael Smith, Michael E. Smith, Stephan Stetter, Lori Thorlakson, Ben Tonra, Simon Tormey, Jordi Vaquer Fanes, Pieter Van Houten, Brian White, Richard Whitman, Stefan Wolff, Reuben Wong, and Harald Wydra.

The book has benefited from extensive and fascinating insights from approximately a hundred interviewees, who kindly shared with me their knowledge, hopes, and frustrations on the functioning and future direction of European foreign policy. I am especially indebted to those connected with the Council of the European Union, who met with me on several occasions, and who gave me a clear picture of the complex backstage workings of the EU's CFSP negotiation process. In particular, my thanks go to Guy Milton, William Shapcott, Andreas Strub, Wolfgang Ploch, and Stephan Mueller. I would also like to thank all my undergraduate and postgraduate students at the Universities of Pittsburgh and Nottingham, who were very critical of EU foreign policy during the Iraq war and the crises in the Democratic Republic of the Congo, Darfur, and Zimbabwe, and who helped make this book useful for their own research on the way EU foreign policy *really* works.

For their advice, constructive criticism, and enthusiasm, I am grateful to Amy Verdun and Jeffrey Kopstein, the University of Toronto Press's editors of the new series European Union Studies; Daniel Quinlan, acquisitions editor; Wayne Herrington, associate managing editor; and the anonymous reviewers of the original typescript.

Finally, I would like to thank my close friends and family for their patience and unfailing support. Devon Curtis's friendship is significant and valuable beyond words. Anaïs Feuga, Giovanni del Brenna, Simona Santoro, Ivana and Antonio Santoro, Viviane André, Raquel Cortes, Hakim Boulhares, Daniela Passolt, Margret and Annette Bauer, Karen Crequer, Catherine Turner, Francesco Colomba, Elisabetta Cervone, Gert Westermann, Teresa Yun-Chung Li and the Cambridge group, Elinor Payne, Houshang Ardavan, and Aldo Faisal have all been there to support this project. Special thanks go to Jennifer Birkett, my aunt, who scrupulously commented on late drafts of the manuscript. My parents are the foundation of all my work. This book would not exist without the extraordinary and constant help and prodding of my mother, Gillian, my father, Michel, and my sister Nathalie, and the encouragement of my grandmother, Elsie Birkett.

Abbreviations

ACP	Africa Caribbean Pacific
AMIS	African Mission in Sudan/Darfur
CESDP	Common European Security and Defence Policy
CFSP	Common Foreign and Security Policy
CHR	Commission on Human Rights (UN)
CIVCOM	Committee for Civilian Aspects of Crisis Management
Coreper	*Comité des Représentants Permanents*
COREU	*Correspondance Européenne*
CPCC	Civilian Planning and Conduct Capability
CSCE	Conference on Security and Cooperation in Europe
DG E	Directorate General E (Council of the EU)
DG Relex	Directorate-General for External Relations (European Commission)
DRC	Democratic Republic of the Congo
EC	European Community
ECHO	European Commission's Humanitarian Aid Office
ECMM	European Community Monitoring Mission
ECOWAS	Economic Community of West African States
ECSC	European Coal and Steel Community
EDC	European Defence Community
EEC	European Economic Community
EPC	European Political Cooperation

ESDI	European Security and Defence Identity
ESDP	European Security and Defence Policy
EU	European Union
EUBAM Rafah	EU Border Assistance Mission in Rafah
EUFOR RD Congo	European Force in the Democratic Republic of the Congo
EUJUST LEX	EU rule of law mission in Iraq
EUJUST THEMIS	EU rule of law mission in Georgia
EULEX Kosovo	EU rule of law mission in Kosovo
EUMC	European Union Military Committee
EUMCWG	European Union Military Committee Working Group
EU NAVFOR Somalia	EU maritime operation in Somalia
EUPAT	EU police mission in Macedonia
EUPM	EU police mission in Bosnia and Herzegovina
EUPOL Afghanistan	EU police mission in Afghanistan
EUPOL COPPS	EU police mission in the Palestinian territories
EUPOL Kinshasa	EU police mission in Kinshasa
EUSEC RD Congo	EU security mission in the Democratic Republic of the Congo
FAC	Foreign Affairs Council
FRY	Federal Republic of Yugoslavia
FYROM	Former Yugoslav Republic of Macedonia
GAC or GAERC	General Affairs and External Relations Council
JAT	Former Yugoslav Airlines
KFOR	Kosovo Force (NATO)
LCD	Lowest Common Denominator
NAC	North Atlantic Council
NATO	North Atlantic Treaty Organization
NGO	Non-Governmental Organization
OHR	Office of the High Representative in Bosnia and Herzegovina
OSCE	Organization for Security and Co-operation in Europe
PMG	Politico-Military working group
Poco	Political Committee
PSC	Political and Security Committee
QMV	Qualified Majority Voting

RELEX Group	Group of External Relations Counsellors
RRF	Rapid Reaction Force (EU)
SACEUR	Supreme Allied Commander Europe (NATO)
SFOR	Stabilization Force in Bosnia and Herzegovina (NATO)
SitCen	Joint Situation Centre (EU)
TACIS	Technical Aid to the Commonwealth of Independent States
TEU	Treaty on European Union
TFEU	Treaty on the Functioning of the European Union
UAV	Unmanned Aerial Vehicle
UK	United Kingdom
UN	United Nations
UNAMID	United Nations / African Union Mission in Darfur
UNMIK	United Nations Interim Administration Mission in Kosovo
US	United States
WEU	Western European Union

EUROPEAN FOREIGN AND SECURITY POLICY:
STATES, POWER, INSTITUTIONS, AND AMERICAN HEGEMONY

Introduction:
Deciding Foreign and Security Policy in the European Union: A Brief Account of CFSP

The framework of the European Union (EU) that was set up in 1992 with the signing of the Maastricht Treaty consists of three pillars: the first pillar relates to the European Community (EC), the second to Common Foreign and Security Policy (CFSP), and the third to Police and Judicial Cooperation in Criminal Matters. Engagement with security and military matters takes place within the CFSP pillar.[1]

State diplomats, military personnel, foreign affairs ministers, defence ministers, and the High Representative meet on a regular basis in the Council of the EU in order to discuss foreign policy and associated highly sensitive political issues, such as defence matters. The EU can deploy troops within and outside European territory.

However, in terms of actual decision-making, there does not seem to be any move towards European integration. The officials of member states guard their powers jealously, and limit those of officials in EU institutions to prevent them from influencing policy decisions in the CFSP system. CFSP, like its predecessor European Political Cooperation (EPC), seems to work in a strictly intergovernmental framework, where unanimity is the rule.

No decisions, or Lowest Common Denominator (LCD) decisions, are the most likely outcomes of policy discussions, and this limits the impact of CFSP on the world. European leaders, for instance, did not reach an agreement on the policy to adopt towards the war on Iraq in 2003, or towards the conflict in the Democratic Republic of the Congo (DRC), where approximately three million people were killed, or towards Darfur between 2003 and 2007. In Darfur, 200,000 victims have been counted since 2003. Declarations on human rights, or policies towards North Korea or South Caucasus, have had very little impact.

Is it really not possible for EU policy-makers to reach anything more than a LCD decision? If not, why not? And if or when better than LCD decisions are reached, under what conditions does this happen? In other words, what prevents EU states from agreeing on common policy in foreign and security matters, and what enables the EU to adopt CFSP decisions?

This book shows how the CFSP system works both in theory, and, especially, in practice. It shows how policy decisions are made by states, and in particular by the big EU states, and how these decisions are often influenced by two unexpected players, the European Commission and an outsider, the United States. The Commission can play a role in CFSP, by using its knowledge of EU institutional rules and by acting as a policy entrepreneur. The United States acts as an observer, a stimulus, and an authority, and holds a de facto power of veto. A further important element, the weight of past decisions (the *acquis* of the European Union), can also have an impact on the CFSP decision-making process, because of the legal constraint it exercises on new CFSP outcomes.

The rules of decision-making are of paramount importance. Whether nine or twenty-seven or more EU state officials are sitting around the negotiation table, the rules determine the effectiveness of policy-making. It is obviously harder for states to agree if unanimity, rather than qualified majority voting, is the rule. It is also harder for a group of states to make a decision, rather than just one person, whose job is to represent all of them. In the history of European foreign policy, EU leaders have been constantly concerned with making the rules: that is, defining the actors and institutions responsible for making policies. They oscillated between creating a supranational European political and military community within the European Communities framework, and establishing an intergovernmental system in which state leaders would retain their national powers of veto over all European foreign and security policy decisions.[2] The history of the progressive setting up of European institutions responsible for security and military affairs shows a demand for a '*Europe puissance*' (Europe as a power in its own right), but it also reveals the reluctance of state leaders to delegate their national foreign policy powers to European institutions.

From Schuman to the High Representative for Foreign Affairs and Security Policy

After the Second World War, European leaders wanted to lay the foundations for a federation of Europe, or a supranational political community, starting with economic integration. The then French Minister for Foreign Affairs Robert Schuman made his famous declaration on 9 May 1950 that 'Europe will not be made all at once, or according to a single plan. It will be built through concrete achievements which first create a *de facto* solidarity' (EU Document, accessed 11/11/09). For him, the pooling of coal and steel production was the first step to setting up common foundations for economic development, and then political development. In a letter to Robert Schuman, one of the founders of the European Union, Jean Monnet, argued:

> The Schuman plan would be a failure if current negotiations came to nothing or led to a purely technical agreement on coal and steel, with no political significance and no future. The Schuman plan was supposed to be, and can be the beginning of the creation of a Western Europe organised on France's initiative, as well as being the only solution to the German problem through the political and material incorporation of Germany into a supranational community comprising also France, Italy and the Benelux. (1950, 59)[3]

At the same time as discussions were taking place to establish the European Coal and Steel Community, in 1950, Jean Monnet also suggested to the French President of the Council, René Pleven, that soldiers from different European countries be merged to form a common European army. This led to the Pleven Plan of 24 October 1950, which proposed the creation, for the purpose of common defence, of a European army tied to the political institutions of a united Europe. The plan failed, but its implementation would have created a supranational Europe in the military field.

The main reason for this plan was to avoid the rearmament of Germany through the North Atlantic Treaty Organization (NATO), as sought by the United States, and to create instead a supranational European structure in which German rearmament would be controlled by the ruling powers of Europe. British and American leaders pushed for German rearmament. In August 1950, the then British leader of the opposition Winston Churchill asked the Assembly of the Council of

Europe to call for the immediate creation of a unified European Army, subject to proper European democratic control and acting in full cooperation with the United States and Canada. In September 1950, the U.S. Secretary of State, Dean Acheson, was in favour of German rearmament, and he wanted it straightaway. The French government was reluctant to agree with immediate German rearmament, which was a very sensitive issue in France. This was why they offered the alternative of the Pleven Plan.

The French government would have preferred a progressive process of integration, rather than a direct and immediate transfer of sovereignty in the defence field; but René Pleven was aware that world events left France no option, and his plan went further in its proposals for the creation of a European army than any proposal made since. First, a united European army, made up of forces from the various European nations, would, as far as possible, pool all its human and material components under a single political and military European authority. This army would be financed from a common budget. Second, a minister for defence would be appointed by the member governments, and would be accountable both to those appointing him and to a European Assembly. He would have the same powers over the European army that a national minister for defence had over his country's national forces. Participant states which already had national forces would retain their authority over those elements of their existing forces that were not incorporated into the European army. This plan was incredibly bold, as it would have led to European institutions being responsible for a key area in the domain of high politics: the field of defence.[4]

The European Defence Community (EDC) Treaty, based on the Pleven Plan, was ratified by Germany and the Benelux countries, and was supported by the United Kingdom and the United States. The EDC Treaty was accepted mostly by nations who thought that Europe could not and should not refuse to do what the United States had demanded, that is, rearm Germany (Hoffmann 1995, 109n15). But in 1954, France, paradoxically, rejected the treaty that it had initiated and proposed to its partners, and for which it had secured U.S. agreement (Gerbet 2004). The French Prime Minister, Pierre Mendès-France, could not fully support the treaty, as his government was split on whether to ratify it. He did not make ratification of the treaty an issue for a vote of confidence in the French Assembly, and the treaty was rejected there, mainly by the Communist and Gaullist parties. This vote marked the end of discussions to create independent European military structures for the next forty years.

Negotiations for the development of a political Europe, including common European foreign policy, nonetheless continued among European leaders. In 1955, at Messina, they agreed to relaunch the European integration process through the development of common institutions, the progressive fusion of national economies, the creation of a common market, and the gradual harmonization of social policy. In the 1957 EEC Treaty, the signatories declared that they were determined to lay the foundations of an ever closer union among the peoples of Europe.

In the late 1950s, French President Charles de Gaulle, who had rejected the EDC Treaty, wanted to reform the European Communities in order to establish a Europe of States, in other words, an intergovernmental system of states. In 1961, European leaders under the chairmanship of Christian Fouchet drew up a draft treaty, which would establish an indissoluble union. It proposed cooperation among states in the areas of foreign policy and defence, science, culture, and human rights protection. In particular, it proposed, alongside existing community treaties, the adoption of common foreign policy and common defence policy, which would strengthen the security of member states faced with aggression.

The members of the European Communities opposed this draft treaty. The main problems were the absence of Britain from the European Communities, and the intergovernmental character of the union. The Belgian Minister for Foreign Affairs, Paul-Henri Spaak, wanted the political commission, which was an instrument of the member states in the Fouchet Treaty, to become an independent power (de Gaulle 1970, 209). Another draft treaty was then submitted, but this one was rejected too, as it infringed on the rights established within the Treaty of Rome: the economic powers of the communities would have been passed over to the Union. After the failure of these talks to create a political union, the heads of state or government did not meet again for seven years. It was not until 1969, once de Gaulle had stepped down as head of state in France, that EC states agreed at the Hague Summit to create a European Political Cooperation framework with the aim of establishing a United Europe capable of assuming its responsibilities in the world, that is, a Europe with foreign policy responsibilities. Unlike the EC, which had supranational characteristics, EPC worked in a purely intergovernmental framework: EPC was not linked to the EC framework, and unanimity was required for EC states to reach a common EPC agreement.

Between 1969 and the signature of the Maastricht Treaty in 1992, the representatives of the various European states attempted to improve the functioning of the EPC system. In the early 1970s, the Commission's role in high politics was 'non-existent' (Sjostedt 1977), because France opposed the presence of the Commission within the EPC system. However, Commission representatives were present in EPC meetings at the Conference on Security and Cooperation in Europe (CSCE) in 1972, and in 1981, the London Report, which aimed to encourage a common approach to European foreign policy, made the Commission fully associated with EPC procedures. This same report made it possible for the political committee, which was the main EPC body charged with preparing the meetings of foreign ministers, to convene within forty-eight hours, and for the EPC system to answer quickly to crises in the world.

In 1983, representatives of member states adopted the Solemn Declaration of Stuttgart, which stated that, in foreign policy issues, it was necessary to increase consultation between state representatives, to take into account the positions of partners, to define common principles and objectives, to identify common interests, to coordinate positions of member states on the political and economic aspects of security, and to increase contacts with third countries outside Europe. This led to the creation of the Single European Act in 1986, which codified the procedures developed since the early 1970s. States accepted to consult one another before a final position was formalized, and a permanent Political Secretariat was created.

Nineteen-ninety-two was a crucial year for the development of a European Foreign Policy, both politically and institutionally. The European Union, created by the Treaty of Maastricht, became responsible for security matters. Article 17 stated that 'the common foreign and security policy shall include all questions relating to the security of the Union.' The treaty, that is, allowed for the eventual framing of a common defence policy. The Treaty of Amsterdam, signed in 1997, introduced a new figure into the CFSP system, the EU's Secretary General/High Representative, whose task is to represent the EU abroad. She or he is answerable to the member states. The responsibilities of this office changed with the ratification of the Treaty of Lisbon on 1 December 2009, but the former High Representative, Javier Solana, carried out tasks which are part of this treaty. For instance, the treaty makes the High Representative legally responsible for contributing, through proposals, towards the preparation of the common foreign and security policy, and for ensuring the implementation of the decisions adopted by the European Council and the Council (article 13a, Treaty of Lisbon).

In the field of security and defence, successive European Councils have taken measures to reinforce the EU's capabilities and its institutional structures. In December 1999, the Helsinki European Council stated that a European Rapid Reaction Force (RRF), comprising 60,000 troops, deployable within sixty days, should be in place by 2003. In May 2000, the Council decided to establish a Civilian Crisis Management Committee. The Feira European Council in June 2000 created new institutional structures: the interim political and security committee, the military staff, and the military committee. These were made permanent in January 2001. A Police Unit was created at Nice in 2000. EU states also agreed to deploy up to 1,000 police officers within thirty days when needed. In 2004, the defence ministers adopted a plan known as the 'Headline Goal 2010' to enable the EU to launch crisis management operations. EU states offered contributions to fifteen EU battle groups at the Military Capabilities Commitment Conference. The EU presented the European Security Strategy in December 2003. The document set out three strategic objectives for the EU: addressing threats, building security in the EU's neighbourhood, and developing an international order based on multilateralism.

Despite early attempts in the 1950s to create supranational institutions in the defence field, and the apparent desire of states to provide European institutions with the military capacity to project European power abroad, states still have an exclusive right to initiate policies, and retain their powers of veto when all types of CFSP decisions are taken. This book addresses the most important puzzle in the study of European foreign and security policy: why and how CFSP decisions, taken in what appears to be an intergovernmental system of considerable complexity, can nevertheless be made and implemented.

Enquiring into CFSP: Some Working Definitions

This book brings a distinctive blend of empirical research and a varied range of theoretical perspectives to the complexities of CFSP decision-making. The question it asks invokes a fact-finding exercise: in the EU CFSP system, under what conditions is common policy reached on issues which are of major importance to one or more big member states? In the process of answering this question, I hope to show whether common policy is in fact an achievable goal, and to analyse, through the study of specific cases, the reasons why it does or does not emerge. The situation I hope to explain is the one that currently obtains, in which CFSP decision-making outcomes vary from a higher than Lowest Common Denominator outcome among existing preferences to the complete absence of a decision.

In this book, the term CFSP has been given a wider interpretation than in most previous academic studies. Three types of issues considered within the CFSP pillar are examined: exclusively CFSP issues, such as declarations, common positions, joint actions, and common strategies; mixed CFSP–EC issues, which are CFSP issues legally requiring EC decisions in order to be implemented; and European Security and Defence Policy (ESDP) issues, which relate purely to security and military affairs.

As indicated above, I have limited my investigation to issues which are of major importance to at least one big member state. Big EU states are to be understood here as the UK, France, Germany, and Italy. These are the most powerful in terms of economic, political, and military weight. They all are part of the G8, and the size of their armed forces is superior to that of the other EU states. In 2007, France had 354,000 troops, the United Kingdom 190,000, Germany 247,000, and Italy 298,000. Defence expenditure in each state was between 1.3 and 2.4 per cent of GDP (NATO, 'NATO–Russia Compendium of Financial and Economic Data Relating to Defence,' accessed 21/12/07).

By 'an issue which is of major importance to at least one big member state,' I mean that the issue is such that the consequences of an EU decision will have major political or economic impact on this state.[5] Major political impact arises when a state's own national foreign policy is changed, and risks being challenged or opposed by citizens and political parties within the state or by traditional friends of the state. Major economic impact occurs when the job market is affected positively or negatively in a member state. Such issues are easily recognized, as they are usually discussed over a long period of time at the level of ministers for foreign affairs. It can take months or years until an agreement is reached at EU level, or there may be no final EU agreement.

Preferences are of major significance here. A state has both strategies and preferences, which are fundamental elements in its negotiations at

EU level, when discussions are being held about action vis-à-vis a third party. The preferences of a state depend on the following aspects of its situation: its own economy (risk of reducing the wealth of citizens: business, contracts, and jobs); its civilian and military population (risk of casualties); its values (risk of infringement); its territory (risk of reduction); its reputation and future influence (risk of damage); its sovereignty (risk that the autonomy of the state as regards foreign policy could be transformed into shared competence with the EU on institutional or policy issues).

For intergovernmentalists, a state's strategy might change during the negotiation process, but its preferences never change. For sociological institutionalists, both strategy and preferences can change. A distinction is therefore made in this book between a change in a state representative's preference and his or her final position, and a change in his or her final position without a change in his or her preference.

CFSP outcomes include no EU decision, an LCD decision, a higher than LCD agreement, and agreements with or without implementation. By seeking to understand the way CFSP decisions are taken at the operational level, I hope to offer testable hypotheses on the patterns of behaviour that direct decision-making. This could make it possible to identify which actors most influence the CFSP decision-making process, and to predict how future decisions could be made on sensitive foreign policy issues.

Agents: Member States, the United States, and the European Commission

My account of how the EU's CFSP system works is actor-based. The players in the CFSP system are defined as 'any individual or composite actor that is assumed to be capable of making purposeful choices among alternative courses of action' (Scharpf 1997, 7).

According to intergovernmentalists, key actors in the CFSP framework are most often the governments of big member states, and these behave as unitary actors. State representatives are assumed to act rationally, with fixed preferences, and always in their own interest. They make cost-benefit analyses when deciding on their state's position, and may also take reputation into account. Common policies are mostly LCD agreements, in which all states are content with the outcome, as they have obtained their initial preference or have made concessions through the use of package deals. For intergovernmentalists, hard bargaining is the only way in which state representatives interact at EU level; they are not influenced by any other actor during the decision-making process. Institutions are not autonomous, and they do not have any power of influence over CFSP outcomes. The national interest of these states is said to relate to economic and geopolitical factors, but in intergovernmentalist theory these are not defined. Common policy, it seems, is reached when the economic consequences of a common policy are not negative for the member states. National preferences and positions are not believed to change under the immediate influence of EU institutions, formal or informal.

The new theoretical argument developed in this book could be termed 'constrained intergovernmentalism'; it represents a revision of the conventional ways of explaining CFSP. Intergovernmentalism, it has been argued, is still the best way to explain CFSP.[6] I seek to show that while this theory is essential, it is insufficient to account for all CFSP operations.

My argument is that most CFSP outcomes on highly sensitive issues cannot be explained without reference to the role of non-member state actors, specifically the United States or the European Commission, and to the role of policy decisions taken in the past (the European *acquis*). Under certain conditions, these actors and past decisions have an impact on discussions, or are able to influence or change the positions of member states, and so they have a constraining, or limiting effect on political outcomes. In terms of theory, realist and rational institutionalist insights help explain the invisible roles of the United States and the Commission. Historical institutionalism is useful for understanding how the lock-ins of pre-existing policy decisions taken both in pillar one and pillar two can shape CFSP decisions.

The United States is an obvious player in the CFSP decision-making process, because an issue of major importance to at least one big member state is likely also to be of major importance for the United States. The economic, military, and diplomatic superiority of the United States in comparison with the EU makes it an actor that cannot be overlooked. It can play four roles in the CFSP decision-making process: indirect observer; de facto veto player; a stimulus; and an authority.

The United States can observe the CFSP decision-making process indirectly, either through the unofficial structure named the Quad or the Quint that brings together the United States and big EU states, or through individual member states, such as the United Kingdom or even France. The United States seems to have a de facto power of veto over CFSP decisions, in the sense that EU governments are disinclined to reach common policies that the United States, at the highest level, strongly disagrees with. However, the United States does not seem to have any de facto power of veto when member states implement a past EU decision. The United States can be a stimulus for EU states to discuss reaching a common policy in the CFSP system. This stimulus can come through U.S. lobbying, or through the EU copying or learning from U.S. foreign policy and strategies. Finally, the United States seems to act as an authority for the EU. EU states appear to ask for U.S. authorization before declaring EU foreign policy towards a state, if the United States is considered a main actor by this state.

These findings are consistent with certain insights from realist theory into the tendency of states to 'bandwagon' with another more powerful state in order to influence it. CFSP outcomes are obviously not all shaped according to U.S. demands, but they seem unlikely to be agreed upon if the United States, at the highest level, opposes them. State representatives try to accommodate U.S. interests in the making of CFSP decisions.

The European Commission has an unexpected role in the CFSP decision-making process. When a CFSP decision legally requires an EC decision in order to be implemented, the Commission can use its 'exclusive' right of initiative in EC matters to modify, delay, or even block the common agreement reached by the member states. In addition, the Commission can use EC prerogatives to initiate proposals on highly sensitive issues which could and even sometimes should be discussed and decided upon in the second pillar. It can do this through its ability to control the implementation of EC law, grey zones in particular, through supplying information weighted in its own favour (this is known as 'asymmetrical' information), and through its manipulation of the lack of communication between state officials working in different areas within the Council. These facts are consistent with institutionalist theory, which argues that institutions can take on a life of their own (Pollack 1996) and can influence EU policy outcomes. The Treaty of Lisbon seems intended to set some limits to the *communautarisation* of CFSP issues (that is, to the progressive incorporation of CFSP matters into the Community framework), by reducing the Commission's powers in the CFSP decision-making process, and in the budgetary field.

Policy decisions taken in the past also have an impact on the development of common policies in the CFSP field. These are decisions taken in both the first and second pillars; they arise from both the *acquis communautaire* and the *acquis politique,* that is, the entire accumulated body of legislation within the European Communities and the European Union. Their role in CFSP decision-making is acknowledged by historical institutionalism, which recognizes the impact of both formal and informal institutions on actors' preferences and on decision-making processes over time.

When the United States and the Commission are not involved, intergovernmentalist theory holds true: common policy seems to be reached when all the big member states agree, and when the economic consequences of that policy are not negative for member states.

Design and Methodology

My hypotheses on the conditions under which states reach policies within the CFSP system are drawn from intergovernmentalist theory. CFSP is legally considered an intergovernmental institution; unanimity is the general rule of its decision-making, and the Commission plays a limited role within the process.[7] I have chosen to test these hypotheses in particularly difficult cases, where issues of high politics are involved. I have also used selected insights from realism and institutionalism to assess whether and how the United States and the Commission have constrained states to reach a particular CFSP outcome. In the process, I have tried to determine whether intergovernmentalism, as a theory to describe CFSP, 'flunks completely, needs repair and restatement, or requires a narrowing of the scope of its explanatory claims' (Waltz 1979, 13).

To test out my hypotheses, I undertook a number of case studies on a range of issues, and compared policy outcomes with the initial positions of member states. Cases were selected according to the following criteria. At least one big member state must have considered the issues discussed of major importance. Between them, the case studies had to represent the whole spectrum of the EU's CFSP decision-making: exclusively CFSP decisions, mixed CFSP and EC decisions, and CFSP–ESDP or pure security decisions. By selecting cases which had operated according to different institutional rules, it would be possible to see whether these rules have no impact on member states' positions, as expected by intergovernmentalism, or whether they do have an impact, as expected by institutionalism. In each study, there needed to be several occurrences of states' reaching or failing to reach a common position. At the beginning of the study, the outcome of the negotiation process must have been uncertain: I wanted to observe the evolution of a state's position throughout the negotiation process. The three main cases chosen all start in the mid-1990s. These cases were thus dealt with under the Maastricht Treaty rules, which were by then in full use: so the CFSP machinery can be considered past its running-in period.

Each of the three cases I selected is analysed in a separate chapter. The first case study focuses on successes and failures in reaching common EU policies against China for presentation to the Geneva Human Rights Commission, in the period 1997–2005. This is the exclusively CFSP case study. The next study looks at instances of agreement and absence of agreement in relation to action to be taken against the Federal Republic of Yugoslavia (FRY) between January and April 2000: the non-modification of the oil ban, the lifting of the flight ban, and the reinforcement of financial sanctions. This is the CFSP–EC case study. The last case study concentrates on successive agreements on the issue of links between NATO and the EU from 1998 until 2008. This is the CFSP–ESDP case study.

The first case study on the EU's position with regard to China at the Geneva Human Rights Commission (1997–2005) shows mainly how difficult it was to reach common policy, mostly because of the positions of the French and German governments. In 1997, France, after long negotiations with the other member states, refused to agree on a common EU policy condemning China. In the following years, when resolutions against China were proposed in Geneva, all EU states succeeded in reaching common policies. These were LCD agreements. Here, intergovermentalism seems to explain every change in position on the part of the states in the process of reaching, or failing to reach, a common policy: big states generally followed their national interests. However, these interests were limited by U.S. policies.

The second case study provides a structured narrative of the decision-making process leading to a CFSP outcome which required an EC decision for implementation. I explain how first a CFSP decision, and then a second EC one on how to implement the former came about, despite much scepticism on the part of the negotiators. Intergovermentalism alone does not apply here, as big member states were constrained by the United States, the Commission, and past decisions.

The final case study, in the CFSP–ESDP field, concerns the establishment of close European links with NATO during the elaboration of the

Common European Security and Defence Policy (CESDP).[8] The creation of ESDP over the period 1998–2001, which made a force of 60,000 persons available to the EU, was an event in itself: it marked a major change of position for Britain, which had always previously refused to allow the EU to deal with security matters. The United Kingdom accepted the creation of an ESDP, and France accepted proposals to 'NATO-ize' the EU. Successive decisions to launch military missions, such as Concordia in the former Yugoslav Republic of Macedonia in March 2003, Artemis in the Democratic Republic of the Congo in June 2003, and the Althea operation in Bosnia and Herzegovina in 2004, and the support of the African Mission in Sudan (AMIS) in Darfur between 2005 and 2007, show divisions between Atlanticists and Europeanists. Here again, intergovermentalism is insufficient to describe the processes involved, as the United States has to be taken into account in order to understand the making of these decisions. In addition, past decisions may have influenced the agreements that were reached.

In each of these three case studies, a narrative of the decision-making process is followed by a test of the adequacy of intergovermentalist hypotheses to explain them. Where intergovernmentalism does not explain the outcome, alternative theories are suggested (see table I.1). Building on the three case studies, two chapters concentrate specifically on analysing the conditions under which the United States and the Commission have effectively constrained EU member states to produce particular outcomes in CFSP decision-making. Out of these studies, with the help of insights adapted from realist and institutionalist theory, I have developed a set of hypotheses which will, I hope, explain future CFSP outcomes.

The evidence gathered for this book goes well beyond that which is available in existing secondary literature. As Moravcsik (1998, 13) notes, 'even prominent historians of European integration today, among them Alan Milward and Peter Ludlow, complain that diplomatic histories have yet to provide a reliable "social history" of European integration.' My arguments draw on five kinds of sources: literature on the CFSP and EU foreign policy and on related theory; newspaper articles; official Council documents; interviews in Foreign Offices in Paris, London, and Brussels (1999–2008) with officials belonging to Permanent Representations of EU states and various EU institutions (European Commission, Council, and European Parliament); and participant observation during a four-month internship (January–May 2000) at the Secretariat General of the Council of the

Table I.1
Cases and Findings

Type of decisions	Case studies	Big member states that consider the issues discussed of major importance	Findings
Exclusively CFSP decisions	EU policies on the condemnation of China at the United Nations Commission on Human Rights from 1997 until 2005	France and Germany	The United States: partial influence Commission: no influence Past decisions: no influence
Mixed CFSP and EC decisions	EU sanctions policies against the FRY from January until April 2000	United Kingdom, France, and Germany	The United States: influence Commission: influence Past decisions: influence
CFSP–ESDP or pure security decisions	EU policies on the links between NATO and the EU from 1998 until 2008	United Kingdom and France	The United States: influence Commission: no influence Past decisions: influence

European Union. I conducted more than eighty interviews. Interviewees asked to remain anonymous.

Interviews and personal observations are essential for a study of this kind. Official documents are insufficient. They give only the result of negotiations; they show neither the real processes of negotiation, nor the disagreements among member states. And foreign policy is a special realm: at all levels, whether within a state, the EU, or an international organization, it is kept secret. This is known as the DDS syndrome, 'indicating that foreign policy is characterised by Discreet, Discretionary and Sovereignty-related activities' (Wessels 1995, 230). Diplomatic action takes place behind the scenes, away from the public eye. Data is thus hard to collect, as there is a 'closed government ethos' (Clarke and White 1989, 8). The researcher must grasp the effective decision-making process that takes place within the member states and in Brussels, not only during the meetings but also before and after, in the corridors, over the phone, and by emails, in each others' offices, and during informal meetings and dinners.

Interviews give a better picture of the whole decision-making process, but they need careful handling. They cannot be trusted: interviewees can lie, not fully understand a process, remember it incorrectly, or be biased. To overcome the problem of trustworthiness, it is important to carry out regular interviews, as this enables the researcher to be permanently aware of the different positions held by representatives during a negotiation process. It is also important to interview the actors who did not change position, because the ones that did do not usually admit it. If information is required about a change in the UK position, having first asked British representatives, it is also necessary (and often more informative) to ask French, German, or Italian representatives. If there are two main actors opposing one another, the researcher must also interview actors who are not directly involved in the debate. Finally, if the researcher herself is a direct observer in the negotiations, she can personally verify the positions of the member states. As Putnam has noted:

> Soaking and poking requires the researcher to marinate herself in the minutiae of an institution – to experience its customs and practices, its successes and its failings, as those who live it every day do. This immersion sharpens our intuitions and provides innumerable clues about how the institution fits together and how it adapts to its environment. (1993, 12)

By focusing on the informal relations and negotiations among state, Council, and Commission officials, not merely on the formal rules and processes of the system, I hope to shed more light on and bring into sharper focus the current analyses of how CFSP works.

In the larger perspective, the aim of this study is to bring fresh insights to academic accounts of European foreign policy and European integration, and to theories of International Relations. Current literature on the mechanisms of CFSP focuses mainly on the development and expansion of CFSP institutions and the Brusselization of the CFSP (that is, the fact that EU governments have permanent staff in Brussels dealing with EU policies in the CFSP field). This book sheds light on the actual making of foreign policy within these institutions. My analysis of the way the decision-making process works makes it possible to understand who the actors involved are, and how and under what conditions they interact. As Clarke (1996, 22) says, it is important to 'determine where decision-making power lies, among how many people, among which institutions, and how widely it is dispersed.' The book also highlights the importance of power politics and leadership in the CFSP system. Whether the EU has nine, twenty-seven, or more member states, CFSP outcomes on highly sensitive issues are likely to be negotiated and decided by big member states outside the EU framework.

Understanding the way CFSP works should enable us to examine the effectiveness of the CFSP system. According to Ginsberg (1999, 449), 'by offering ... a set of evaluative criteria or conditions for pooling sovereignty, theorists have begun to shift the focus from identifying the EU as an international presence to evaluating the effectiveness of European foreign policy actions.' It should also provide some insights into the future nature of the EU. Researchers believe that the European integration process and the evolution of EU foreign policy are closely related (Sjursen 2001b, 188; Elgstroem and Smith 2000). Heisbourg (2000, 111) says that 'the debate on the development of the ESDP is linked to the EU's *finalité politique* [political future].' On the evidence offered in this book, the EU is not on its way to becoming a fully-fledged federation. CFSP is likely to remain intergovernmental, and is unlikely to be integrated into the EC system.

Finally, in the context of International Relations theory, this research offers a synthesis of intergovernmentalist, realist, and institutionalist approaches to explain the making of CFSP decisions, and looks to provide a via media between contending mainstream approaches.[9] In terms of its engagement with mainstream theory, my study tends to support what Hasenclever, Mayer, and Rittberger (1996) call 'neo-liberal' or 'interest-based' theories of regimes rather than cognitivist or constructivist ones. In international forums where highly sensitive foreign policy issues are discussed, certain insights from realism and rational institutionalism need to be considered seriously and system-atically, while sociological institutionalism only has a marginal rele-vance. My model of 'constrained intergovernmentalism' could help guide future research into the CFSP and European Foreign Policy systems, and more generally into the ways states cooperate in both formal and informal institutional settings. The conclusions I set out in my final chapter, with regard to the role in the CFSP system of big member states, the United States, the Commission and past decisions, are valid both now and for the future, with or without further enlarge-ment of the EU and with the ratification of the Lisbon Treaty. They are extremely important tools for predicting the outcome of CFSP deci-sions. Furthermore, the findings on the role of the Commission in the CFSP system contribute to the institutionalist literature on the condi-tions under which the Commission is an autonomous actor in EU affairs.

To summarize, the material that follows is divided into three parts. Part One explains in detail the theoretical framework of the study and the mechanisms of the CFSP system: its actors, capabilities, and aims, and the shape of the decision-making process. Part Two comprises three case studies, in which I discuss the relative influence of various actors. Part Three draws conclusions from the evidence established in the two earlier parts, and discusses the extent to which this evidence can be generalized to all CFSP outcomes. Two thematic chapters are developed, on the respective and major roles in CFSP discussions of the United States and the Commission – two actors whose agency is not considered in intergovernmentalist theory. A model for a theory of 'constrained intergovernmentalism' is offered in the conclusion.

PART ONE

CFSP – Theory and Practice

1 Foundations for 'Constrained Intergovernmentalism': A New Theoretical Approach

This chapter sets out the bases for my theory of 'constrained intergovernmentalism,' which brings together aspects of intergovernmentalism, realism, and institutionalism in order to provide a more comprehensive explanation of how CFSP decisions are made.

Intergovernmentalism and CFSP

Intergovernmentalism is a theory which highlights the importance of relations among states, along with state sovereignty and interests, in negotiations within the European Community and European Union. Intergovernmentalism is part of European integration literature. It is regarded, together with neofunctionalism, as a grand theory, in the sense that it helps us understand the dynamics and the future of the EU, as opposed to middle range theories, which concentrate on what the EU is as an entity.[10]

The concept of intergovernmentalism was created by Hoffmann (1966, 1995), in reaction to Charles de Gaulle's promotion of the French national interest to the detriment of supranationalism. De Gaulle's motivation was made apparent in the early 1960s, with the Fouchet plans for the creation of intergovernmental European foreign policy. De Gaulle's policy had a negative impact on the European integration process in 1965–6, when he decided not to participate in meetings of the Council of Ministers, in reaction to the Commission's proposal to give more budgetary and decision-making powers to the European Community. This episode was known as 'the crisis of the empty chair.' Intergovernmentalism was revived in the 1990s by Moravcsik, who focused on the negotiations that led to the signing of all the treaties relating to the development of the European Union.

The theoretical origins of intergovernmentalism are to be found in realism. Intergovernmentalism uses the same assumptions as realism. Both intergovernmentalists and realists assume that the state is the most important actor in international relations. They also assume that a state is a unitary actor and acts rationally, and that its aim is to defend and enhance its self-interest. However, they explain policy outcomes differently. Realists argue that, in an anarchical international system, states are faced with a security dilemma, and as a result, they base their decisions on their wish to influence the balance of power; cooperation among states is consequently difficult. Intergovernmentalists do not think that states are more concerned with their security and survival than with the development of their economy. Rosamond (2000, 76) emphasizes that Hoffmann 'sought to advance a rather deeper notion of interests than the standard realist view that treats interests as derivative of structural balance of power calculus.' Furthermore, intergovernmentalists do not assume that state representatives care about relative gains, that is, the gains made by other states as a result of a negotiation process, or that representatives aim to maximize the relative gains of their own states.

The following intergovernmentalist assumptions, drawn from Hoffmann's and Moravcsik's theories, will be tested in this book: that the main actor is the state, and not international institutions or transnational groups; that the state acts as a unitary state, in the sense that governments pursue coherent national strategies; and that there may be disagreements among national officials from the same country, for instance between two ministers, but the national position will remain the same.

Intergovernmentalist theory holds too that a state has a set of preferences, which are decided upon before negotiation starts at EU level, and which are not changed by the negotiation process. Preferences are an ordered and weighted set of values placed on future outcomes. They are 'not simply a particular set of policy goals but a set of underlying national objectives *independent* of any particular negotiation to expand exports, to enhance security vis-à-vis a particular threat, or to realise some ideational goal' (Moravcsik 1998, 20; my emphasis). Governments first define a set of interests, and then bargain among themselves in an effort to realize those interests (Moravcsik 1993, 481). Preferences are constant in the long term, and Moravcsik expects to find this specifically in the CFSP field:

It is the stability and continuity of preferences, not their instability, that stands out ... The relative positions of major governments on core issues such as ... foreign and defence policy ... have hardly changed in forty years. Germany has consistently sought a common European foreign and defence policy consistent with NATO ... France has sought a more independent common foreign and defence policy ... Britain has sought a modest foreign and defence policy. (1998, 493)

Preferences are unaffected by the norm of the promotion of European integration. During negotiations at the European level, state representatives follow a 'logic of diversity' rather than the logic of integration advocated by Jean Monnet. For Hoffmann (1995, 84), 'state leaders prefer the self-controlled uncertainty of national self-reliance, to the uncontrolled uncertainty of the blending process.'

Intergovernmentalists believe that a state acts rationally and strategically. A rational actor examines his or her preferences, and then calculates the course of action that would have the best consequences in the light of these preferences. For intergovernmentalists, actors make cost-benefit analyses of their foreign policies. They are self-interested and self-serving utility maximizers. They do their utmost to satisfy their own interest, and do not care about the interests of other states. They only care about absolute gains.

Intergovermentalists would not believe that state representatives might have no clear idea of the outcome of a negotiation process, nor that they might misinterpret other states' bargaining moves, or that there might be unexpected consequences of a decision. They agree that state representatives can be dissatisfied with an outcome: representatives, they believe, are fully aware that, at some point, they might have to accept an outcome that does not correspond to their national interest, as a result of an earlier decision they have agreed to. But for intergovernmentalists, there are no unintended consequences. A government can predict patterns of bargaining. For Moravcsik and Nicolaidis:

Though governments have often issued spurious denials, developments such as ... the tendency of qualified majority voting to impede opposition by governments with extreme preferences were far from unforeseen or unintended. The primary purpose of European integration was to bring about just such results. (1999, 175)

Table 1.1
Intergovernmentalism and CFSP

Major characteristics	Intergovernmentalist assumptions
Role of the state in the CFSP decision-making process	Crucial actor Unitary actor, in the sense that the national position is unique
Characteristics of the national interest	Preference formation precedes negotiation Preferences are unaffected by norms and inter-state bargaining
Rationality of a state's representative	A state's representative is: – goal-oriented – a utility maximizer: he or she calculates the costs and benefits of an agreement – committed to a hierarchy of preferences
Concern of state's representative with gains that can come out of a negotiation process	A state's representative is exclusively concerned with absolute gains: he or she is a rational egoist and cares only for his or her state's own gains, and he or she is indifferent to what others do
Role of previous decisions	A state's representative is aware of the consequences of the decisions he or she takes: unforeseen consequences are either impossible, or only limited to secondary matters

Table 1.1 gives an overview of intergovernmentalist assumptions about the major characteristics of the CFSP system. On the basis of these assumptions, the intergovernmentalist hypothesis on the reaching of a common policy, which will be tested in this book, is the following:

A common policy in the CFSP system is more likely to be reached, when it presents an economic, personal, or geopolitical advantage for the leaders and governments of big member states. It is likely to be an LCD agreement.

This intergovernmentalist hypothesis can be broken down in two sub-hypotheses in order to make analysis more precise. In the first subhypothesis, a distinction is made between a common policy in the CFSP field, which has economic consequences for member states, and one which has no such consequences:

> A common policy with no economic consequences for one or more big member states will only exist if it corresponds to the ideologies and personal commitments of leaders, and if it is perceived by leaders as having positive geopolitical implications for these states. A common policy with economic consequences for one or more big member states will only exist if the economic consequences are positive for these states, and the geopolitical consequences are not negative.

Although Moravcsik's aim in his book of 1998 was not to analyse foreign policy but the 'grand bargains' that led to the creation of treaties, he does allude to foreign policy. He (1998, 478) believes that 'geopolitical considerations tended to be important where issues had no immediate economic impact, as in foreign policy coordination,' and he also states it is right in such cases to 'predict the predominance of concerns about security and sovereignty.' It is worth noting that Moravcsik seems, over a period, to have changed his mind about the factors that influence states' preferences. In 1993, he wrote that, in the CFSP field, 'preferences reflect the ideologies and personal commitments of leading executives, *as well as* interest-based conceptions of the national interest' (494; my emphasis). But in 1998, he states clearly that 'significant geopolitical factors are more ideological than objective and often connected with prestigious national leaders' (478). In the end, Moravcsik seems to be more convinced by the liberal constructivist argument, which underlines the importance of the way leaders perceive the world, than the realist argument, which highlights the will of states to balance or bandwagon with other stronger and threatening states. In either case, he does not define these geopolitical factors.

The second subhypothesis is the following:

> A common policy will only exist when all the big member states agree. No other actor plays a significant role in the making of this common policy. The policy outcome is likely to be an LCD agreement.

For intergovernmentalists, actors within the EU system do not play any role in the CFSP decision-making process. These actors, that is, EU institutions, are considered to be the instruments of states. They have been created in order to help member states attain their goals. Supranational entrepreneurship is thought to play no role at all in the CFSP decision-making process. The role of supranational institutions 'tends to be futile and redundant ... and ... their influence has been limited' (Moravcsik 1998, 8). For intergovernmentalists, the European Commission does not influence policy outcomes.

A common policy is based on the gradual process of preference convergence among the most powerful member states, which strike central bargains amongst themselves and offer side-payments to smaller, reluctant states (Moravcsik 1991, 25). For intergovernmentalists, big states are the most important actors.

An LCD agreement is one that satisfies all the states. For Nuttall (1992, 314n35), an LCD agreement is produced when 'all the national positions are put on the table and whatever coincides becomes the European position.' When discussing the CFSP provisions of the Maastricht Treaty, Nuttall (2000, 11) qualified them as sedimentary, 'in the sense that they were all that was left when everything else had been washed away by the objections of one or the other member state.' The LCD agreement reached can be seen as resulting from a 'Christmas tree' attitude. For instance, the presidency can present a one-page text, and delegates treat this like a Christmas tree: each one adds his or her own version, and the text becomes as long as three pages, but remains too general to be effective. Governments, it is argued, have no interest in making concessions beyond their conception of their national interest.

For Moravcsik (1993, 500–1), states must compromise with the least forthcoming government, and this can be preferable to the vetoing of an agreement. Moravcsik's analysis focuses on benefits in domestic political terms, and not, for instance, in terms of preserving good relations with partners at the negotiation table (1998, 482). He argues that in the case of the Maastricht Treaty negotiations:

> The compromises [the big states] reached reflected the perceived relative costs and benefits of exclusion. In an area such as the Maastricht social protocol, the British government perceived advantages from non-participation and welcomed exclusion. In areas such as tariff and monetary policy, it perceived disadvantages in exclusion and sought to compromise. (1998, 483)

An EU agreement which includes an opt-out clause for one or several states is considered an LCD agreement. In the view of Moravcsik and

Table 1.2
Intergovernmentalism and Policy Outcomes

CFSP policy outcome	Position of member states
1. No final common policy	states oppose one another openly *or* states are discreet about the disagreements between themselves
2. A final LCD common policy	all states obtain their initial preferences *or* some states, instead of vetoing a proposal, compromise somewhat, after having made a cost-benefit analysis of failing to agree to this proposal, and after taking into consideration the benefits of possible package deals through side-payments or issue linkages
3. A final higher than LCD common policy	one state gets its preferences through, while the other states do not have intense preferences on the issue discussed *or* a state changes position under isolation, a credible threat of exclusion, or a threat of being left behind

Nicolaidis (1999, 75), commenting on the Treaty of Amsterdam and the movement of peoples, Britain accepted an opt-out rather than veto the arrangement, because it wanted in return to obtain satisfaction on other issues.

Intergovernmentalism does, however, allow the possibility of outcomes higher than LCD. Moravcsik argues:

> The only tool that can impel a state to accept an outcome on a major issue that it does not prefer to the status quo is the threat of exclusion ... If two major states can isolate the third and credibly threaten it with exclusion, and if such exclusion undermines the substantive interests of the excluded state, the coercive threat may bring about an agreement at a level of integration above the lowest common denominator. (1991, 26)

Intergovernmentalists would therefore envisage the possible situations in relation to the outcome of policy discussions outlined in table 1.2.

Sociological institutionalism, or constructivism, presents an alternative set of assumptions and hypotheses to intergovernmentalism, concerning the factors which might make states change their preferences in order to reach a common policy.[11] This theory studies the impact of formal and informal institutions, such as norms of behaviour, intersubjective understandings, ideas, culture, and identity, on actors' identities and preferences.

For sociological institutionalists, actors' preferences are considered endogenous, that is, they have an internal cause or origin, and are liable to change under the influence of changing norms and rules. The preferences of state representatives follow a logic of appropriateness, rather than a logic of consequentiality. According to March and Olsen:

> The logic of appropriateness [corresponds to action which] is often more based on identifying the *normatively appropriate behaviour* than on calculating the return expected from alternative choices … [T]he logic of appropriateness is associated with obligatory action and the logic of consequentiality with anticipatory choice. (1989, 22–6; my emphasis)

Actors are believed to behave according to the expectations of appropriate behaviour within the social context in which they are placed. Actors look at the domestic and international environment of the negotiation. They consider what appropriate role they should play with respect to this environment and their options.

A number of academics have focused on the impact of these features on the EU's decision-making process. In particular, they have used sociological institutionalism to show that the state representatives' identities and preferences are transformed by the socialization of these representatives at the EU level. European institutions are said to have a 'socialisation power' (Checkel and Moravcsik 2001). Christiansen et al. (2001, 2) note that 'European integration has a transformative impact on the European state system and its constituent units.' M.E. Smith (2004, 263) also thinks that 'the EU has fundamentally changed the way its member states define and pursue their interests.'

There is, these theorists argue, not only a transformation of strategies but also of preferences. For Risse-Kappen:

> International institutions and norms are key structures of international relations, they *condition* the preferences of the member states; they do not merely influence the cost-benefit calculations of actors and constrain their behaviour. (1995, 6; my emphasis)

State representatives are socialized through the norms of institutional culture within the EU (Bulmer 1998, 375–6). Their national affiliations are 'often thwarted by the affiliations with the councils' (Kerremans 1996, 232). In their deliberations, they can be persuaded by good arguments, and by a powerful actor. Their negotiation technique is problem-solving, not bargaining (Risse 2000; Johnston 2001). Five main features of the decision-making process are distinguished by Lewis (2000): diffuse reciprocity (mutual concessions and self-restraint to facilitate bargains and help build credit for the future); thick trust (mutual respect, confidence, and close interpersonal relations); mutual responsiveness; consensus-reflex; and a culture of compromise. For Lewis, there is no room for the hard bargaining described by intergovernmentalists, in which the member states care only about their own interests.

This phenomenon of a state changing its preference under the influence of institutional culture within the EU differs from the simple learning process put forward by intergovernmentalism, whereby new information alters strategies but the state pursues its predetermined preference. Table 1.3 gives an overview of the differences between intergovernmental and sociological institutionalist assumptions.

For sociological institutionalists, an EU common policy in the CFSP field can be reached, even when one or more big member states disagree. State representatives can change their preferences due to transgovernmentalism, which is the socialization process that operates at EU level among state and EU institutions' representatives. When this occurs, an agreement higher than the LCD is reached. Wallace defined the concept of transgovernmentalism in 1976, stating:

> The distinction between intergovernmental and transgovernmental is between those contacts which, following the formal and traditional patterns of international diplomacy, flow through the regular channels for conducting and co-ordinating foreign policy – embassies, foreign ministries, and prime-ministerial and presidential offices – and those which are conducted directly between ministers and officials in particular ministries without detailed clearance by the central core of governmnent. (168)

Sociological institutionalists have refined this definition. According to Risse-Kappen:

> Transgovernmental networks among state officials in sub-units of national governments, international organisations and regimes fre-

Table 1.3
Intergovernmentalism versus Sociological Institutionalism

Characteristics	Intergovernmentalist assumptions	Sociological institutionalist assumptions
Role of the state in the CFSP decision-making process	Crucial actor Unitary actor, in the sense that the national position is unique	Crucial actor, but relevance too of trans-governmental actors
Characteristics of the national interest	Preference formation precedes negotiation Preferences are unaffected by norms and inter-state bargaining	Preferences vary with endogenous changes: they are affected by norms and EU negotiations
Rationality of a state's representative	A state's representative is a rational actor; he or she is: – goal-oriented (his or her aim is to enhance security if threats are present, to realize ideational goals, to expand economy) – a utility maximizer (he or she calculates the costs and benefits of an agreement) – committed to a hierarchy of preferences – self-interested	A state's representative is a sociological actor. He or she undergoes a learning process whereby he or she can consider European solutions to be better than national ones
Concern of a state's representative with gains that can come out of a negotiation process	A state's representative is concerned with absolute gains (he or she is a rational egoist and cares only for his or her state's own gains, and he or she is indifferent to what others do)	A state's representative cares both about his or her state's and other states' interests

quently pursue their own agenda, independently from and sometimes even contrary to the declared policies of their national governments. (1995, 4)

In the first pillar framework, Lewis (1998a, 484) argues, socialization has an impact on state positions. He identifies the existence of what he terms the Janus-face phenomenon: a state's representative needs to deliver the goods both at home and in the Brussels community. Lewis (1998a, 490–1) believes that intergovernmentalism is challenged by his findings. For him, institutional networks and frameworks can have an impact on state preferences, under a range of different conditions. At the negotiation table in Brussels, for instance, officials can put their national instructions aside, give their provisional assent to the EU proposal, and recommend changes back to their national government. The member state can signal to its representative that a margin of manoeuvre exists, and that he or she effectively is the decision-maker. The state can feel that it is a political need to minimize confrontation and let the representative agree with the issue at a low level, that is, in a working group or in a political directors group, instead of in a group of ministers for foreign affairs. Finally, the national capital cannot make up its mind on the instructions to give, and the representative can make up his or her own instructions.

Checkel (2003, 213) also proposes a range of conditions under which state representatives can be convinced by the argument of their peers. For him, argumentation is more likely to be effective when the person to be persuaded is in a novel environment, of which he or she is uncertain, and has few prior or ingrained beliefs; when the persuader is an authoritative member of the group, but does not lecture or demand and instead deliberates with his or her peers; and when deliberation occurs in in-camera settings which are less politicized and more insulated.

Socialization might occur at two levels. It could be observed when the prime minister or the foreign affairs minister changes his or her state's preference as a result of prolonged interchanges with European colleagues, or of being convinced by colleagues who work in Brussels at other levels – political directors or working groups. It could also be seen in the form of a state official who yields to persuasion from an authoritative member in the Council, for instance, the president of the European Union or the High Representative, in an in-camera setting and decides to take a decision in Brussels that goes against his or her national instructions. The sociological institutionalist hypothesis that will be tested in this book is the following:

> The more state officials, from the lowest to the highest level of the deci-
> sion-making process, meet one another on a regular basis and discuss
> their positions within the EU setting, the more likely it is that a higher
> than LCD decision will be reached.

This hypothesis will be tested in cases where officials have clear instructions. Obviously, any demonstration that socialization has a real impact on state positions would establish a hard case against the validity of intergovernmentalism. So far, however, theorists have failed to show that socialization has any impact in the CFSP field. Glarbo, for instance, who concentrates on the institutional environment of diplomats, not on the impact of the socialization process, writes that there is 'an institutionalized imperative of "concertation"' vividly evident from the interaction within political cooperation' (1999, 650). He alludes only briefly to the prospective impact of the socialization process on the CFSP decision-making process:

> The diplomats of present-day CFSP, besides being affected by the struc-
> tural surroundings of political cooperation and national diplomacies, are
> also aware of the deep social demands levelled at them for conducting
> both 'national' and 'European' foreign policies. In the future, this
> enhances the ability of diplomats to control reflexively their own diplo-
> matic undertakings and, in turn, to manipulate the political cooperation
> environment itself. Highly interesting implications for the future of CFSP
> may be drawn from this. (1999, 650)

Jorgensen (1997a, 168) shows only that officials communicate on a regular basis at the EU level. He suggests that 'although Political Directors meet less frequently than Coreper [the *Comité des Representants Permanents* – the committee of permanent representatives who are based in Brussels], one could expect an esprit de corps among Political Directors' (1997a, 175). However, Jorgensen's analysis does not demonstrate that the socialization process has an impact on EU decisions.

Theories of International Relations and CFSP

The theory of intergovernmentalism must be supplemented by other schools of theory in order to apprehend more clearly the way CFSP works.

Realism: On Bandwagoning

Realism needs to be brought back into the study of the CFSP system for its assumption that states respond to external events or factors, such as the presence of a hegemon. Pijpers (1988) is one of the few analysts of European foreign policy to have said that EPC was not unique, and that its functioning was best understood by applying realism, and thereby taking into account the pre-eminence of security, the relevance of the concept of balance of power, the marginal impact of domestic politics, and the role of the state as an international actor. Holland (1995, 3) also believed that 'although not sufficient in themselves, realist assumptions need to be incorporated in any composite theory dedicated to conceptualising European foreign policy-making.' One particular insight provided by realism, namely, the concept of bandwagoning, will be used here to cast light on the invisible role of the United States in the CFSP system.

Not all realist assumptions are equally useful.[12] My study does not accept the following realist propositions: (a) the EU is in itself a non-viable entity. Mearsheimer (1990), for example, asserts that the EU would break up in the absence of the Former Soviet Union; (b) a state is unitary; (c) a state's policy is only determined by the structure of the international anarchical system, which is characterized by the absence of a world government to organize relations among states, and by the desire to expand power and security; (d) international institutions play no role; (e) cooperation among states is difficult; and (f) states are concerned with relative gains, that is, gains obtained by other states as a result of a negotiation.[13]

Realists are unclear as to how a state should act in the international system. Some realists argue that states balance one another, others that they bandwagon one another. They do not give detailed explanations about the conditions under which actors would decide to balance or bandwagon, and they make indeterminate predictions about the likelihood of states balancing and bandwagoning with other states. Hyde-Price (2006, 231), for instance, while arguing that the EU responds to U.S. hegemony, presents a vague characterization of what this response consists of: 'EU member states are likely to pursue a variety of strategies towards America, from balancing to bandwagoning.'

The concept of balancing is not a useful addition to any hypothesis about how CFSP outcomes are produced. Balancing involves states interacting to assure their survival within the anarchy of international politics, by preventing the empire or hegemony of any state or coalition of states (Waltz 1979; Doyle 1997, 162).[14] It is unlikely that the EU could balance the U.S. hegemon, as its military power is vastly superior to that of Europe.

Realists themselves disagree as to whether the EU can balance the United States. Some realists assert that the EU can indeed do so. They argue that states are 'edging away' from the United States in order to provide a counterweight to its power (see Waltz 1993; Mastanduno 1997, 54; and Layne 1996). Huntington (1999, 45) believes that the creation of the EU represents the single most important move towards an anti-hegemonic coalition. Other realist authors (Posen 2004, 2006; and Paul 2005, 58) prefer the term 'soft-balancing' to that of balancing, in order to describe moves to build EU foreign policy. They define soft-balancing as the pursuit of 'limited, tacit, or indirect balancing strategies largely through coalition building and diplomatic bargaining within international institutions.' However, other realists, such as Gray (2006, 234) or Wohlforth (1999), assert that it is impossible to balance the United States, which is a superpower. Wohlforth (1999, 37), for instance, believes that states, whether in Europe or in Asia, use the rhetoric of balancing, and give the impression they are acting according to precepts of realpolitik and power politics, but that they are in fact incapable of balancing the United States.

In any event, the realist proposition that states might seek to balance the United States is not part of my argument. This book focuses instead on the realist concept of bandwagoning, in order to describe the way in which CFSP can be influenced by the powerful external agency of the United States. Bandwagoning is about siding with a stronger party, usually for one of two motives: either to align oneself with the source of danger, or for profit. First, a state seeks security, and protection from a stronger and possibly threatening power. A state aligns itself with the source of danger; it gives in to threats.[15] Walt gives a comprehensive definition of bandwagoning, seen in this light:

> Bandwagoning involves unequal exchange; the vulnerable state makes asymmetrical concessions to the dominant power and accepts a subordinate role ... Bandwagoning is an accommodation to pressure ... Bandwagoning suggests a willingness to support or tolerate illegitimate actions of the dominant ally. (1991, 55)

Secondly, a state may already feel secure enough, as it finds itself in a world in which survival seems to carry few risks, and it wishes to pursue absolute gain and profit (Schweller 1994). In this perspective, states are assumed to be offensive and to aim for power; they do not need to aim for security. Schweller (1994, 89) believes that, in a conflict, states are 'lured to the winning side by the promise of future rewards.' In adopting this definition of bandwagoning, focused on the desire for profit, Schweller (1994, 81) rejects Walt's definition based on fear and threat. He considers Walt's definition as coming close to the concept of capitulation, as states have to comply involuntarily with the policies of the stronger ally. Schroeder (1994) also seeks to show that states, especially small powers, are more likely to bandwagon with other states than to balance other states.[16] In the same vein, Wohlforth (1999, 37) thinks that states seek 'the best bargains for themselves given the distribution of power.'

Adopting a loose interpretation of Schweller's 'bandwagoning for profit' concept and of Wohlforth's argument, one would expect the EU would align itself for profit, as the United States is not a threat to the EU. The EU should aim to obtain the best bargains from the United States. The EU should either let itself be directly lured into future rewards by the United States, or expect to obtain rewards even without any U.S. promise.

Bandwagoning implies that the EU has a subordinate role, whereby it accepts pressure, and supports most policies conducted by the United States. According to this concept, the EU is likely to reach a common policy when it does not go against U.S. interests, and when the policy in question is of interest to the United States. Conversely, it is unlikely to adopt a policy which is contrary to U.S. interests: the United States can effectively be considered a de facto veto player by EU states. These hypotheses will be tested in order to clarify the role played by the United States when higher than LCD agreements in the CFSP field are reached.

Rational and Historical Institutionalism:
Entrepreneurship and Path-dependency

Rational institutionalism shares many assumptions with intergovernmentalism. The state is seen as the principal actor, and also as a unitary actor. It is a goal-seeking actor with interests that derive from its position in the international system. Rational-choice institutionalists, as opposed to sociological institutionalists, believe in the logic of consequentiality, which means that how an actor acts depends on what consequences an action will have on his or her goals. The actor first establishes those goals, then looks at the positions of the other member states, and finally looks for the best action. The question asked is: 'How I can achieve my goals?' or 'What is the best for me?' For rational institutionalists, as for intergovernmentalists, the preferences of a state are exogenous to EU institutions, that is, they are independent from any negotiation process within these institutions, and they are not changed by the fact that the state is part of a larger institution.

The main difference between intergovernmentalism and a rational-choice institutionalist approach is that the former focuses on relations among states and institutions in intergovernmental conferences, while the latter observes the day-to-day workings of institutions. The second difference is that intergovernmentalism believes that formal or informal institutions play a role which is expected by states, that is, institutions create credible commitments for states, and are used as instruments by states to pursue their national policies, whereas rational institutionalists argue the opposite, that is, institutions can take on a life of their own, and influence EU policies against the will of some of the states (Pollack 2001, 233). In short, rational institutionalism believes the state is the main actor, but that it can be constrained by institutions, which can develop more knowledge, information, and expertise than states, and which can use these to influence policy outcomes.

Rational-choice institutionalists assume that the Commission can be an entrepreneur and that it engages in agenda-setting activities (Peters 1994). Pollack (1997, 121–31) argues that it is able to play a role in the decision-making process under both qualified majority voting and unanimity rules. Rational institutionalists distinguish between the Commission's formal and informal agenda-setting power.

Formally, the Commission has limited means to influence an EU policy outcome. It is unlikely to play a role when unanimity is the rule. It must take states' preferences into consideration when it makes a proposal. Informally, however, the Commission can influence an EU policy outcome under a range of conditions (Pollack 1997; Pollack 2003, 51–2; Tallberg 2000, 849). These include when there is information asymmetry in favour of the Commission; when state representatives are uncertain of their positions; and when the Commission appeals to the values and beliefs of state representatives (Tallberg calls this 'framing' and 'cooptive justification'), rallies sub-national actors, links unpopular measures to popular ones ('packaging'), or asks specific governments to present its proposal as their own ('camouflage').

Rational institutionalists who have worked on EU issues have concentrated on analysing the effects of institutions on interstate behaviour in the first pillar framework, not in the second pillar framework. According to them, in the CFSP system, the Commission is unlikely to pursue its own interest rather than, or to the detriment of, that of the states (Pollack 2003, 26). The Commission's influence is considered to be limited because unanimity is the rule, and states have strong preferences in highly sensitive issues. In addition, before the ratification of the Lisbon Treaty, the Commission had a co-right of initiative with the states, and after Lisbon it has an indirect right of initiative through the High Representative who is also vice-president of the Commission. This means that it is not the only body responsible for setting the agenda; its proposals can be ignored, and other agendas may be proposed by states.

Nonetheless, the rational institutionalist hypothesis, which could be relevant in the CFSP field, is the following: the more there is information asymmetry in favour of the Commission, or the more the Commission can use packaging and camouflage methods, the more likely it is that a policy outcome will be influenced by the Commission, and a more than a LCD policy outcome will be reached.

Historical institutionalism explains the impact of formal and informal institutions on actors' preferences and decision-making processes over time (Hasenclever et al. 1996, 178; Powell 1994, 341). It posits that there can be a gap between the institutions state representatives want to create, and those they effectively create (Pierson 1996). States may become prisoners of their past actions (Keohane and Hoffmann 1990). As Pierson says:

> Actors may be in a strong initial position, seek to maximise their interests, and nevertheless carry out institutional and policy reforms that fundamentally transform their own positions (or those of their successors) in ways that are unanticipated and / or undesired. (1996, 131)

As a result, institutions do not always perform the way they were intended to when they were created. Pollack (1997, 107) argues that, for example: 'the Commission ... might gradually take on new roles that were not foreseen at the time of the creation.'

For historical institutionalists, once an institution is created, it is difficult for states to regain control of it. Institutions can 'lock-in,' or take

Table 1.4
Theories of International Relations and CFSP

Theory	Hypotheses
Intergovernmentalism	A common policy with no economic consequences for one or more big member states will only exist if it corresponds to the ideologies and personal commitments of leaders, and if it is perceived by leaders as having positive geopolitical implications for these states
	A common policy with economic consequences for one or more big member states will only exist if the economic consequences are positive for these states, and the geopolitical consequences are not negative
	A common policy will only exist when all the big member states agree, and it is likely to be an LCD agreement. No other actor plays a significant role in the making of this common policy
Sociological Institutionalism	A common policy can be reached when state officials are socialized and/or persuaded, especially by an authoritative member in the Council and in an in-camera setting. They change their preferences, and as a result also change their state's position: – Low level officials decide to take a decision in Brussels that goes against national instructions, and – High level officials change their state's position
Realism: On Bandwagoning	A common policy is reached when it does not go against U.S. interests, and when it is of interest to the United States
	Conversely, a policy which is contrary to U.S. interests is unlikely to be adopted: the United States can effectively be considered a de facto veto player by EU states
Rational Institutionalism	A common policy can be influenced by the Commission when: – there is information asymmetry in favour of the Commission – the Commission can use packaging and camouflage methods
Historical Institutionalism	A common policy can be constrained by past decisions. A path-dependency effect is created, whereby state representatives not only accept past formal and informal institutions, but also perpetuate them even if they go against their preferences

on a life of their own. This can happen for a number of reasons. The decision-making process usually requires unanimity to change an existing EU rule (Pierson 2000 refers to this as the 'inertia' of institutions); actors themselves often resist changes to institutions (Pollack 1996–7); a path-dependency effect can be created, whereby state representatives not only accept the authority of past formal and informal institutions, but will seek to perpetuate those institutions even if they go against their preferences.[17]

The historical insitutionalist hypothesis, which will be tested in this book, is the following: in the creation of a common policy, options can be constrained by past decisions. A path-dependency effect is created, whereby state representatives not only accept past formal and informal institutions, but also perpetuate them, even if they go against their preferences.

Table 1.4 sums up the main hypotheses presented in the theoretical approaches which have been discussed in this section.

This book tests the assumptions of intergovernmentalism, and draws on selected insights from realism and institutionalism, in order to demonstrate the deficiencies of intergovernmentalism as an explanation of how higher than LCD decisions are reached in the CFSP field. Appropriate alternative hypotheses will be put forward in the conclusion, which will give a comprehensive explanation of CFSP outcomes.

2 CFSP:
The Machinery of Decision-Making

This chapter aims to set out how CFSP works in practice: how the machinery in Brussels engages with Foreign Offices and Ministries of Defence in the capitals of Europe, how it works in tandem with institutional actors such as the Foreign Affairs Council, the Political and Security Committee and the High Representative, and how the military institutions of the EU and member states are called into play to carry out the policies it produces. The first section describes the status and function of CFSP within the policy-making structures of the EU. The second section highlights the difficult relations between states when making and implementing EU foreign and security policies, and the strains that process puts on EU solidarity.

The Place of CFSP within EU Policy-Making

The CFSP system is legally defined as a part of the EU's external action system (Title V, Treaty of Lisbon). The EU's external action system is itself part of the European foreign policy system, which is defined as encompassing EU external relations, member states' foreign policy, and the foreign policy of candidate countries.[18] It is important to note that the existence of policies produced within the CFSP system does not mean that the EU has a common foreign policy. Wallace defines a common foreign policy in the fullest sense as involving

> an integration of the different instruments of diplomacy, political, military, economic and cultural, with common financing and a decision-taking centre with the authority to guide and direct the whole structure – which would take the participating governments straight back into the embarrassing debate about transferring authority to a new European Union. (1983, 6)

Figure 2.1: CFSP and European Foreign Policy

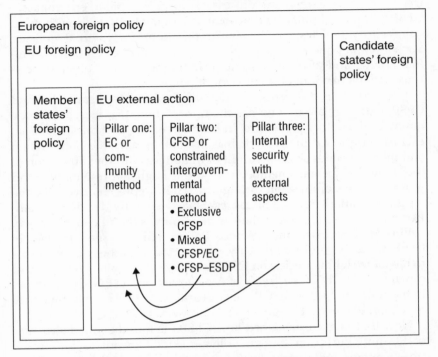

Note: The arrows represent the *passerelles* (bridges) between the three pillars: some pillar two and pillar three decisions can only be implemented in pillar one.[19]

A single foreign policy would require the following mechanisms: a single Ministry of Foreign Affairs and diplomatic service, with common missions abroad, a single intelligence service, a single set of armed services, a single development policy, and a single cultural policy. According to Hill (1993), the common policies developed within CFSP are of such a kind that the individual foreign policy arms of EU states remain independent, and will continue to do so. States continue to pursue their own national foreign policies in other forums.

The EU external action system covers external relations, security, and economic and development policies. These are created according to different decision-making rules, depending on which of the three pillars the Treaty on the EU sets them in. Figure 2.1 shows how the CFSP system fits into the broad framework of European foreign policy.

The first pillar deals with EC matters, that is, trade policies, aid policies, and the enlargement process. The second pillar encompasses
CFSP.[20] The third pillar (and to some extent the first) deals with internal security policies which have implications for external policies.
Such internal policies focus on police and judicial cooperation in criminal affairs, and also visas, asylum, immigration, and other policies
linked to the freedom of movement of peoples.

The two main differences in decision-making as regards EC and
CFSP matters relate to who has the right to initiate policy, and to the
nature of the voting procedure. In EC matters, the Commission has an
exclusive right of initiative, whereas in CFSP matters, the Commission
and member states share the right of initiative. With the ratification of
the Treaty of Lisbon, member states, the High Representative, and
indirectly the Commission through the High Representative, all have
a right of initiative for CFSP issues. States generally decide by qualified majority in pillar one, whereas unanimity is the rule in pillar two.

European Security and Defence Policy (ESDP) issues are legally
CFSP issues. No revision of treaty was necessary for the member states
to have the right to decide on ESDP issues, as that right is already laid
down in article 17 of the Treaty of Amsterdam on the European Union.
In the Treaty of Lisbon, ESDP is an integral part of CFSP, and the whole
of section two of that Treaty is taken up with it.

Now that I have established how CFSP fits into the broad structure
of EU and European foreign policy-making, I want to look more
closely at the CFSP system itself. A system is characterized by an interdependence of actors, regularities of interaction, the presence of formal
and informal rules/institutions, and processes which sustain or alter
the flow of demands and products of the system as a whole.[21] Table 2.1
covers these aspects under the following heads: actors, capabilities,
aims, and decision-making mechanisms. I shall take each of these categories in turn, beginning with the actors: member states acting at all
levels within the Council, Council Secretariat, High Representative,
and Commission.

Actors

The member states are the most important actors in the CFSP framework. For Patten (2000), 'foreign policy remains primarily a matter for
democratically elected member state governments.' This remains true
within the framework of the Treaty of Lisbon. A state is represented by

Table 2.1
The CFSP System

Actors	The European Council and the Council of the European Union, composed of – member states and the president – Secretariat, including the High Representative – the Commission
Capabilities	Military Economic Diplomatic: – information – planning – representation – negotiation – intelligence operations – leadership
Aims	A Common Foreign and Security Policy (CFSP) A Common European Security and Defence Policy (ESDP)
Decision-making mechanism	Decision-making process Rules Decisions: – Exclusively CFSP decisions: Actions, positions, and arrangements for the implementation of these actions and positions in the Treaty of Lisbon (previously known as declarations, common positions, joint actions, common strategies) – CFSP decisions followed by EC decisions – ESDP decisions

a multitude of different bodies and actors, based both in Brussels and in the national capitals.

The European Council stands at the apex of the CFSP system. It was created by the Paris Summit meeting in 1974, in order to 'ensure progress and overall consistency in the activities of the Communities and in the work of political cooperation.' It consists of the heads of state and government, together with the president of the Commission. With the ratification of the Treaty of Lisbon, the president of the Commission is joined by the president of the European Council, who serves for a term of two and a half years, renewable once, and by the High Representative. Under Lisbon, the task of the European Council is to identify the strategic interests and objectives of the Union. The European Council meets at least twice every six months, and under Lisbon, when the situation so requires, the president also is entitled to convene a special meeting. The Lisbon Treaty, then, strengthens the powers of the president as against those of the member states. This is precisely what small member states are uneasy about. Alexandr Vondra, the Czech Deputy Prime Minister for European affairs, explained that, with a permanent European President and Foreign Minister, 'people fear ... this power management' (*New York Times*, 14/02/09). The appointment of Herman Van Rompuy, former Belgian prime minister, as first president of the European Union seems to show that Big Member States might also be uneasy with the idea of a strong president, precisely from a Big Member State.

Within the Council, the General Affairs and External Relations Council (GAC or GAERC), or under Lisbon, the Foreign Affairs Council (FAC), is the body which usually decides on CFSP matters.[22] It meets once a month. The GAC/FAC consists of a Minister for Foreign Affairs from each member state. Issues discussed there rarely go, at least formally, to the European Council level. The GAC/FAC either merely accepts decisions taken at a lower level, or decides on contentious issues that could not be agreed upon at the lower level. Under the Treaty of Lisbon, the High Representative presides over the Foreign Affairs Council, which consequently becomes a more important body. This council is responsible for elaborating the Union's external action on the basis of strategic guidelines laid down by the European Council, and for ensuring that the Union's action is consistent.

There are three major levels below the GAC/FAC, that is, the Political and Security Committee (PSC), the group of External Relations Counsellors (the RELEX Group), and all the working groups. First and foremost, there is the PSC, which consists of the member states' ambassadors in Brussels.[23] The PSC deals with the difficult points of foreign policy issues, such as security matters. Under the Lisbon Treaty, it exercises, under the direction of the FAC and of the High Representative, political control and strategic direction of crisis management operations. It is, up to a point, the driving force and the guiding body behind EU foreign policy. However, in practice, it can never take a decision, as all sensitive issues not agreed on must be sent up to be dealt with by the FAC. The PSC meets at least twice a week and its members are based permanently in Brussels. It also meets once every four months in a wider framework, with three non-EU NATO states, Turkey, Iceland, and Norway. The *Comité des Représentants Permanents*

(Coreper), composed of the permanent representatives of the member states, is the body which advises on all EU policies, including legal, financial, or institutional matters, before they are sent to the FAC/GAC. However, there is a tacit understanding that the Coreper plays no role in CFSP issues.

Beneath the PSC, the RELEX Group, formerly known as CFSP counsellors, plays a crucial role. RELEX counsellors prepare PSC meetings by taking the temperature of issues, and they implement FAC decisions. They discuss institutional, legal, and financial points. They have two hats: political and economic. Defining policy is not a part of their role: according to one of my interviewees, 'the political issues should be decided elsewhere, through the COREU network or at the PSC.'[24] But in practice, they can. They meet on a more or less daily basis.

Finally, under the RELEX Group, numerous working groups discuss foreign affairs issues, help prepare PSC meetings, and implement GAC/FAC decisions.[25] The frequency of their meetings depends on the issue discussed; they too can meet once a day.

In parallel with these structures that deal with traditional foreign policy issues, the GAC also created institutions in the ESDP framework, in order to address issues of crisis management. EU defence ministers have met at the Council of the European Union since 2002. Their meetings have always been chaired by the EU's High Representative and not by the state holding the EU presidency, and they can include non-EU states.

Under the level of defence ministers, state officials who work on civilian and military issues also meet at the Council of the European Union. In the civilian sphere, the Committee for Civilian Aspects of Crisis Management (CIVCOM) was created in May 2000. This committee gives advice on the political aspects of non-military crisis management and conflict prevention. In June 2007, the Council decided to establish the Civilian Planning and Conduct Capability (CPCC). CPCC provides assistance and support to CIVCOM in the planning and implementation of civilian ESDP operations.

In the military sphere, the Feira European Council of June 2000 created the following institutional structures: the European Union Military Committee (EUMC), which meets once a week; the military committee working group (EUMCWG), which meets twice a week; and the Politico-Military working group (PMG), responsible for examining the politico-military aspects of all proposals within the framework of the CFSP, and for assisting the PSC, which meets once a week.

The European Union Military Committee is composed of the chiefs of defence, represented by their military officials. It is responsible for providing the Political and Security Committee with military advice and recommendations on all military matters within the EU. The Chairman of the EUMC attends meetings of the GAC/FAC when decisions with defence implications are to be taken. The EUMC exercises military direction of all military activities within the EU framework, including the EU Military Staff. This last body, composed of more than 200 officials, provides military expertise and support to the military working group and the Military Committee. It supports the conduct of EU-led military crisis management operations. It also performs early warning operations, situation assessment and strategic planning for Petersberg tasks, including identification of European national and multinational forces and implementation of policies and decisions as directed by the EUMC.[26]

The head of all of the above groups in the Council is the presidency, which is held by a member state. The Treaty of Lisbon introduces two exceptions: a president elected for two and a half years who chairs the European Council, and the High Representative who chairs the Foreign Affairs Council. The presidency acts as a mediator. It takes initiatives, convenes meetings, sets the agenda, builds a consensus, acts as a spokesman for the member states, manages and conducts consultations with third countries outside the EU, and implements decisions taken (see Hayes-Renshaw and Wallace 1996). Its role is very similar to that of the Commission under the first pillar. A presidency has a chance to show its efficiency, to impose its priorities for developing a European foreign policy, and to have more visibility vis-à-vis international actors. In CFSP issues, my study will show that the presidency can play a role in determining the agenda and in constraining state positions, by giving its own interpretation of the implementation of general CFSP decisions.

Figure 2.2 shows the actors who take decisions in the CFSP system, and the paths of decision-making. The general orientations of the CFSP are first given by the European Council (indicated in thick lines). Thereafter, foreign affairs ministers instruct their national officials to discuss foreign affairs with their European colleagues. Policy is first negotiated at the lowest level (working group) before progressively seeking acceptance at the higher levels and finally GAC level (and sometimes at the European Council level, in the case of disagreements among the foreign affairs ministers).

Figure 2.2: Decision-Makers in the CFSP System

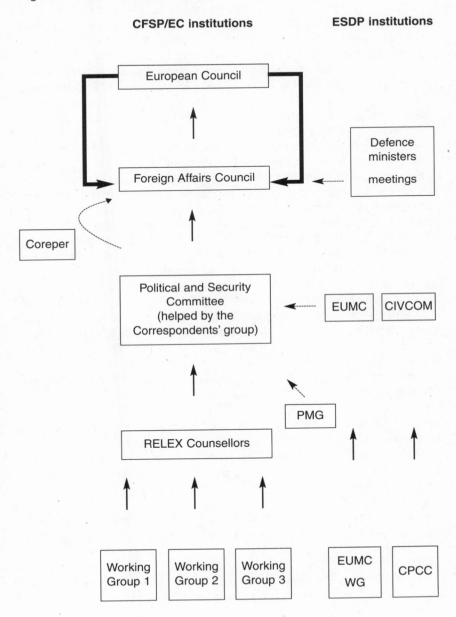

Three bodies help state representatives when they negotiate CFSP issues at the Council: the Directorate General E (DG E), the office of the High Representative, and the Policy Unit.[27] The principal Secretariat for CFSP issues is the DG E, which is composed of both EU staff and seconded officials who have been temporarily lent by states to the EU institutions. DG E is divided into two: one half deals with economic external relations, and the other with CFSP matters. DG E is responsible for drafting the texts of the presidency. It also deals with foreign policy, the defence aspects of external relations, and civilian crisis management and coordination.[28]

The High Representative enables the EU to have a 'phone number.' The U.S. Secretary of State, Henry Kissinger, apparently requested a phone number from Europe in the early 1970s, at a time when Denmark, a small state, was holding the presidency. What mattered to him less was who he could talk to than what the person at the other end of the line could tell him and the influence this person could wield (De Schoutheete, 25/03/01). As early as 1981, Altiero Spinelli, who founded the European Federalist Movement, had already called for the appointment of a high-ranking statesman to represent the EC in discussions with Washington and Moscow. In 1999, the choice of Dr Solana as the first High Representative of the European Union showed the will of the states to appoint an influential personality, as he had been Secretary General of NATO from 1995 until 1999, during the Balkan crisis.[29] (One of my interviewees referred to Dr Solana as 'Mr Bomb.') The post of High Representative has, then, 'heightened the element of diplomatic personality' (Hill 2001, 328). The Treaty of Lisbon states:

> The High Representative shall represent the Union for matters relating to the common foreign and security policy. He or she shall conduct political dialogue with third parties on the Union's behalf and shall express the Union's position in international organisations and at international conferences. (article 13a)

His or her telephone number is still only one of many, and a clash of phone numbers to call for information on European foreign policy is still likely. Article 9b stipulates:

> The President of the European Council shall, at his or her level and in that capacity, ensure the external representation of the Union on issues con-

cerning its common foreign and security policy, without prejudice to the powers of the High Representative of the Union for Foreign Affairs and Security Policy.

A clash is also possible with the European Commission, as it is responsible for ensuring the Union's external representation, though with the exception of CFSP issues. The Lisbon Treaty may create yet more numbers, as the High Representative has to share the representation of EU foreign policy with three other authorities: the Heads of States of the major EU states, the president of the Commission, and the president of the European Council. The High Representative should at least have more political visibility than the previous High Representative, who had to compete for leadership in foreign affairs with a President who changed every six months. However, the current High Representative nominated in 2009, Baroness Cathy Ashton, might find it difficult to take the leadership of the EU's foreign policy for the following reasons: she was trade commissioner for one year, she has never been elected to any office, and she does not have political legitimacy.

With the ratification of the Treaty of Lisbon, in addition to representing the EU abroad, the High Representative is required to preside over the Foreign Affairs Council, act as one of the Vice-Presidents of the Commission, and take part in the activities of the European Council (articles 9b and 9e). The task of the High Representative, accountable both to the member states and to the Commission, may well be an impossible one. For Wallace:

> [The High Representative cannot] gain and retain the trust of national foreign ministers in the Council while also respecting the different collegial loyalties of the Commission. Both the Commission president and the Council president will demand the foreign minister's respect and attention. (*Financial Times*, 11/11/03)

The High Representative is responsible for contributing proposals towards the preparation of the common foreign and security policy, and for ensuring implementation of the decisions adopted by the European Council and the Council (article 13a, Treaty of Lisbon). Under the Treaty of Lisbon, the European Council could ask the High Representative to design a policy which would only require a qualified majority to be accepted.

The Policy Planning and Early Warning Unit, commonly shortened to the Policy Unit, is extremely small compared to the Pentagon's planning centre, which employs 400 officials. When first created, it was composed of four members from the Council of the European Union, one from the European Commission, one from the Western European Union, and fifteen seconded officials from the member states.[30] It has now grown into eight task forces: Mediterranean and Middle East; Africa; Eastern Europe and Central Asia; Asia and Oceania; Western Balkans; UN and Latin America; Horizontal security issues and conflict prevention; and ESDP.

The Policy Unit is regarded as the Political Cabinet of the High Representative. It represents an added-value to DG E, as it receives more information from the member states and the Commission's delegations than DG E does. The Policy Unit is in very close contact with the European capitals. It receives not only material sent through the COREU but also national telegrams sent by the embassies of the member states, which include summaries, reports, and analyses. It produces reports: it made, for instance, a list of all the financial aid given by EU states to the Balkans. However, it has not always been prepared for international crises. It had no report ready on Afghanistan, for example, when the terrorist attack on the the World Trade Center took place on 11 September 2001.

The EU Joint Situation Centre (SitCen) was set up on 1 January 2003 by the Policy Unit in order to address the issue of readiness. SitCen brings together the expertise of civilian and military staff from the Policy Unit and the military Situation Centre. It monitors and assesses crises worldwide on a twenty-four-hour basis. It provides support for the EU High Representative, the PSC, and the EUMC. It also aims to improve cooperation between member states in the field of intelligence.[31]

The High Representative also is helped by a network of special representatives, who provide expertise, policy formulation, and visibility to the EU. The work of the special representatives relates to the following areas and issues: the African Union (since 2007); the South Caucasus and Central Asia (2006); Sudan and Moldova (2005); Afghanistan and Bosnia and Herzegovina (2002); the Former Yugoslav Republic of Macedonia (FYROM), and the Stability Pact for South Eastern Europe (2001); Kosovo, and the coordination of the process of stability and good neighbourliness in South-East Europe, known as the Royaumont Process (1999); the Federal Republic of Yugoslavia (1998); the implementation of the EU assistance program for the Palestinian authority (1997); the Middle East Peace Process; and the African Great Lakes (1996).

With the Treaty of Lisbon, the High Representative is able to rely on a European External Action Service. This service 'shall work in cooperation with the diplomatic services of the member states and shall comprise officials from relevant departments of the General Secretariat of the Council and of the Commission as well as staff seconded from national diplomatic services of the member states' (article 13a).

Finally, the European Commission is associated with the work carried out in the CFSP framework. The Commission has its own crisis room, equivalent to the Council's situation centre. The Directorate-General for External Relations (DG Relex) has a CFSP Directorate, with a Security Unit and a Crisis Management and Conflict Prevention unit. It also has a CFSP counsellor and a European Correspondent's unit.

The European Commission has been associated with political cooperation at all levels since the London Report in 1981. It has been linked with the COREU network since 1982. The Commission participates at all levels of the CFSP decision-making institutions, that is, in all the committees. Its presence in ESDP structures has not always been evident. It was not invited to the first meeting of the military committee (EUMC), and it had to be content with receiving only the agendas of the meetings of the military bodies, despite the fact that the military committee's policy can have a marked effect on the rest of EC policy, and that the Commission itself argued strenuously for its own participation. Germany, Italy, and Spain agreed with the Commission, but France and the United Kingdom did not. They argued that the Commission had no military expertise, and that there was no need for a civilian body to sit in the room. However, since 2005, following the wording of the Treaty and previous Commission involvement in EPC and CFSP issues, the Commission participates fully in all EUMC meetings (Spence 2006, 374).

The Treaty of Lisbon might give the Commission the opportunity to represent the EU as a whole, as under this Treaty, the High Representative for Foreign Affairs and Security Policy is responsible for the conduct and coordination of all aspects of the Union's external action.

The role attributed to the Commission in the CFSP decision-making process by successive EU Treaties is not the same as the role it has in the EC decision-making process. There are two main differences.

First, while in EC affairs the European Commission has an exclusive right of initiative, in the CFSP field the Commission has an indirect right of initiative via the High Representative which is shared with the member states, and has no effect on CFSP decisions, as unanimity is the rule, and as states can make their own proposals. According to article 15a of the Treaty of Lisbon:

> Any member state, the High Representative of the Union for Foreign Affairs and Security Policy, or the High Representative with the Commission's support, may refer any question relating to the common foreign and security policy to the Council, and may submit to it initiatives or proposals as appropriate.

Second, the Commission enjoys important prerogatives in EC matters when it implements EC decisions, as it is responsible for the execution of EC law. In the CFSP field, the Commission only implements CFSP decisions when EU states make a specific demand.

The European Commission contributes ideas into the non-military areas of CFSP. It has no military or nuclear means, expertise, or responsibilities. It is a civilian body, as it is not the responsibility of the president of the Commission to send troops abroad. However, the Commission has been developing its military knowledge. Both Jacques Santer, then president of the Commission, and Emma Bonino, EU Commissioner for Humanitarian Aid (ECHO), visited NATO Headquarters in the mid-1990s. This was surprising, as the Commission was, by its nature, not supposed to be involved in military matters. This led to the presence of the Commission in NATO exercises on the prevention of weapons of mass destruction, and to collaboration between the Commission and NATO on matters such as the funding of Internet communication infrastructure in countries outside the EU (NATO Documents, 02/05/07, 15/04/08).

Capabilities

The CFSP system has few financial means of its own. In 2006, approximately 60 million were spent under the CFSP budget (European Union Document 2006 General Budget), divided as follows: conflict prevention and crisis management (3.5 million); non-proliferation and disarmament (17 million); conflict resolution, verification, support for the peace process, and stabilization (32 million); emergency measures

(1 million); preparatory and follow-up measures (400,000); and European Union Special Representatives (7 million). At the same time, the EC budget for external affairs was 5.33 billion. The resources for action lie either with the EC or at the national level. The Commission is responsible for most of EU foreign policy financing, whereas member states have most of the military structures. The EU has civilian, economic, and diplomatic resources, and is developing its own military capabilities.

In 2000, EU states decided to equip the EU with civilian crisis management capabilities, that is, capabilities to deal with police-related matters, with strengthening the rule of law and civilian administration, and with civil protection. The first crisis management operation was a police mission (EUPM), which was sent to Bosnia and Herzegovina in January 2003 to follow up on the United Nations International Police Task Force. Following this, the EU conducted police and security missions in Macedonia (EUPAT), in the Democratic Republic of the Congo (EUPOL Kinshasa and EUSEC RD Congo), in the Palestinian territories (EUPOL COPPS), in Afghanistan (EUPOL Afghanistan), and in Guinea-Bissau (EU SSR Guinea-Bissau). It also conducted Rule of Law Missions in Georgia (EUJUST THEMIS), in Iraq (EUJUST LEX), and in Kosovo (EULEX Kosovo). Other EU-led missions were the Support mission to AMIS II in Sudan/Darfur, the Aceh Monitoring Mission, the Border Assistance Mission in Rafah (EUBAM Rafah), and the autonomous civilian monitoring mission in Georgia (EUMM Georgia).

In 2008, member states undertook to provide the EU with more than 5,000 police officers, 631 officers responsible for strengthening the rule of law (prosecutors, judges, prison officers), 565 experts on civilian administration, approximately 5,000 staff for civilian protection, and 500 officials for the monitoring of crises areas (EU Factsheet, June 2008). Furthermore, EU states have agreed to deploy a military operation against acts of piracy and armed robbery off the Somali coast in 2008 (EU NAVFOR Somalia or operation ATALANTA).

In order to improve the crisis management capability in sensitive areas, Spain, Italy, France, the Netherlands, and Portugal created the European Gendarmerie Force in 2004. This European Gendarmerie Force has an initial reaction capability of about 800 men within 30 days. The CFSP has succeeded in conducting military missions both within and outside Europe, but member states and EU military capabilities remain limited. The EU has undertaken five military missions since 2003: two in the Balkans (Operation Concordia in Macedonia in 2003, and EUFOR Althea in Bosnia and Herzegovina since 2004), and three in Africa (in the DRC, operation Artemis in 2003 and EUFOR RD Congo in 2006; and in Chad and Central African Republic, EUFOR TCHAD/RCA in 2008–9). However, all these military missions relied on EU states' own capabilities. They were paid for on an ad hoc basis by direct contributions from EU states. The paradox here is that the states which agree with an EU operation and send their own troops abroad, therefore facing a potential human cost, are also those which have to finance this operation, agreeing to taking on a financial burden.

The EU has limited military equipment, especially for long-term missions and for missions which take place in countries geographically far from Europe. At the national level, the defence budgets of France and the United Kingdom, the two major EU states in terms of military expenditure and capability, increased only slightly in the period 2003–7. In 2003, the EU's Artemis operation in the Democratic Republic of the Congo relied on Ukrainian Antonov transport aircrafts. In 2006, however, the European Force EUFOR RD Congo deployed the following military resources: eight cargo planes C-130 and C-160, and a Turkish Hercules in Gabon; three German CH-53 helicopters and four Belgian Unmanned Aerial Vehicles (UAVs) at Kinshasa-N'Dolo; and three French f1CR Mirage planes based in N'Djamena (see Gegout 2007). In 2007 and 2008, EU operations, such as those in Chad and the Central African Republic, suffered from a lack of helicopter availability.

The EU is still struggling to find the necessary equipment to deploy troops. Currently, there is no lack of medium-sized transport aircraft, with about thirty A-340s and KC-10s, and about 270 C-130s and C-160s, and appropriate maritime transport vessels are available; but the EU still has to use the Ukrainian Antonov 124-100 for heavy transport duties. This should change when the UK's Royal Air Force Boeing C-17 cargo planes enter into service, and when European states acquire the long-range air transport Airbus A 400M, which should be in service in 2010. It has to be noted, however, that states can be reluctant to supply resources to the EU. For instance, this was the case with the United Kingdom and Germany, who did not provide airlift capability for the European mission in Chad. Up-to-date intelligence is still needed, despite the development of new optical and radar satellite equipment (Helios II, Sar-Lupe, and Cosmo-Skymed).

At the EU level, member states have committed themselves to creating independent EU capabilities. Following the signature of the Amsterdam Treaty, the Helsinki European Council in December 1999 created the headline goal of a European Rapid Reaction Force, to be set up by 2003, comprising 60,000 troops deployable within sixty days for a mission of at least a year. EU states revised their ambition in 2004, and decided on EU capabilities on a smaller scale, with the setting up of fifteen battlegroups for the EU to use whenever necessary. Full operating capability of the battle groups, made up of 1,500 ground forces, was achieved in 2007. Two battlegroups are now on permanent call, and the states taking part in them change every six months. However, these battlegroups were used neither in the DRC in 2006, when they were already operational, nor in Chad and the Central African Republic (CAR) in 2008–9.

EU operations can be managed by one of five EU Operational Headquarters in Paris in France, Potsdam in Germany, Larissa in Greece, Rome in Italy, and Northwood in the United Kingdom. As well, the EU can rely on the EU Operations Centre based in Brussels.

Diplomacy, of course, comes before military action. While economic instruments, such as trade and aid, are developed strictly under the first pillar framework, states decide within the CFSP framework upon the setting or lifting of sanctions, as well as economic and arms embargoes against a third party.

In terms of diplomatic capability, the EU is progressively acquiring the elements of a ministry for foreign affairs. With the Lisbon Treaty, the EU is creating a European diplomatic service. This is likely to facilitate coordination between the Council Secretariat and the Commission. It could also help rationalize EU states' diplomatic services; already in 2002, the former High Representative Javier Solana remarked that there were more than twice the number of diplomats in five times the number of embassies compared to the United States. There is a clear effort to coordinate action between foreign affairs and defence ministers at EU level. The EU is developing military planning capabilities through the use of European headquarters. There is also apparently some cooperation and information exchange between member states' military intelligence services.

Diplomacy is not only about institutional structures; it is also about action and implementation. The EU uses dialogues, confidential démarches and Troika missions, and has a monitoring role on issues such as elections, human and minority rights, and freedom of the press. The Troika, established by the Treaty of Amsterdam, brought together the minister for foreign affairs holding the presidency, the High Representative, and the European commissioner in charge of external relations. The presidency can also be assisted, where necessary, by the representative of the future presidency. This Troika has disappeared with the Lisbon Treaty, as the High Representative is the only representative of the Union for matters relating to the common foreign and security policy. The role of the High Representative and his or her staff in CFSP outcomes can be considerable. The High Representative has a role both within the EU's institutional structure and in the external world that goes beyond his or her official role.

Internally, the High Representative is considered the twenty-ninth person at the table, in addition to the twenty-seven states and the Commission. She or he acts as a kind of secretariat for the member states. She or he has to give assessments of crisis situations. For instance, former High Representative Javier Solana gave advice to EU states on the policy to adopt towards Iran in 2006. He recommended targeted sanctions such as visa bans on political leaders, tighter controls on exports of technology that could be used to develop nuclear weapons, and an arms embargo. The High Representative also acts as a thermometer within the EU, as she or he is in the unique position of understanding each EU state's positions on foreign policy issues. Before European Councils, former High Representative Dr Solana visited all the EU capitals with the president to discuss all informal and formal agendas. Finally, the High Representative plays a motor role, acting like a minister for foreign affairs in the sense that a minister for foreign affairs 'tends to take the initiative, to outline proposals and to invite responses from colleagues' (Hill 2003, 57). According to an interviewee who worked directly for Javier Solana, 'He change[d] the perspectives of the EU's foreign policy.'

In the external world, the High Representative contributes to the creation of a European diplomatic presence outside the European Union. Former High Representative Dr Solana developed three main axes of negotiation at both formal and informal levels: with the big EU states and the United States, towards the Balkans and the EU neighbourhood, and towards the Middle East.[32] Dr Solana established specific links with the big EU states and the United States; he had an informal seat at the United Nations Security Council, and this was institutionalized through the Treaty of Lisbon. In the Balkans, he had a mediation role in Macedonia, and brokered an agreement under the auspices of the EU, the United States, and NATO in 2001. He also thrashed out a settlement between Serbia and Montenegro in March 2002.

As regards EU neighbourhood policy, Dr Solana was especially active in promoting close links between the EU and Ukraine, and in solving the Orange Revolution crisis. In winter 2004–5, the Ukrainian presidential election was considered unfair, and contested by the opposition. It led to large-scale demonstrations. Ukraine's Supreme Court ordered a new vote, the elections were then declared fair and free by international observers, and the leader of the opposition, Viktor Yushchenko, became president. The former U.S. Ambassador to Ukraine, Steven Pifer, argued in October 2007 that 'the presence of European negotiators proved key to launching the negotiating process, kept pressure on the Ukrainian negotiators to make progress, and provided a strong disincentive against the use of force' (Woodrow Wilson International Center for Scholars, 15/10/07). The advantage provided by Dr Solana, he said, was credibility. This credibility was due to two factors: pre-existing personal relationships, and the attraction power of the EU, as the EU is 'an institution that all Ukrainian roundtable participants agreed they wanted to see Ukraine join.' (Kopstein [2006, 92] argues, however, that the role of EU diplomacy in Ukraine must not be overstated. He sees civil society and non-governmental organizations [NGOs], mainly funded by the United States, as the main actors in the Orange Revolution.)

Javier Solana was particularly active in the Middle East Peace Process. He was part of the Sharm el Sheik fact-finding committee (the Mitchell Commission), which investigated the origin of the crisis in the Middle East following Sharon's visit to Temple Mount in September 2000. The other members were the U.S. former Senator, George Mitchell; the former Head of State of Turkey, Suleiman Demirel; the Norwegian Foreign Affairs Minister, Thorbjoern Jagland; and the former U.S. Senator, Warren Rudman. On 30 April 2001, this committee stated that 'the Sharon visit did not cause the second intifada. But it was poorly timed and the *provocative effect* should have been foreseen; indeed it was foreseen by those who urged that the visit be prohibited' (Mitchell Committee Report, 30/04/01; my emphasis).

Dr Solana was also at the origin of the creation of the Quartet, developed for reviews and close consultations on the Middle East. The Quartet is composed of the United Nations Secretary General, the Russian foreign minister, the U.S. Secretary of State, and for the EU, the foreign minister of the state holding the presidency, the High Representative for European Common Foreign and Security Policy, and the European Commissioner for External Affairs. The High Representative was also part of the EU delegation sent to the Middle East in early January 2009 in order to re-establish a ceasefire between Israel and Gaza.

Informally, Dr Solana insisted on the importance of discreet negotiations. He had negotiators who worked in the field and who seemed to have an impact on crisis resolution. As early as 1998 in the Middle East, a British security expert, Alistair Crooke, was appointed counter-terrorism liaison officer between the Palestinian Authority and the European Union. Alistair Crooke provided an exceptional link between Israel and Hamas. He mediated an end to the Israeli army's sieges of both Yasser Arafat's compound in Ramallah and the Church of the Nativity in Bethlehem in 2002. This was a rare example of EU intelligence activity and action at a time when neither the EU states nor the United States were visible on the ground.

Dr Solana also became, together with the Big Three states of France, the United Kingdom, and Germany, a major mediator in Europe's relations with Iran since 2004. He presented the following three advantages. Internally to the EU, he represented all EU states and not just the Big Three. This was a major issue for small states, which asked for the inclusion of the High Representative in the negotiations (Sauer 2007, 10). In Iran itself, he was seen as a neutral actor as opposed to a negative actor such as the United States (Chubin 2006, 66). Vis-à-vis all international actors, he had credibility based on his connections with Iranian negotiators. As a consequence, he represented not only the EU but also the entire international community when he discussed the nuclear issue with Iran. For instance, in 2006, he presented Iran with a proposal agreed on by the five permanent members of the UN Security Council and Germany. There are, however, drawbacks to the involvement of the High Representative. He or she can give no guarantees, and there is no certainty that the EU will back his or her promises. Another problem is that '[o]ne voice could represent a loss of subtlety, a need to choose a single European policy. A pluralistic approach, perhaps more difficult to manage, gives Europe the potential to play a more subtle game' (Weiler 1988, 253).

To conclude: the High Representative, by drafting policy proposals, can induce member states to discuss issues they would not themselves have put on the agenda. But he or she cannot force states to reach a common position on these issues. The High Representative's main form of autonomous action is as a mediator in third countries outside the EU. This kind of action gives visibility and the possibility of diplomatic success to the EU. However, the High Representative's mediatory role can only be limited; one person cannot mediate all the world's conflicts on behalf of the EU. Third countries might not always be willing or interested in having the High Representative as a mediator. Moreover, the High Representative 'has no authority of his own' (Crowe 2003, 542). Member states can always limit or oversee the mediatory role. This is still true within the framework of the Lisbon Treaty and with the current High Representative, Baroness Cathy Ashton.

The EU is regularly criticized for the slow process of its CFSP operations. Former High Representative Dr Solana (House of Commons document, 20/01/08), for instance, admitted that in his years in this post, he had 'been frustrated by the difficulty in delivering and the rhythm with which the European Union delivers.' The next section highlights the constraints under which EU states work in their formal and informal negotiations within the CFSP system, in relation to its aims and decision-making process.

Aims

The aim of CFSP was spelled out in the European Security Strategy of 2003. This strategy addressed the concern of Javier Solana (Solana, EU document, 23/05/02), who emphasized that 'a more effective Europe in the foreign policy field requires that we clearly identify our common interests, that we have a consistent and clear message, and that we have the policy instruments to support this message.'

According to article 10a of the Treaty of Lisbon, the objectives of the Common Foreign and Security Policy are as follows:

1. ... to seek to advance in the wider world: democracy, the rule of law, the universality and indivisibility of human rights and fundamental freedoms, respect for human dignity, the principles of equality and solidarity, and respect for the principles of the United Nations Charter and international law.
2. to: (a) safeguard its [of the European Union] values, fundamental interests, security, independence and integrity; (b) consolidate and support democracy, the rule of law, human rights and the princi-

ples of international law; (c) preserve peace, prevent conflicts and strengthen international security, in accordance with the purposes and principles of the United Nations Charter, with the principles of the Helsinki Final Act and with the aims of the Charter of Paris, including those relating to external borders; (d) foster the sustainable economic, social and environmental development of developing countries, with the primary aim of eradicating poverty; (e) encourage the integration of all countries into the world economy, including through the progressive abolition of restrictions on international trade; (f) help develop international measures to preserve and improve the quality of the environment and the sustainable management of global natural resources, in order to ensure sustainable development; (g) assist populations, countries and regions confronting natural or man-made disasters; and (h) promote an international system based on stronger multilateral cooperation and good global governance.

However, in practice, despite this effort to agree on common EU aims, it appears that reaching CFSP decisions together remains a difficult task.

The EU also has an explicit aim in the ESDP field. At the Cologne European Council in June 1999, EU leaders agreed that 'the Union must have the capacity for autonomous action, backed by credible military forces, the means to decide to use them, and the readiness to do so, in order to respond to international crises without prejudice to actions by NATO' (Cologne European Council, 04/06/99).

The EU does not have a common long-term defence objective. The defence of a political entity means ensuring, in all circumstances and against all forms of aggression, the security and the integrity of a territory and the life of the people (Perret 1995, 83). The Lisbon Treaty stipulates that there is 'an obligation of aid and assistance [to other member states facing an external security threat] by all the means in their power, in accordance with article 51 of the United Nations Charter.' However, still according to the treaty, 'this shall not prejudice the specific character of the security and defence policy of certain member states' (article 28a). The treaty adds a 'solidarity clause,' according to which 'the Union and its member states shall act jointly in a spirit of solidarity if a member state is the object of a terrorist attack or the victim of a natural or man-made disaster' (article 188r).

CFSP–ESDP aims are broad and vague. There are no clear guidelines for foreign policy on highly sensitive matters, such as military intervention within or outside EU borders.

The Decision-Making Process

White and Clarke (1989, 2) believe that 'an understanding of the way in which policy is made is central to an understanding of the substance of foreign policy.' To understand EU policy-making, the decision-making process and different types of rules and decisions must be analysed.[33]

In the CFSP decision-making process, systematic cooperation, exchange of information, and consultation on all foreign policy subjects are required during all phases between the actors, both institutions and states. No unilateral decision on the part of EU actors is expected. The basic rule in the CFSP decision-making process is unanimity: all EU states therefore have a right of veto. There are, however, four cases where qualified majority voting (QMV) is the rule: (1) when adopting a decision defining a Union action or position on the basis of a decision of the European Council relating to the Union's strategic interests and objectives; (2) when adopting any decision implementing a decision defining a Union action or position; (3) when appointing a special representative; and (4) since the Treaty of Lisbon,

> when adopting a decision defining a Union action or position, on a proposal which the High Representative of the Union for Foreign Affairs and Security Policy has presented following a specific request from the European Council, made on its own initiative or that of the High Representative. (article 15b)

Qualified majority has been used several times since the Treaty of Amsterdam came into force. It was used for the first time for a decision concerning Russia, on the issue of nuclear disarmament. It was also used for a visa ban policy towards the Balkans. According to one of my interviewees, the threat of the use of qualified majority is a positive instrument. When state representatives discuss a draft text, they have to be extremely careful about what they want to exclude from it, and about letting vague terms slip in. Once a text has been voted on under the rule of unanimity, its implementation might subsequently be voted on simply by qualified majority: as a result, representatives would no longer have the possibility of vetoing the final policy outcome. The initial text might, for example, have failed to specify a time frame with deadlines, or to give clear definitions; with a negotiation which requires a qualified majority vote, member states no longer have the power to determine these crucial items.

The unanimity rule prevails when a state declares important reasons of national policy are at stake in a particular issue, and when decisions to be taken have military or defence implications. The requirement for unanimity is considered counterproductive by both academics and EU officials: a state has no incentive to compromise if it knows it has a right of veto, and it blocks the decision until it succeeds in securing its own position.[34] Young states that '[t]he operation of unanimity rule, by itself, engenders incentives for ambitious or greedy actors to hold out in the hope that others will offer significant concessions to avoid stalemate and the resultant outcome of no agreement' (1991, 284). As a result, a decision is either not taken at all, or it is reduced to the lowest common denominator, 'where the most reluctant actor determines the pace and level of achievement' (Elgstroem and Joensson 2000, 690).

CFSP decisions are categorized in this study into three groups: exclusively CFSP decisions, mixed CFSP–EC decisions, or CFSP–ESDP decisions. My categorization is different from that found in the treaties. The Treaty of Lisbon proposes three categories of decisions: a decision which defines a Union action; a decision which defines a Union position; and a decision which implements previous decisions. These replace the following terms of previous treaties, none of which had any clear definition: declarations, common positions, joint actions, and common strategies.

Declarations (not defined under Amsterdam) covered all the geographical regions of the globe. They were issued before or after a crisis, that is, pre-emptively or in reaction. The Treaty of Amsterdam defined joint actions and common positions: joint actions addressed specific situations where operational action was deemed to be required (article 14), and common positions defined the approach of the Union to a particular matter of a geographical or thematic nature (article 15). Joint actions were used for support and aid to third countries, creation of posts of special envoys to third countries or regions, and action in the field of security issues. Common positions were issued for the creation of embargoes concerning third countries; the encouraging of third parties to either sign or ratify international treaties; and the specification of internal CFSP mechanisms (for instance, the EU link with the Western European Union). Common strategies were decided upon by the European Council by unanimity, and implemented by the Council by qualified majority. Three common strategies were created: the first concerns Russia (June 1999), the second Ukraine (December 1999), and the third the Mediterranean region (June 2000). They were widely criticized because they were merely declaratory.

All these types of decisions are either exclusively CFSP decisions, mixed CFSP–EC decisions, or CFSP–ESDP decisions. Exclusively CFSP decisions are taken by either the European Council or the General Affairs Council. Mixed CFSP–EC decisions require the use of first pillar instruments to implement a CFSP decision, either for sanctions against third countries (article 188k, previously article 301) or for the financing of CFSP operations (article 28 TEC). Finally, CFSP–ESDP decisions are taken by either the European Council or the General Affairs Council. They concern such decisions as the creation of a European crisis management force or a police force.

In the context of the decision-making process, the question of financing CFSP operations raises its own problems. Since the Amsterdam treaty, most CFSP operations are financed by the Union budget, previously known as the budget of the European Communities: the first pillar is therefore responsible for both first and second pillar external relations' expenditure, except for such expenditure arising from operations having military or defence implications. The Treaty of Lisbon (article 28.3) introduces the possibility for EU states to allocate funds for foreign policy issues without having to use the Community method, which is a procedure mainly conducted by the European Commission. It gives the EU the possibility of accessing the Union budget for urgent CFSP issues, and in particular preparatory activities for ESDP missions. It also allows for the creation of a start-up fund, made up of member states' contributions. States can authorize the High Representative to use this fund in cases where CFSP tasks cannot be charged to the Union budget. According to the House of Commons' report of 20 January 2008: 'Dr Solana suggested that, in particularly in situations requiring rapid or changing action, it was problematic that the priorities in the use of resources are sometimes so fixed that when a crisis comes it is very difficult to adopt the structure and deploy them rapidly.'

Solidarity among States: Rhetoric and Reality

As described above, the EU has in appearance all the elements of a fully fledged system of foreign policy. The provisions of the treaties encourage solidarity among states. Article 11 of the Treaty of Nice stipulated that the member states shall: '... support the Union's external and security policy actively and unreservedly in a spirit of loyalty and mutual solidarity' and 'work together to enhance and develop their mutual political solidarity, and refrain from any action which is contrary to the interests of the Union.' Article 16 added: 'Member states shall inform and consult one another within the Council on any matter of foreign and security policy of general interest in order to ensure that the Union's influence is exerted as effectively as possible by means of concerted and convergent action.' The rhetoric in the Treaty of Lisbon is stronger than this. Article 11c stipulates:

> The Union shall conduct, define and implement a common foreign and security policy, based on the development of mutual political solidarity among member states, the identification of questions of general interest and the achievement of an ever-increasing degree of convergence of member states' actions.

Also, article 16 follows with: 'Member states shall consult one another within *the European Council* and the Council on any matter of foreign and security policy of general interest in order to *determine a common approach*' (my emphasis).

In practice, however, despite some progress towards more dialogue between states at EU level, states still act independently from the EU, seldom reach agreements that are higher than LCD, and do not systematically implement CFSP decisions. They act in this respect according to intergovernmentalist expectations, and this despite the institutionalization of CFSP since 1992, that is, the increase of institutions created to make multilateral cooperation among states systematic (see M. Smith 2004; Jones 2007). Table 2.2 sums up the various stances taken by states when dealing with some important foreign policy issues, either at national or EU level.

This section analyses the examples given in this table. They are not exhaustive, but together they give a good reflection of how member states behave within the CFSP system. They are mainly based on information collected in interviews I carried out in Brussels at the Permanent Representations of the member states, and within EU institutions (the European Commission and the Council of the European Union).

Unilateral policies established without EU consultation, which appear in the first section of the table, are very rare. The Treaty on the

Table 2.2
Stances of EU States on Foreign Policy Issues

Type of attitude of member states	Examples
Unilateral national policies established without EU consultation	Mururoa 1995 and nuclear issues related to EU states
	Iraq 1991, 1998, 2001
	Terrorism and African issues until 2000
Discussions on most international affairs, but:	
Open clashes among states	Iraq 2003
Open clashes between one state and all the others	Recognition of Slovenia and Croatia 1991
Discreet clashes among states	Indian/Pakistani nuclear tests 1998
Agreement at EU level for states to act unilaterally	Sierra Leone 2000, Côte d'Ivoire 2002
Agreement at EU level for states to act multilaterally, independently from the EU	Sanctions against Israel 2002 Sending troops to Lebanon 2006
Decisions at EU level, but:	
LCD agreements, and discretion on major issues of contention	Rwanda 1994, common strategies on Russia 1999 and the Mediterranean region 2000
Some more-than-LCD CFSP decisions	Recognition of FYROM 1993 Code of Conduct 1998 Non-Proliferation Treaty 1999
Selective implementation of CFSP decisions, and limited co-operation between some Member States and the EU	Visa bans and arms embargoes Policies towards Zimbabwe in 2003, Georgia in 2008, Nagorno-Karabakh since 2006 Recognition of the sovereignty of states

European Union stipulates that states 'shall refrain from any action which is contrary to the interests of the Union or likely to impair its effectiveness as a cohesive force in international relations,' and that 'before undertaking any action on the international scene or entering into any commitment which could affect the Union's interests, each member state shall consult the others.' Article 16 in the Treaty of Lisbon reiterates this. Theoretically, states should always consult the other EU states before they act unilaterally. Given that the European Court of Justice has no competence in this field, there is nothing that could effectively prevent them from acting unilaterally. But in practice, policies related to nuclear issues are generally the only ones that are not discussed at EU level. These are still perceived as national foreign policy issues, and respected as such. When the French unilaterally decided to resume nuclear testing at Mururoa atoll in June 1995, very few countries officially regretted the French action.

One issue kept off the EU agenda by some states until 2002 was the Iraqi question. In 1991, in the run-up to the Gulf War, EU states openly disagreed with one another. President Mitterrand was trying to negotiate with Saddam Hussein, Berlin was paralysed in the face of anti-American demonstrations, and London was in favour of intervention. Then, in late 1998, the British government joined the American government in bombing Iraq instead of negotiating alternative policy options with the other EU states (Forster 2000, 55; CNN, 17/12/98). This happened even though the British had held the presidency of the EU in the first semester of 1998, and it was only two weeks after the St Malo agreement between France and the United Kingdom, which seemed to indicate close relations between the two countries. Again unexpectedly, in February 2001, the British in consultation with the Americans took a unilateral decision to bomb Iraq, for the first time since December 1998, despite all the other member states being against such action.

Terrorism and African issues are themes that used to be regarded as belonging to the exclusive sphere of competence of individual EU states. They are now high on the EU agenda. However, discussions at EU level on African affairs have led neither to the disappearance of unilateral policies, nor to the creation of a systematic EU approach towards African crises. Nevertheless, there is still validity in Hill's (1997, 7) contention that 'the 1968 crises over Cuba and Czechoslovakia passed without the merest glimpse of European coordination. Today this would not be possible.'

As the second section of the table indicates, the general expectation is that discussions of foreign policy issues will take place at EU level. But these discussions do not necessarily lead to agreement, and in fact, they can lead to clashes among states. The biggest recent clash was that on Iraq in 2003, when EU states disagreed on whether to support the United States in its war on Iraq. Big EU states actively and publicly fought against one another, whereas usually they would keep any disagreements in low profile. The British openly supported the United States, and the French and Germans opposed U.S. policy.

The absence of solidarity among European states is also illustrated by the German reaction to the declaration of independence by Slovenia and Croatia in 1991. After having agreed to a common position with the other EC state representatives against early recognition, the German government unilaterally decided to recognize the independence of these two countries. Such behaviour is perceived by some researchers as an exception in the CFSP decision-making process (M. Smith 1998; Glarbo 1999; Ginsberg 1999). For them, CFSP is evolving towards more solidarity among member states. However, of the forty-three interviewees who answered the question 'Do you think this kind of attitude, on the part of a state, could happen again?' twenty-five said they did not believe it would, eight said they did not know, and ten said they thought it was possible. These figures show that solidarity among states is far from obvious, and that one state alone can block the successful creation of a common policy.

Even after discussions, then, states will not hesitate to adopt unilateral national policies rather than EU policies which do not correspond to their preferences. For instance, in 1998, the French and the British representatives opposed one another in the discussions to sanction India and Pakistan, which were carrying out nuclear tests. They agreed to disagree, and respected their divergences. No sanctions were established.

States can decide to carry out unilateral policies with the consent of their fellow EU states. British officials made it known to their partners that the United Kingdom would intervene militarily in Sierra Leone in May 2000. France apparently called its European partners for help when it intervened militarily in Côte d'Ivoire in 2002. In November 2004, when French forces were attacked by the Ivorian forces in Bouaké, there was EU action in support, albeit of a minimal kind: phone calls were made by the High Representative and the presidency of the EU to the President of Côte d'Ivoire, Laurent Gbagbo, in an attempt to halt military operations.

Surprisingly, some EU states may prefer to act together or with similar policies, but independently from the EU. When EU states discussed the possibility of sanctioning Israel at EU level in April 2002, no EU decision was taken, and instead, big EU states took national foreign policy decisions against Israel. For the first time since the invasion of Lebanon in 1982, Britain imposed a de facto arms embargo on Israel. France also quietly suspended sales of certain arms. Germany refused export licences for military equipment. In August 2006, EU states presented to Kofi Annan their national military contributions to the United Nations Interim Force in Lebanon within the EU framework at a Council meeting. Dr Solana played an important coordinating role between the states, but they clearly preferred to deploy their troops to Lebanon in the form of an ad hoc multilateralism, rather than any collective EU policy.

As the last segment of the table shows, CFSP outcomes are mostly LCD agreements. As regards Rwanda, for instance, where 800,000 people were killed in the spring of 1994, a declaration was issued expressing the dismay of the EU states. State representatives may discuss controversial issues, but often the final outcome does not even refer to these discussions having taken place. The common strategy on Russia of 1999 was quite vague: it was in favour of the consolidation of democracy and cooperation with Russia. Javier Solana himself considered this negotiation a bureaucratic exercise. In the drafting of the Mediterranean common strategy, as London and Berlin were extremely cautious, agreement was finally reached in 2000 by excluding from it the Middle East Peace Process.

States can sometimes reach higher than LCD positions: diplomatic pressure and use of threats can eventually lead to an EU agreement. When the Greek government refused to recognize the Federal Yugoslav Republic of Macedonia (FYROM), other state representatives tried to influence the Greek position, over the period from 1991 until 1993. An interviewee who took part in the EU negotiations and was extremely angry with the Greeks, told me 'big member states had to threaten Greece with stopping the creation of the cohesion fund for Greece.'

When the Code of Conduct to limit arms exports was signed in June 1998, French officials gave the impression of having conceded an EU agreement closer to the British view on some of the articles. However, France appears not to have given in on all its preferences, as 'the section governing the export of arms to repressive regimes and a noundercutting requirement were watered down largely at French insistence' (Cooper 2000, 150). This corresponds to the intergovernmentalist assumption that states will make some compromises in order to reach an EU position. A similar example is that of the French government's eventual acceptance of an EU common position for the Conference on the revision of the Non-Proliferation Treaty. An intergovernmentalist explanation can be given: France did not have a strong preference on this issue.

States implement CFSP decisions selectively. State leaders may ask for authorization from their EU colleagues to sell arms to countries which are under an arms embargo, such as Sierra Leone or Nigeria, or temporarily withdraw certain persons from visa ban lists. They may also decide not to follow EU policies. This was the case for France when it invited the President of Zimbabwe, Robert Mugabe, to the African summit in Paris in March 2003. Likewise in 2008, under pressure from France, the EU appointed a French official, Pierre Morel, as EU special representative for Georgia. He undermined the work carried out since 2006 by EU Special Representative for the South Caucasus, Peter Semneby. This is because 'member states start from very different perceptions of, and responses to, Russia' (Akçakoca et al. 2009, 34). Member states can also exclude EU officials from multilateral negotiations. The EU special representative for the South Caucasus has to 'beg France for information' about negotiations organized by the Minsk group, which is an OSCE group headed by a Co-Chairmanship consisting of France, Russia, and the United States, and responsible for issues related to the crisis in Nagorno-Karabakh (Wolff, personal communication). State leaders can decide to act unilaterally towards a third party without informing their EU colleagues, and this despite the existence of a common EU approach. For instance, states adopted different policies towards Chechnya and towards the recognition of North Korea and Kosovo.

Some progress has been made in the CFSP field, in the sense that EU states now discuss practically all national foreign policy issues at EU level and show they take EU decisions seriously by implementing them. Intergovernmentalist hypotheses seem to be validated, in that most CFSP common policies appear to satisfy EU states, that is, they are LCD policies, and states are content not to press for common policies if this could harm their national interests. Higher than LCD policies are sometimes reached, but they are the result of a bargaining process whereby states link issues either in different policy fields, for instance, a foreign policy decision with a decision in matters relating to agriculture, or over time, for instance, a foreign policy decision today with another one tomorrow. They can also be the result of a threat; for example, the majority of states might threaten a dissenting state that they will take measures within the EU to sanction its unilateral behaviour.

In summary, the institutionalization process in the CFSP field does not seem to have had an impact on the creation of common policies when issues of vital importance are discussed. Despite thirty years of European Political Cooperation and CFSP cooperation and policies, EU state representatives still seem to act solely in their states' interests.

PART TWO

Case Studies in CFSP – The Mechanism in Action

3 A Pure CFSP Case:

The Condemnation of China's Human Rights Policy (1997–2005)

This chapter looks at the way member states succeeded or failed to agree on a common EU policy for presentation at the United Nations Commission on Human Rights (CHR), during the period 1997–2005. As intergovernmentalist theory would predict, states apparently only agreed to reach a common policy on condemning China's human rights record when they had no motivation to prefer some unilateral policy of their own. However, this is not the whole story, since hostile U.S. foreign policy towards China seems to have been an underlying condition for states to reach agreement on an EU policy of condemnation. If the United States did not put forward a resolution condemning China, the leaders of EU states did not even think of putting forward a resolution of their own.

The Commission on Human Rights, consisting of fifty-three members, was created in 1946 and was replaced in 2006 by the United Nations Human Rights Council.[35] The CHR has been described as the single most important institution of the global human rights regime (Donnelly, quoting K. Smith 2002, 7). It held an annual six-week session in the spring of every year, and commented on the human rights records of all the states in the world.

At the CHR, the Rules of Procedure for condemning a state's human rights policy were as follows. A resolution to condemn a state could be put forward by one or several states. Thereafter, any state, including the one which was condemned, could propose a no-action motion on this resolution, in order to counter the possibility of voting on the resolution to condemn it. The vote on the no-action motion in any one year depended on the composition of the CHR in that year. The fact that a no-action motion was passed had the effect of preventing the

CHR from debating the resolution's subject matter, and of blocking any attempt to formulate a critical resolution.

Every time a resolution against China was put forward at the CHR, a no-action motion was proposed by China or one of its allies. No other nation under human rights review, including Cuba, Iran, Iraq, Russia, or the Sudan, used this tactic. They generally preferred to debate or dispute resolutions about them on their merits. In 2002, a no-action motion on Cuba was proposed by China, and it was defeated. The UN's Commission on Human Rights is an excellent test site to observe the conditions under which common policy can be reached as a different EU common policy was presented there every year from 1997 until 2005 – despite the fact that throughout that time, China's human rights record remained very poor.

This chapter describes the evolution of EU positions at the UN CHR, and shows how member states had no qualms about breaching European solidarity. It then goes on to explain why it was so difficult for EU states to reach a common policy every year at the CHR, and concludes by highlighting the usefulness of intergovernmentalism, completed with the concept of bandwagoning, for constructing this explanation.

Reasserting Unilateral National Foreign Policy

After the Tiananmen Square massacre by the Chinese army in June 1989, EU states decided to use the UN framework to condemn China's attitude to human rights. Between 1990 and 2005, under the CFSP framework, the General Affairs Council (GAC) discussed what should be the official position of the EU at the CHR on the condemnation of China's human rights record. This section shows how this position evolved over time, while the following section will analyse the reasons why it changed.

From 1990 until 1995, the EU and the United States presented a project of resolution every year, condemning the situation in China. Western diplomats argued that the mere fact of having a debate on China forced the issue into the open and put pressure on China to reform. Every year, the resolution was never voted on, because China always proposed a no-action motion, and the motion was passed, as many developing countries on the CHR voted in favour because they did not want to be similarly condemned.

The first and only time Europe and the United States succeeded in putting China on the CHR's agenda was 1995, an unusual year for that reason. A resolution was presented and defended by France in the name of the EU, with strong support from the United States, which was a cosponsor. China lost its first attempt to prevent a resolution from being introduced, with its usual no-action motion. On 8 March 1995, the EU-United States resolution was ultimately defeated by China. China avoided condemnation, but the critical resolution was at least publicly debated.

In 1996, the EU and the United States presented another resolution condemning China. China successfully rallied support from the developing nations and no resolution was passed. The United Kingdom was ambiguous on the position it would adopt, and France apparently did not want to take any part in the project. However, the French Ministry for Foreign Affairs eventually declared its wish to show solidarity with its European partners (*Le Monde*, 19/03/96).

The period 1997–2005 is an interesting one to focus on, as some EU state representatives felt less inclined to criticize China's human rights record than they did before 1997, and the discussions at EU level became difficult. The worst year for EU unity in general was 1997, and for the creation of a Common Foreign and Security Policy in particular.

In China, the human rights situation was worsening. China imprisoned thousands of dissidents, set up a vast network of forced-labour camps, and would not tolerate either a free press or free speech. Hans van Mierlo, the Dutch foreign minister, then holding the presidency of the EU, voiced open criticism of China in a speech to the CHR on 12 March 1997. At that time, according to one of my interviewees, all EU states seemed to agree provisionally that the EU should sponsor a resolution condemning China. The sensitive issue of human rights in China was debated by EU Foreign Ministers during a two-day meeting on 6 April 1997 in the Dutch coastal town of Noordwijk.

However, several member states broke consensus. There was open argument within the EU on the question of whether or not to support a resolution against China. EU states failed to back an EU resolution on this subject for the first time in seven years. This was a big setback both for EU human rights policy and for CFSP. France suddenly announced it was not going to join in sponsoring an EU resolution, and that effectively blocked the EU from signing a proposal for a resolution.[36] Germany, Spain, and Italy then adopted a similar attitude.

As a result, at the 53rd session of the CHR in Geneva, EU states were split. On 10 April 1997, a resolution condemning the human rights situation in China was tabled by Denmark, together with a large number of cosponsors, including the United States. Britain and the Netherlands, acting at the national level, joined in the condemnation. China, as it had done in the previous years, tabled a no-action motion, which was approved.

In early 1998, in China, violations of human rights were widespread. The Chinese government continued to use a repressive policy towards Tibet, to run laogai labour camps, to allow the trading in organs of executed criminals, and to promote the one-child-per-family policy. On 23 February, EU foreign affairs ministers nonetheless decided not to support a resolution to condemn China. The British Foreign Affairs Minister, Robin Cook, holding the presidency of the EU, justified this leniency by the need to maintain unity among EU members. Neither the United States nor the EU submitted a resolution on China, as they argued that Beijing's record had improved, and they wanted to pursue dialogue with China. According to diplomats, the American decision not to sponsor an anti-China resolution was intended to smooth the path for President Clinton's visit to Beijing in June. It was the first visit by a U.S. president since the 1989 suppression of the Tiananmen Square pro-democracy demonstrations.

In December 1998, China asserted itself. President Jiang Zemin declared that China would never copy the political systems of Western countries. Subsequently, long prison sentences were passed on dissidents, in contravention of the UN Covenant on Civil and Political Rights that Beijing had signed in early 1998. In March 1999, China was continuing its oppression of Tibet. China's attitude did not lend any substance to claims by the EU states that 'constructive engagement' was the solution for improving the situation. In March 1999, the United States announced it would seek censure of China at the UN. This decision was taken despite the fact that the Chinese Prime Minister, Zhu Rongji, was due to visit the United States in April 1999, in order to discuss China's accession to the World Trade Organization (WTO). EU states decided not to condemn China: no official EU position was adopted on the attitude the EU should take at the UN. Finally, China blocked the U.S. resolution by twenty-two votes to seventeen.

In 2000, the United States proposed a resolution condemning the continuing crackdowns in Tibet and on the followers of Falun Gong, who drew attention to China's abuse of human rights. The U.S. Secretary of State, Madeleine Albright, attended the CHR session and gave a speech urging the United Nations to confront China over its wide-spread denials of basic freedoms. This was the first time a U.S. Secretary of State had addressed the Commission on Human Rights. The European Union refrained from taking any position on the U.S. resolution, or on a possible no-action motion by China. The GAC merely concluded: 'The Council will continue to keep EU policy on China under regular review.' China, yet again, succeeded in having its no-action motion adopted.[37]

From 2001 onwards, EU states decided to condemn China only if a resolution was set by another state, that is, the United States, and passed. On 19 March 2001, the GAC agreed to a strangely lukewarm position:

> That the EU should adopt and make public the following approach:
> - If the resolution is put to a vote, EU members of the Commission will vote in favour, but the EU will not co-sponsor.
> - EU members of the Commission will vote against a no-action motion, should one be presented, and the EU will actively encourage other Commission members to do likewise, since in the EU's view, the very notion of no-action is in itself contrary to the spirit of dialogue.

Thus, 2001 showed an improvement in respect to the 2000 position. The EU publicly announced its decision to oppose a motion of no-action, but it still did not cosponsor the U.S. resolution. In April 2001, the resolution against China sponsored by the United States was blocked by a no-action motion by China.

In 2002, the EU declined to sponsor a resolution on China, but did leave open the possibility of an individual EU member sponsoring a measure. The Council stated:

> If a draft resolution on human rights in China is tabled at the 58th session of the UN Commission on Human Rights, the EU will study its contents carefully. The Council has agreed that the EU should adopt and make public the following approach:
> - If such a draft resolution is put to a vote, EU members of the Commission will consider favourably voting for its adoption;
> - EU members of the Commission would vote against a no-action motion, should one be presented, and the EU would actively encourage other Commission members to do likewise, since, in the

> EU's view, the very notion of no-action is in itself contrary to the
> spirit of dialogue. (GAC Conclusions, 11/03/02)

No resolution was tabled by either the EU or any of the EU states. As the United States had no seat on the CHR in 2002, no resolution condemning China was tabled at all. On 10 April 2002, China escaped once more scrutiny of its human rights record at the CHR, despite an increase in its human rights abuses.

In 2003, the GAC (18 March) decided that 'the EU at the UN Commission on Human Rights would convey its deep concern over the serious violations of human rights in China and the lack of progress in a number of areas.' It nevertheless fell short of taking action on its concern. It adopted the same position as in the past: if a resolution had been tabled by a state, namely the United States, then it would vote in favour of this resolution. But it did not take responsibility for initiating the tabling of a resolution. This position was heavily criticized by Human Rights Watch (25/04/03), which declared:

> The United States and to a lesser extent, the European Union have not
> exerted positive leadership ... The Commission appears to be in a really
> serious decline ... Governments this year were even less outspoken in
> criticizing the worst human rights violators worldwide.

The difference between 2004 and the previous two years was that the United States decided to put forward a resolution. Like the EU, it deplored the human rights situation in China, but unlike the EU, it took action on its concern. As the United States had put forward the resolution, the EU voted in favour of it. It was defeated by a no-action motion.

In 2005, an EU representative made a statement at the CHR. Despite a request from the European Parliament that it sponsor or cosponsor a resolution on China's human rights record, the EU merely acknowledged the improvement of the situation in China. No U.S. resolution was tabled, and China was not condemned.

To conclude this section, table 3.1 summarizes the EU positions both on the sponsoring of a resolution against China and on China's no-action motion.

Human Rights and Economic Interests

All the policy outcomes of the EU on China's human rights record can be explained in terms of intergovernmentalist theory: big states were

Table 3.1
EU Positions towards China (1990–2005)

Years	U.S. resolution	EU cosponsoring of the U.S. resolution	EU voting in favour of a resolution tabled by a third party	EU position on China's no-action motion	China's no-action motion	China condemned
1990–1994	Yes	Yes	Yes	Against	Succeeded	No
1995	Yes	Yes	Yes	Against	Failed	No
1996	Yes	Yes	Yes	Against	Succeeded	No
1997	Yes (cosponsored the Danish resolution)	No	No	Not mentioned (EU states voted against it)	Succeeded	No
1998	No	No	No	Not applicable	Not applicable	No
1999	Yes	No	No	Not mentioned	Succeeded	No
2000	Yes	No	Yes (informally)	Not mentioned, but against informally	Succeeded	No
2001	Yes	No	Yes	Against publicly	Succeeded	No
2002	No	No	Yes	Against publicly	Not applicable	No
2003	No	No	Yes	Against publicly	Not applicable	
2004	Yes	No	Yes	Against publicly	Succeeded	No
2005	No	No	Not mentioned	Not mentioned	Not applicable	No

the main actors, they did not act in the European spirit of solidarity, and they favoured their economic interests. But they seem to be much more conditioned by the foreign policy of the United States towards China. Up to 1996, EU states could all agree on their policies towards China without much discussion. However, 1997 was a bad year for the idea of solidarity. States began acting in accordance with their own economic interests, and their own evaluation of the importance of human rights in relation to these. The French government decided in March that dialogue with Beijing was better than confrontation. According to an interviewee, 'The EU policy conducted until 1997 had not led to any result in China. France wanted to try a new policy towards it.' French leaders thought that this new policy would certainly not have any harmful economic consequences for France. As early as December 1996, President Jacques Chirac had announced:

> When I travel abroad, I hear criticism from certain quarters. People say, 'Why is he going there?,' as if I were going on a holiday. I go to sell France. I have no qualms about this, no more than others do. Traditionally, Americans, British or others do this. I go abroad to sell French products, because we need a higher growth rate. We have to look for where it exists, in Asia, South America, and Eastern Europe. That is where we have to sell. It is also the role of a politician to do this ... Do you really think that, when China decides to buy Airbus planes and to make a plane with us, seating a hundred people, which is an important contract, even though Boeing is making them interesting offers, there is no political factor influencing the outcome? You see, one billion French Francs in contracts is equivalent to 2,000 jobs. Today, for the first time in 1996, we had a surplus in our trade balance; we will probably make 140 billion French Francs in excess. That is 280,000 jobs. (*Le Monde*, 14/12/96)

The press and the academic world echoed Chirac's words. According to *L'Humanité* (15/05/97), France wanted to increase its exports to China, and sell more Airbus A 320s, for a total of $1.2 billion. Academics (Cabestan 1997; Holzman 1997) believed that France wanted only to improve its economic relations. France also wanted to appear as a credible political power to China, especially as diplomatic relations were being strengthened. The Chinese Premier Zhu Rongji visited France in early April 1997, and President Jacques Chirac visited Beijing in May. France preferred a unilateral national policy to European unity. According to one French interviewee:

European solidarity comes in addition to French foreign policy. If EU states are willing to follow French policy, that's good. If not, France goes it alone ... otherwise, it will cease to exist. France prefers acting unilaterally, as this makes it more credible for China, as it is effectively capable of acting alone, without referring to the EU. The EU is viewed as an extra instrument of French diplomacy.

Germany apparently remained especially quiet during the 1997 EU negotiations, but eventually supported France's determination not to condemn China. Germany's Minister for Foreign Affairs, Klaus Kinkel, said: '[I]t is more important to achieve specific progress than to agree on resolutions which have no success' (*The Independent*, 08/04/97; *Le Monde*, 09/04/97). Germany also believed it was more important to discuss the human rights situation directly with China, at national level, rather than try to reach a common EU policy for public condemnation of the Chinese leadership. This new position would have positive economic consequences for Germany, which now does more trade with China than any of its European competitors. The French position was also supported by Italy and Spain.

In 1997, the presidency, held by the Netherlands, failed to make France, Germany, Italy, and Spain change position. Before the absence of a common policy on the condemnation of China was made known publicly, the Dutch officially announced that they disagreed with these four states' positions. In a letter dated 31 March, the Dutch Minister for Foreign Affairs and President of the Council, Hans van Mierlo, told his EU partners that the refusal of four of them to back a resolution on China was 'a serious setback for the perspectives of a foreign policy of the Union. Even more serious is the fact that the essence of the human rights policy of the Union is at stake.' He added:

> I am deeply convinced that a change of policy such as the present one with regard to the China resolution directly affects the credibility of our policy vis-à-vis other countries. I am therefore of the opinion that the European Union – as a union – should refrain from any initiative to obtain comparable condemnations of other countries where human rights are being violated. (*The Daily Telegraph*, 04/04/97)

Hans van Mierlo then announced that he would not transmit to the CHR all the other EU projects of resolution supporting the condemnation of the human rights situations in Iraq, Iran, Burma, the Palestinian territories, Zaire, and Timor. However, he did eventually transmit them all, and there was still no EU common policy on China. The threats made by the Dutch presidency did not make the four countries change position.

The readiness of Britain, the Netherlands, and Denmark to condemn China at the national level shows that states have no hesitation in opting, when they wish, for unilateral action rather than action within the EU framework. This is exactly what intergovernmentalist theory states: a common policy is only possible if a state has good reason to prefer an EU policy to a unilateral national policy. There were two strong reasons for these states to decide to condemn China, although other EU states did not do so. They had always condemned China, and there was no cause to change that preference in 1997, as for them, the political and economic context had not changed. And they were not acting alone in the world arena, as the United States was willing to sponsor a resolution.

To sum up the events of 1997: once France decided to act unilaterally, for economic advantage, all the other states adopted the same attitude, and acted according to their national interest. The fact that the United States held to its existing policy of condemning China was a further incentive for some states to maintain an anti-Chinese position.

In 1998, the EU decided not to condemn China. This time, all states were protecting their own economic interest, and in so doing, they gave the impression of EU unity and solidarity. In 1998, all EU state representatives believed that a new policy of dialogue with China should be launched. The United Kingdom had strong reasons for changing its position. In May 1997, a new Labour government had been elected. In early 1998, the United Kingdom took over the EU presidency, and wanted to restore dialogue with China. At the beginning of January, the Foreign Secretary, Robin Cook, decided not to meet Wei Jingsheng, the leading Chinese dissident released in November 1997, and made a visit to China. After his visit, Cook explained in Brussels that he had secured the first-ever invitation for the UN High Commissioner to visit China, that Beijing had also agreed to allow three European ambassadors to visit Tibet for the first time, and that China had signed, but not yet ratified, the covenant on economic, social, and cultural rights. The political covenant that Beijing said it would sign covered freedom of expression and religion, peaceful assembly, participation in public affairs and elections, freedom of movement, and equality before the law. Apart from some relaxation in internal travel, the other rights did not exist in China. The decision not to sponsor a resolution against China came just ahead of the first EU–China summit in Britain in April 1998, during which no comment was made on the issue of human rights. EU states clearly privileged their economic relations with China over their human rights principles.

The whole episode re-established the image of a unified EU. According to *Le Monde* (25/02/98), 'the EU Foreign Affairs Ministers decided not to support a resolution to condemn China ... so as not to show intra-EU disagreements.' EU policy did not conflict with U.S. policy, as the United States, for the first time since the Tiananmen events, did not sponsor a resolution against China. The EU position seems to have been taken in full cooperation with the United States. Both EU states and the United States expressed publicly their belief that there had been progress in the human rights dialogue with China.

In 1999, EU states adopted the same position as in 1998, and the EU issued no project of resolution against China. Individual states all had strong positive motivation to produce a common policy: they all wished to continue their dialogue with China, and to show their unity. For instance, British representatives reiterated that dialogue with China was a better way than condemnation to improve the human rights situation. And British ministers knew, as they had known in 1998, that everything had to be done to avoid what had happened in 1997: one interviewee emphasized to me that 'an impression of EU unity had to be given, even at the expense of not defending human rights.' According to the *Daily Telegraph* (22/03/99), 'Derek Fatchett, the Foreign Office minister with responsibility for Asia, believes it is better for Britain to stick with an EU consensus against advancing a condemnatory resolution than to break ranks and speak out against Chinese oppression.' The British government was criticized in 1999 for subordinating its ethical values to commercial interests (Wickham-Jones 2000, 25). The United Kingdom agreed, with the other member states, not to condemn China formally, despite the fact that Prime Minister Tony Blair had addressed criticism to China's leaders on human rights grounds during his visit in October 1998. The 1999 EU position went against the U.S. position. This was possible because the United States apparently did not lobby intensively for its resolution to be sponsored.

In 2000, the EU officially adopted a very mild position. The GAC of March 2000 merely concluded that 'the Council will continue to keep EU policy on China under regular review, including at CHR 56th.' The EU did not disappoint China, as there was no vote on a U.S. resolution. The collective decision was an LCD position, which did not put states at risk in terms of negative economic consequences. Germany and Denmark showed signs of wanting to be cosponsors of the U.S. resolution, but according to my interviewees, they decided not do this in order to ensure the appearance of unity among EU states. In fact, German Minister for Foreign Affairs Joschka Fischer was apparently the only high-level official in favour of sponsoring the resolution. German Chancellor Gerhard Schroeder was not, and the final EU outcome reflected the chancellor's position. The United Kingdom argued against cosponsorship, claiming that support for the U.S. resolution would damage its dialogue process with China. The Foreign Office did not believe that a return to the previous position would serve the United Kingdom or the cause of human rights in China. The final EU outcome, therefore, also corresponded to the British position. On this occasion, the United States did not have a strong preference for the EU to adopt a policy similar to its own. It did not, at the highest level, lobby the EU. EU policy was correspondingly neutral: it did not condemn China and it refused to consider a condemnation. It did not follow U.S. policy, but did not totally oppose it, either. Intergovernmentalist theory is insufficient to explain the official position taken here, because it takes no account of the influence of the United States on the positions EU states feel able to take up.

The unofficial version of the EU position that came to light in the course of my research shows a change in attitude on the part of some member states and a higher level of agreement. Informally, France agreed to condemn China, if the U.S. resolution was put to a vote, and Germany and Denmark agreed not to cosponsor the U.S. resolution on a national basis. There was a new element in 2000: if the U.S. resolution had been put to a vote, that is, if the Chinese no-action motion had failed, EU states had made the commitment to vote in favour of the U.S. resolution. One interviewee stated that the French position was not clear at the beginning of the 2000 negotiation process but that, eventually,

> France has accepted to vote against China. It was reluctant to have an EU resolution. No one believed it would be successful ... If there is a critical resolution, France included, will agree on voting. 1997 was a bad experience: there was no commitment and in the end, France voted against it. It is now more difficult for France to vote against it.

There had been a change in the French position. The French felt that they could not act as they had done in the past, and that their position within the EU had to appear more flexible. This could be interpreted as a product of socialization. However, a French interviewee explained that 'it did not cost France anything to agree with an informal EU position, as there was little chance for the resolution to be voted on, and there would always be time to change position.' In 2000, France did not want to make this EU position public. It opted to show solidarity with other European states within the EU, but at the same time give China the impression that it was not condemning China. Intergovernmentalist theory would describe France's unofficial position as a strategy to obtain a common policy that would reflect French interests. The British apparently agreed not to make the informal EU position public, in the interests of solidarity with France.

The official final agreement reached in 2000 appears to resemble the 1999 agreement. It can be defined as an LCD agreement, which was reached because the interests of the member states were all protected. Dialogue with China and the defence of EU states' economic interests were preferred to support of the U.S. position. The unofficial agreement was also an LCD decision, as France, the United Kingdom, and Germany all eventually agreed to a position which corresponded to their preferences. EU states agreed informally to show European solidarity and unity. However, adopting an informal position was cost-free: it was highly unlikely that a U.S. resolution would be eventually put to a vote, and the EU's informal position would never have been communicated to the public.

In 2001, an extra step was taken, compared to 2000: all states made some compromises rather than fail to present a common EU position to the Commission on Human Rights. EU states made public the fact that they would vote in favour of a resolution condemning China, if this were put to a vote. This time, the EU states opposing one another, that is, those in favour of a common policy versus those in favour of unilateral national policies, were mostly the small ones. Surprisingly, France was not part of the dispute. France no longer opposed making the EU position public. One of my interviewees believed this was purely because France had already signed its contracts with China. Other reasons can be given: it was unlikely a resolution would be put to the vote, and even if it were, an interviewee said, 'we could always tell the Chinese that they themselves were the ones responsible for this policy.'

At the beginning of the 2001 negotiation process, Denmark and the Netherlands totally disagreed with one big state, namely, Italy.

Denmark wanted China to be criticized. Italy was against the EU cosponsoring the U.S. resolution, and also against the idea of a public statement that the EU would vote in favour of a condemnation of China, if a resolution was passed. Eventually, at the GAC, the Netherlands and Denmark agreed that the EU would not cosponsor the U.S. resolution, and Italy finally agreed to making the declaration public.

EU officials expected these countries to give in, as they were isolated, in the sense that they were the only ones resisting a common policy. This analysis corresponds to intergovernmental theory: the final outcome reflected a middle ground between the Italian and the Danish-Dutch positions and states compromised somewhat. The small states decided to favour their own economic interest, and, especially, EU solidarity, at the expense of the principle of defence of human rights.

As in 1998, the fact that the United States did not sponsor a resolution had an impact on the EU's ability to formulate a common policy. And again, although intergovernmentalism explains the 2002–3 agreements, as it explains all the previous agreements, it must also be said that states seem constantly to be taking U.S. foreign policy into consideration.

The 2004 position recalls the 2001 position: EU states are ready to support the United States, but not to cosponsor the U.S. resolution. The EU bandwagons with the United States, and it adopts a low profile towards China. Finally, the 2005 position is coherent with the previous ones. The GAC of March 2005 merely stated that 'the fact that human rights dialogues are held does not prevent the EU from expressing its views in an appropriate manner in the CHR.' The EU was again ready to express its disagreement with the human rights situation, but not to take the lead to sponsor a resolution against China.

Bargaining and Power Politics

Discussions among EU states on the attitude to adopt towards China show that intergovernmentalism is a useful theory to understand the persistence of national unilateral foreign policies, the focus on economic gain, and the reliance of EU states on the U.S.

States were the most important actors in this process, as they were the only ones with the legal right to decide on the issue of condemning China's human rights record. They could be seen to act as unitary bodies: their national positions were never self-contradictory.

Germany presented a unitary position at EU level, although there seem to have been differences of opinion between the Minister for Foreign Affairs, Joschka Fischer, and the Prime Minister, Gerhard Schroeder. The United Kingdom always presented a unitary position, despite intrastate divisions in the United Kingdom between Whitehall and the Foreign Office.

Intergovernmentalist theory says that preference formation mostly takes place prior to the negotiation process, and that states rarely change their preferences during the negotiation process. This was generally the case here. The French change in preference in 2000 is an interesting exception. France was the main EU state against an EU policy that would support the condemnation of China, and it suddenly agreed to unofficially support a resolution against China. This attitude could be interpreted as a result of a socialization process: French officials could have felt in 2000 that they could not act again as inappropriately as they had in 1997, when they completely ignored both the preferences of all other EU states and all previous EU decisions on China since 1989, and could have decided instead to present a common position in the name of European solidarity. But French officials had nothing to lose by accepting an unofficial agreement to condemn China, in certain circumstances, as China would not have been aware of this unofficial EU decision.

EU states did not look at the gains other states might make out of EU positions. They were only concerned with their own national gains, that is, in intergovernmentalist terms, with their absolute gains. For instance, France did not consider the negative economic impact its decision to reject a common EU position in 1997 could have on Denmark, the Netherlands, or the United Kingdom. As intergovernmentalist theory notes, state representatives acted rationally, with due regard to the consequences for them of decisions taken at EU level. For instance, Danish officials knew there would be economic retaliation on the part of China. Denmark was being threatened financially and politically by China (*New York Times*, 08/04/97; Yee and Storey 2002, 123). Technically, EU decisions did not have a path-dependency effect, as every year, the negotiation process started from scratch.

In the long term, the intergovernmentalist hypothesis on states' commitments to their own economic interests to the detriment of European solidarity is verified. Economic interests were of high importance in this process, as intergovernmentalist theorists would indicate (alongside, of course, most other commentators). China has major economic significance for EU states. In the 1990s, the EU was China's third trading partner, and China was the EU's fourth trading partner. In the 2000s, China is the EU's second largest trading partner after the United States, and the EU has been China's largest trading partner since 2004.

France constantly took decisions at EU level that, it hoped, would not go against its economic interest. France always preferred unilateral national action to a CFSP agreement, and to EU solidarity, and protected its economic interests. China was and is an important partner for France; in 2005, China was ninth in the list of countries to which France sent exports, and seventh for imports received. Airbus, in particular, was an important industry for France, as most of Airbus employees are located in France (11,500), followed by Germany (10,000), United Kingdom (7,000), and Spain (2,000). Sales of Airbus to China increased sharply over the period, in comparison with Boeing. In the late 1990s, Airbus only represented 7 per cent of the Chinese market, which Boeing dominated. By 2006, Airbus had captured almost 50 per cent of sales to China. This may well have been in the mind of James Rubin, spokesman for the U.S. State Department, when he complained on 20 April 2000 that 'some countries seemed to care more about interfering with their commerce with China than standing up for human rights.' The European Commissioner for External Relations, Chris Patten (2005, 14), noted that France, in particular, was not going to let anything interfere with the aims of its commercial diplomacy in China.

The concerns of EU leaders were justified, as economic figures show that the 1997 clash of national interest at EU level did have an impact on their trade relations.[38] Exports to China by Denmark, Italy, the Netherlands, the United Kingdom, and even France were reduced from 1997 until 1998. At first glance, EU leaders were right to consider the impact of their political decisions on their trade relations. Nevertheless, figures also show that until 1997, the EU position on China's human rights record did not affect European economies. The flow of trade between EU states and China was constantly rising during the 1990s. It was only when the EU was split on its policy that China acted against Europe in economic terms.

The EU no longer risks jeopardizing its trade relations with China. It used to be very vocal against China before 1997, but, at best, from 2000 onwards, it would agree to vote in favour of a resolution put forward by a third party, instead of sponsoring or cosponsoring a resolution on its own behalf. Even so, economic factors did not prevent some states from making political statements which could harm their states' economies. Surprisingly, in 1997, some EU states (in 1997, Denmark, the Netherlands, and the United Kingdom; in 2000, Germany and Denmark; and in 2001, Denmark and the Netherlands) condemned China, despite the clear warnings given by the Chinese government of the negative impact this would have on their trade relations, and in particular on the chances of European companies winning contracts in China. Given the willingness shown here to risk negative economic consequences, future national and EU decisions to act on principle cannot be completely ruled out. However, it would appear that the states which stood up for human rights learned their lesson; in later years, they favoured policies that would not harm their economic interests.

The intergovernmentalist hypothesis on the likelihood of policy outcomes being LCD decisions is partially validated in this case study. Big states which refused to reach a common policy did not change their positions during the negotiation process: the absence of a common policy corresponded to their preferences. When common policies were reached in and after 1997, they were all LCD agreements, whereby no concessions were made. The fact that some EU states avoid condemning China, but agree to condemn smaller states, also confirms the intergovernmentalist assumption that no agreement is generally reached on highly sensitive issues.[39]

Intergovernmentalism predicts that, apart from member states, no other actor plays a significant role in the making of a common policy. However, as an interviewee reported: 'The role of the United States is extremely important. An EU condemnation of China is unimaginable without a U.S. resolution.' EU leaders only considered condemning China when the United States wanted to do so, as it would have been detrimental to the diplomatic and economic relations of EU states with China to condemn China alone. The United States can be said to have exercised here an indirect power of veto.

Until 1996, the United States and the EU adopted the same policy towards China. After 1996, when the United States did not put forward a resolution to condemn China (in 1998, 2002, 2003, and 2005), EU states also all agreed not to sponsor a resolution condemning China.[40] When the United States did put forward a resolution to condemn China, EU states did not necessarily decide to adopt the same position as the United States. However, when the EU chose to adopt a different policy, there was apparently no intense lobbying on the part of the United States for the EU to follow the U.S. position.

As intergovernmentalism acknowledges, the European Commission can have a role in policy-making. The Commission had an occasional say in the formation of the EU's policy towards China, but it did not have any impact on the EU's final position. The Commission's role in the negotiations that led to the absence or presence of an EU position on the condemnation of China was hardly ever noted by the people I interviewed. In 1997, the Commission reacted to the Chinese sanctioning of Denmark, the Netherlands, and the United Kingdom. In order to show solidarity, Endymion Wilkinson, the Ambassador to China for the European Commission, addressed a message of protest to China. However, the Commission had no influential role during the 1997 negotiation process.

In 2000, a new European Commission was nominated. Chris Patten, the European Commissioner responsible for External Relations, replaced Sir Leon Brittan. The attitude of Chris Patten at the 56th UN Commission on Human Rights was new for the Commission. He indirectly criticized the China–EU human rights dialogue in Geneva on 27 March 2000:

> Debating human rights in the abstract can never be an excuse for inaction on the ground. Dialogue cannot substitute for deeds. And signing covenants – welcome though it may be – is not the same as ratifying and applying them. A signature should be an expression of unambiguous intent to implement them fully as soon as possible, and to respect their spirit immediately. It should certainty not be acceptable as a tool for diplomatic delay, rather a commitment to action. Dialogue is not an end in itself ... It is the means to an end. It is neither morally acceptable nor economically wise to believe that closing one's eyes to abuses opens up opportunities for trade. (EU Document, Speech by The Rt. Hon. Chris Patten, 27/03/00)

This position is rather different from the position of European Commissioner Sir Leon Brittan, who had said on 2 April 1998, 'China wants to carry on the process of reform. We want to encourage them. And I think we want to help them, and I think they are interested in having our help as I found out from talking to Zhu Rongji on more than one occasion.'

Whatever the position of Commissioners on China's human rights record, they cannot, apparently, have a direct impact on states' positions. They seem too afraid of damaging their reputations and future possible influence. Chris Patten's spokesman in Brussels, Gunnar Wiegand, said: 'This is certainly an important issue for Mr Patten. He has a well-established personal profile on this which he would not like to endanger in his new job' (World Tibet Network News and *South China Morning Post*, 20/03/00).

It will be clear from this that I disagree with Bourne and Cini (2000, 182), who argue that the European Commission was more likely than the British government to be proactive in setting the EU's agenda on relations with China. Member states, and not the Commission, were the main players here.

To conclude: in terms of lessons learned, the French position in 1997 had a negative impact on the economies of its partners, on its own economy, and on the image of the EU in China. And also, it would appear that European states benefit economically from presenting a unified position. In terms of theoretical understanding, although inter-governmentalism appears to be the most appropriate theory to explain the absence or reaching of EU common policies, it is insufficient. A theoretical framework seeking to explain CFSP outcomes needs to incorporate the role of the United States, as, in this case study, its attitude clearly conditioned EU positions. The EU can usually decide to follow U.S. condemnations or not, but when the United States does not condemn China, it is very difficult for the Europeans to take a harsher line. The United States must be thought of as a player with an indirect power of veto.

4 A CFSP–EC Case:
Sanctions against the Federal Republic of Yugoslavia (Spring 2000)

This chapter analyses the negotiation of CFSP decisions on sanctions against the Federal Republic of Yugoslavia (FRY) from January to April 2000. At the time, the EU was discussing the possible renewal or amendment of its three major types of sanctions targeting the FRY: an oil embargo, a flight ban, and financial sanctions. The procedure for establishing sanctions towards third parties remains unchanged under the Treaty of Lisbon (through article 188k, previously article 301). The findings of this chapter are therefore relevant for any future sanctions policy.

After the war in Kosovo and the end of NATO bombing in June 1999, discussions were held at the Council of the European Union, in order to evaluate the relevance of continuing sanctions against the FRY. EU states all agreed in principle that the sanctions policy had to be adapted to the situation there, and that something had to be done at EU level. The majority of EU state representatives were in favour of lifting the sanctions policy. For them, this policy had been aimed at halting FRY action against Kosovo, and they did not think that main-taining sanctions harmful to the population would harm Milosevic. In addition, the Serbian opposition was asking for support and for the lifting of sanctions. The majority of states, therefore, wanted to help the opposition. However, some EU states, mainly the United Kingdom and the Netherlands, together with the United States, which also had sanctions against the FRY, did not agree with this approach. They argued that, as Milosevic was still in power, by lifting the sanctions, they would be helping his regime. EU sanctions were discussed at length, and in early 2000 states finally reached a common policy: the oil ban was not mentioned, the flight ban was to be lifted, and finan-cial sanctions reinforced.

This chapter sets out to show that the big states involved here, namely, France and Germany versus the United Kingdom, reached no common policy on the oil sanction due to the important role played by the United States. However, these big states reached a more than a LCD common policy when they negotiated the EU flight ban and financial sanctions: they all changed their initial position in order to reach a common policy. The issues discussed in this case study are highly sensitive. State officials were deeply concerned about the lifting of the oil ban, as this would have economic consequences for EU countries as well as the FRY. The fact that this issue was hardly discussed at EU level shows that state representatives do not try to reach common policies on issues that do not correspond to their interests.

Intergovernmentalists would point out that the flight ban and financial sanctions were not important for the big states, as the common policy on these issues did not have an impact on the economic and political situation in the EU; nevertheless, these issues must have been important for the big states, as representatives stuck to their national positions for a very long time, even when the majority of the other states disagreed with them, before agreeing on a common policy. For one interviewee, this was a 'politically strong' negotiation. The issue of the two sanctions was discussed for over six months, and it was still an issue in summer 2000. It was on all the agendas of the Political Committee and the CFSP counsellors group and took up most of the time of every EU meeting. It was an issue discussed daily, if not twice a day, on an official basis, at the working group for the Western Balkans. EU states did not therefore consider the sanctions policy a minor issue; on the contrary, they cared.

I interviewed officials regularly in the course of the 1999–2000 decision-making process. The negotiation was a long and tedious one, and the evolution of the positions of member states is clearly demonstrated in this chapter. This is a hard case for intergovernmentalism to explain.

A Narrative Account of EU Sanctions Policy and the FRY

The history of EU sanctions policy in relation to the FRY can be divided into two periods. From 1991 until 1995, the EU applied sanctions in conformity with UN sanctions. From 1998 until 2000, the EU, like the United States, applied sanctions independently of the UN.

From 1991 until 1995, the EU followed the same policy as the United Nations and the United States. The Slovenian and Croatian conflict started in June 1991. The UN maintained sanctions against the FRY from

September 1991 until the Dayton Agreement of 21 September 1995, when all UN sanctions were suspended. During this same period, the United States applied the same sanctions as the UN, and it suspended them likewise in 1995. As early as 1991, the EU decided to suspend trade and trade preferences with the FRY, to set visa restrictions, and to ban financial, scientific, technical, and cultural cooperation. In 1995, the EU sanctions against the FRY were suspended, except for the arms embargo. EU common policies on the sanctions towards the FRY were easily reached; they were agreed at the beginning of each negotiation.

The second set of sanctions on the FRY addressed the Kosovo crisis, from 1998 until 2000. In 1998, the UN's only sanctions policy against the FRY was an arms embargo. The EU, like the United States, set up its sanctions independently. In 1998, the United States froze FRY assets, banned investment and economic transactions with the FRY, introduced a ban on Yugoslav Airline (JAT) flights, and imposed an oil embargo.

From 1998 until 2000, the EU maintained an active sanctions policy towards FRY.[41] In 1998, the EU cancelled the preferential trade status of the FRY, it restricted certain investments, and it set a flight ban. Then, in 1999, it imposed an oil embargo, banned EU investments, froze assets of government, companies, and individuals associated with Milosevic, set a visa ban, and imposed restrictive measures on export restrictions, although the areas of Montenegro, Kosovo, Nis, and Perot were exempted.

In 2000, seeking to help the Serbian opposition and to remove Milosevic from power, the EU did not manage to reach any agreement on the lifting of the oil embargo, but it did decide to extend the visa ban and, especially, to lift the flight ban and reinforce financial sanctions. The visa ban list was extended from 588 to 800 persons. The extension of the visa ban was easily agreed to by the states, and is therefore not studied here. The reinforcement of financial sanctions meant that there was a general ban on trade, except for Serbian firms on a white list, that is, those that could prove their disassociation from the Serbian regime.

Finally, in autumn 2000, when Vojislav Kostunica was elected president, the EU and U.S. flight and oil bans were lifted, and the FRY was admitted to the Stability Pact for South Eastern Europe (October 2000). It also became a member of the UN and the OSCE (Organization for Security and Cooperation in Europe). Table 4.1 summarizes the actions of the international community in response to FRY policy in Kosovo from 1998 until 2000.

Table 4.1
EU and International Sanctions towards the FRY (1998–2000)

Dates	UN sanctions	EU sanctions	U.S. sanctions
1998 Kosovo crisis	Arms embargo	– Cancellation of preferential trade status – Restriction on certain investments – Flight ban	– FRY assets frozen – Investment and economic transactions banned – Oil embargo
1999	As above	– Oil embargo – Ban on EU investments – Freezing of assets – Visa ban – Restrictive measures on export restrictions	As above
2000	As above	– No common policy on the oil embargo – Extension of the visa ban – Lifting of the flight ban – Reinforcement of financial sanctions	As above
Autumn 2000	– EU and U.S. flight and oil ban lifted – The FRY was admitted to the Stability Pact for South Eastern Europe – The FRY was admitted as UN and OSCE member		

As EU states generally condemned Milosevic's policy in Kosovo, one might think that EU measures to impose or lift sanctions were taken easily, and that EU states agreed from the beginning of the negotiation process on a common policy to help remove Milosevic from power. However, the states did not agree on the type of sanctions to be imposed or lifted; and looking at the daily negotiation process that took place between July 1999 and 5 April 2000, disagreements between states, and the progressive modification of the sanctions policy towards the FRY, are clearly revealed. The July 1999 GAC agreed that measures affecting the population, such as the flight ban, the oil embargo, and the ban on sporting links, would be the first to be lifted. These issues were discussed at every GAC after this, and it was not until February 2000 that states finally came to a common policy on some of them.

In summer 1999, the Serbian opposition made contact with the international community, asking it to help them call for free elections and dismiss Milosevic. The EU decided to send humanitarian aid to Serbia, and to modify its sanctions policy towards the FRY. The first item was easily agreed on, and the project Energy for Democracy provided oil to the opposition towns of Nis and Perot. The modification of the sanctions policy was more difficult to achieve, as member states, and more precisely the big member states, disagreed on the extent of the modifications. The decision-making process between January and April 2000 was a laborious business, completed in two steps. A first negotiation took place under the second (CFSP) pillar, lasting until 14 February 2000, and a second negotiation took place under the first (EC) pillar, ending on 5 April 2000.

Under the CFSP pillar, on 14 January 2000, the Political Committee discussed a text preparing the lifting of the flight ban. The British political director implicitly announced, for the first time since July 1999, that the United Kingdom was about to change its mind on the lifting of the flight ban. On 24 January 2000, at the GAC, the British and Dutch delegations put a reserve on the lifting of the flight ban. These two countries only wanted the ban lifting for European carriers, and not for all carriers, that is, Yugoslavian as well as European. No consensus was reached. On 1 February 2000, at the meeting of the working group for the Western Balkans, member states discussed the possibility of adopting a dual-track approach. First, there would be a freezing of funds and the lifting of the flight ban. Secondly, there would be the lifting of the oil embargo, and a clear, common position on the necessity for the Serbian opposition to have a common platform against Milosevic. On 9 February 2000, at Coreper, the United Kingdom and the Netherlands were reluctant to have a reference to the possible lifting of further measures, which meant to the lifting of the oil embargo. Finally, on 14 February 2000, the GAC decided, after much discussion, not to refer to the oil embargo; to waive the embargo on flights between EU countries and the FRY for six months; and to invite the European Commission to come forward with detailed proposals for strengthening the effectiveness of existing financial sanctions without penalizing the Serbian people. The United Kingdom and the Netherlands succeeded in having their request for the reinforcement of financial sanctions granted.

A package deal, including the lifting of the flight ban and the reinforcement of financial sanctions, seemed to have been agreed on. The discussions then switched to the first pillar. The Council adopted the common position of suspending the flight ban for six months with no difficulty, at first. Then the most sensitive negotiation began. In early March 2000, the European Commission presented a draft Council regulation concerning a freeze on funding and a ban on investment in relation to the FRY. On 9 March 2000, at the CFSP counsellors group, the Commission's proposal was put on the table. According to an interviewee, the serious work then started. The CFSP counsellors working group was the main body responsible for negotiating the conditions of the reinforcement of the financial sanctions. It met eight times in March 2000. The Commission's proposal was extremely strict, and for all states, except for the United Kingdom and the Netherlands, equivalent to a trade embargo, and hence difficult to agree to. But, according to article 301 of the Treaty of Amsterdam, EU states were forced to come to an agreement based on the Commission's proposal, and must do so by qualified majority.

Before continuing the negotiation at CFSP counsellors group level, the counsellors had to wait for the outcome of the meeting of the management committee that was responsible for implementing the financial sanctions.[42] On 10 March 2000, the management committee met. It was in favour of the Commission's proposal. On 13 March 2000, at the CFSP counsellors group, the negotiation became difficult. The United Kingdom announced that the non-acceptance of the Commission's proposal could lead it to take the issue of the financial sanctions to the GAC as a B point, which would mean that the ministers themselves would have to negotiate an agreement on the reinforcement of the financial sanctions, and which would consequently stop the procedure for the lifting of the flight ban.[43]

The GAC of 20 March 2000 represents a turning point in this case study, as it set the framework of the sanctions policy. EU states adopted both the Council regulation suspending the flight ban and the Council conclusions on the modification of financial sanctions: negotiations were ordered to be concluded before the end of the month. EU states implemented and, at the same time, narrowed down the CFSP decision. They agreed to negotiate the financial sanctions immediately, by linking the lifting of the flight ban to the reinforcement of the financial sanctions: and the GAC agreed that the lifting of the flight ban should be simultaneous with the reinforcement of the financial sanctions 'before the end of the month.' This was a surprising agreement, as the majority of the states seemed to have wanted more time to negotiate the reinforcement of the financial sanctions, and as France and Germany finally accepted a policy they had not seemed to want at the beginning of the negotiations. Between 20 March and 5 April, at the CFSP counsellors group, there were tough negotiations between the European Commission and the states, as regards the conditions attached to the implementation of the financial sanctions. Finally, on 5 April 2000, at Coreper, the procedure was launched with no comments. The issue was ready to go to the GAC as an A point.

What was really meant in the final decisions by 'suspending the flight ban' and 'reinforcing the financial sanctions'? Suspending the flight ban was to apply for all carriers, both Yugoslavian, which were not allowed to use EU air space or refuel on EU territory, and European. This decision went against the British position, which wanted a lifting of the ban only for EU carriers. It was also to apply for a limited period of time, not unlimited, as most of the states' officials would have liked. The time factor did correspond, however, to the British position. The decision on the lifting of the flight ban seems to reflect a bargaining process between the United Kingdom and the other EU states.

Reinforcing the financial sanctions meant establishing a white list and not a black one. The white list was a list of all the Serbian companies that were not in contact with Milosevic; Serbian companies that wished to have links with the EU had to prove that they had no contacts with Milosevic to be on this list. The black list was a list of companies that were in contact with Milosevic. According to the Commission, a black list was impossible to make as no firm would denounce itself as being black. According to the majority of state officials, a white list was impossible to make as no firm would want to announce it was against Milosevic. According to the *Financial Times*:

> Serbian companies will be afraid to come forward and present proof that they are not owned by members of the regime, as they will risk being penalised by the Serb authorities (by preventing them from getting raw materials or withdrawing their export licence) ... In addition, the companies have developed fantastic methods to avoid sanctions. (16/06/00)

At the beginning of the negotiation, the majority of state officials were in favour of a black list, whereas in the end, they all accepted the creation of a white list.

Power Politics and Manipulation

Intergovernmentalist theory would seem appropriate to explain the construction of the final common policies towards the FRY in early 2000. Policy outcomes seemed to satisfy all state representatives. There was no common policy on the lifting of the oil ban, as some states opposed it. All EU states seemed to agree with the issue linkage between the lifting of the flight ban and the reinforcement of the financial sanctions, especially as these two sanctions were not very important for EU states in terms of impact on their economy.

Both negotiations and the outcomes of the negotiations were complex. The final decision on the lifting of the flight ban and the reinforcement of the financial sanctions was extremely difficult to implement, and was characterized as ineffective. It was considered a shambles by some of my interviewees: 'The outcome was clearly a mess,' or, 'The agreement is not very clear but every one can say she or he gained something out of it.' According to these interviewees, the decision was an LCD decision.

In addition to being ineffective, this decision mostly addressed an institutional battle: EU states were no longer negotiating about the regulation for implementing the CFSP decision on financial sanctions, but about the European Commission's powers in the implementation process of this regulation. The negotiation that took place in the last days of March was, according to some interviewees, mainly 'institutional.' EU officials told me that 'there are also many institutional issues that are not related to the policy towards the Balkans. France and Germany fear the Commission and they want to prevent it from having too much power,' or that 'France was faced with a different problem: the role of member states within the EU decision-making process. However, the Council legal service accepted the Commission's interpretation.' The final decision in April was also viewed as an LCD. One delegate emphasized, 'We accept this agreement although it looks like an institutional monster.' Another answered, 'We have seen worse!' This negotiation shows that we are far from the description given by the sociological institutionalists Joerges and Neyer (1997a; 1997b) of interactions in committees among national and supranational experts, which they characterize as deliberations and joint problem-solving.

However, reaching common policy on the lifting of the flight ban and the reinforcement of the financial sanctions was an enormous achievement. During the negotiation process, state representatives were concerned that the whole negotiation would fail, and that there would be no common policy at all. The decision revealed a change in the positions of big states. This was confirmed by the fact that in July 2000, several months after the Commission's proposal was passed, some state officials still continued to think that the EU's sanctions policy was not appropriate. According to Agence Europe, 'Several ministers spoke in favour of a review of the policy of sanctions currently being applied against the FRY: Greece, Finland, Sweden, Ireland, Belgium and France judged the situation as not being satisfactory' (10–11/07/00, 7).

I now want to discuss why it was possible to reach common policy on the lifting of the flight ban and the reinforcement of the sanctions policy, but impossible to do so on the lifting of the oil embargo. This will involve a fairly lengthy return to the first step of the debate, under the second pillar, and especially the role of the United States and of peer group pressure. I will then show how the implementation of these sanctions was influenced in the second step, under the first pillar, by the Commission's deployment of its expertise and its ability to manipulate states into agreeing with the position it had already taken up on the policy to adopt towards the FRY.

Second Pillar Phase: U.S. Approval, Peer Group Pressure

From 1991 onwards, the former Yugoslavia was a question of common concern for the United States and the EU states – though they did not always agree on the way to solve the Balkan crisis. European diplomacy failed in the early 1990s, and the lack of U.S. support seems to have been crucial. According to Holbrooke (1999, 51), the European Vance-Owen Peace Plan 'proposed dividing Bosnia into ten "cantons," some of which would be Muslim controlled, and some Croat controlled. It had been attacked by many American commentators as a sell-out, another Munich and precursor to the break-up of Bosnia.' According to Woodward (1995, 324), 'the U.S. Congress and the Clinton administration derided the Vance-Owen plan for appeasing Serbs and rewarding "land grabs."' Gow (1997, 199) said that the Vance-Owen Peace Plan 'was resoundingly rejected in Washington.' Owen himself (1995, 107–8) also mentioned the U.S. negative reaction to his plan. However, he believed that 'had the Clinton administration supported the Vance-Owen Peace Plan, we would have been able to carry it out' (Owen 1995, 38).

In addition, the United States refused to send troops, and wanted to bomb Serbia. EU states opposed this policy. U.S. Senator John McCain, and the UK Foreign Secretary, Malcolm Rifkind, were extremely angry about the policy conducted by each other's government. At a meeting in 1995, Senator McCain apparently came close to slapping Rifkind. For Gow (1997, 156), 'a major difference was between the United States on the one hand and the Europeans and the Russians on the other, more or less from the beginning of 1993 onwards.'

However, there was a need for Europeans to coordinate their policies with the Americans, both on a bilateral level and within NATO, in order to find a solution to the Yugoslav crisis. One would expect the United States to be linked with the EU in the Balkans, as the United States was a major player in the area. The United States had a prominent role in resolving the crises, both diplomatically and at the military level, through NATO. According to one commentator:

> In 1992, the nature of the problems involved in Bosnia, the difficulties already experienced and, not least, NATO's need to establish a role for itself, all contributed to NATO contributing substantially to planning and organising UNPROFOR in Bosnia. (Gow 1997, 112)

More bluntly, Gow also said that 'without U.S. involvement, the European allies in NATO simply did not have enough troops to make sure that a fiasco would be avoided' (Gow 1997, 180). From 1991 until 1999, there were few or no effective EU policies towards the FRY.[44]

In 1999, Kosovo was a major foreign policy issue. EU governments had little choice but to coordinate their policies on Kosovo with the United States. The French and the British had similar views on this coordination, even if they differed on specific proposals. Gow noted:

> France and the UK, traditionally distrustful of each other even as allies, began to form an axis for military-political policy and activity in the European context. This emerged after both countries made sizeable deployments of armed forces to operate with UNPROFOR in Bosnia and with the WEU [Western European Union] and NATO in support of UN Security Council resolutions. (1997, 183)

Of particular interest in this section of my study is the way the United States was effectively linked to the EU, the channels used by the United States to make its point of view known, and the extent to which the U.S. position was taken into account.

The United States was involved directly and indirectly in the EU's policy-making on sanctions. In terms of direct action, the United States contacted the Permanent Representations in Brussels, and shared its expertise. According to an interviewee:

> The documents relative to the U.S. policy towards the Balkans were passed on to the Permanent Representations. For instance, the United States was indicating to the EU which Serbian firms had to be banned from having any links with European firms.[45]

Another interviewee confirmed that 'the United States gave lists of the firms due to be considered black.' The United States was also in permanent contact with the United Kingdom, and used that contact to make its position clearly known. One interviewee said that 'even at the negotiation table, the United Kingdom reminded the other European countries that the United States had to be informed on the evolution of the EU's position.'

The United States had an impact on the EU's common policy on the lifting of the flight ban, by intervening on a bilateral level with the United Kingdom. The United Kingdom appears to have obtained U.S. assent to lift the flight ban at EU level. The British Foreign Affairs Minister, Robin Cook, announced the United Kingdom was ready to lift the flight ban for European carriers, and not for JAT, the Yugoslav airline, during a joint press conference with the U.S. Secretary of State,

Madeleine Albright, in Washington on 9 February 2000. The press (*Financial Times*, 08/02/00; *Le Monde*, 11/02/00, 5) stated that Mr Cook was trying to win U.S. support for the revamped sanctions package. One interviewee was extremely bitter about the British attitude:

> Member states can be very bad, and have no solidarity. As regards the package deal, the United Kingdom blocked any agreement for several months. Then, suddenly, the United Kingdom gave in, but it announced it in Washington with the United States! This is not EU politics. This is about big countries' politics and power politics.

The press also condemned the British attitude: 'In order to take a decision by unanimity, the United Kingdom had to be convinced, and it went to Washington last week to ask for permission' (*Le Figaro*, 15/02/00).

The United States was clearly against lifting the flight ban for all carriers, both European and JAT. One interviewee reported that 'the day preceding the 14 February GAC meeting, Albright was extremely tough, and not ready to give in on the JAT.' Another said categorically that 'the United States did not want to suspend the flight ban for JAT,' and added, interestingly, that for the American administration there was the problem that 'lifting the flight ban would be considered weak by the Republican opposition.' In the end, as shown above, the ban was lifted for all carriers. However, the United Kingdom and the EU did not follow the American position slavishly on all points. The United Kingdom negotiated with the United States in order to secure its own preferred policy. According to one interviewee, 'Cook wanted it on record that the United States agrees with the lifting of the flight ban. If Albright said this in public, she could not get out of it: it came to locking Albright in.'

The EU did not agree with the U.S. point of view, that the flight ban should either not be lifted at all or should be lifted only for European carriers. Instead, the EU made its own policy prevail, of lifting the flight ban for all carriers. However, it is important to add that the United States did not insist on its position; the issue was not brought to presidential level. Some interviewees said that they would not have been surprised if higher intervention on the part of the United States had changed the EU decision (for instance, if President Clinton had decided to speak to the European Union heads of state and governments). They were sceptical about the ability of the EU to stand up to Clinton.

The United States was in contact with other states. Interviewees noted that 'since July, Cook, van Aartsen [the Dutch minister for foreign affairs], and Albright met on a regular basis'; 'there were contacts between the United Kingdom, the Netherlands and the United States,' and 'Albright was in Europe all the time.' Finally, the United States was in contact with EU institutions. According to an interviewee, 'Patten was in contact with Albright on a weekly basis.' The United States also lobbied the Commission during the first pillar phase of the decision-making process, when the implementation of the reinforcement of financial sanctions was discussed. An interviewee revealed that 'when negotiating on the conditions set for FRY firms to be part of the white list, the U.S. representative thought that the Commission had not gone far enough.'

Indirectly, the United States had means of influencing EU states through the Contact Group and the Quint, which are both informal groupings of big EU states and the United States. Russia is also part of the Contact Group. The Contact Group was created in 1994 in order to give a coherent response to the Bosnian crisis. It appeared to be a constant feature linked to the CFSP decision-making process during all the Balkan crises. In the period discussed here, there was an official meeting on 23 February 1999. Another one was organized on 28 March 2000 in Paris, to discuss the rising unrest in Kosovo. Finally, a third took place on 3 May 2000, and the High Representative and the Commission were both represented there. Contact Group meetings might seem to have been rather infrequent for the negotiation of sanctions policy. However, one must be aware of the fact that these meetings are not always publicized.

The Quint was the informal body in which the United States and big EU states discussed matters related to the Balkans. Several interviewees argued that 'it was clear that the decision on the sanctions on the FRY was made in a small committee with the United States.' Despite the difficulty in fully grasping the functioning of the Quint, as it is extremely discreet and does not issue any official documents, it is fairly clear that the existence of this group had implications for the nature of the EU sanctions policy. In particular, in this case, the Quint had an impact in that there was no modification of the oil embargo, which the United States did not want to see lifted. One interviewee said that the 'Quint decided that only the lifting of the flight ban and the reinforcement of the financial sanctions would be discussed at EU level, and not the lifting of the oil ban.' The Quint also had an impact

on the modification of the flight ban and financial sanctions. Interviewees explained that: 'in the Quint and with the EU Presidency, there
were regular discussions'; 'the Quint always "pre-cooked" the EU
decisions, and this prevented the EU from making any other move';
and 'the whole question of the sanctions was negotiated at the Quint.'
The Quint seems to have been at the origin of the EU common policy
on sanctions towards the FRY.

The United States appears clearly here as a major player in the EU
decision-making process. The United States lobbied the EU for it to
adopt the same sanctions policy as itself towards the FRY. As regards
U.S. influence, several interviewees had the impression that the United
States had dictated its own position to the EU. They stated: 'our policy
is clearly dictated by the United States'; 'the package deal [flight ban and
visa ban against the reinforcement of the financial sanctions] was obviously dictated by the United States'; 'the thirteen thought there was no
way out. They changed their opinion because of the United States. They
did not dare to go against the U.S. opinion'; and 'it is not the first time
[speaking of the lifting of the flight ban] a policy is dictated by the
United States; the same happened when the oil embargo was set.'

The United States, in sum, was far from indifferent about CFSP outcomes. Indeed, it cared very much. The United States was present in
the informal CFSP decision-making process, and it also had an impact
on the common policies considered in this case study. The United
States seems to have prevented the EU from lifting the oil embargo. It
also seems to have partially influenced the lifting of the flight ban, in
so far as it allowed it to happen. The United States can be considered
an unofficial player in the EU's decision-making process. If a policy is
not vital to the United States, that is, when the United States does not
insist at presidential level, the EU can have its own policy, and does so.

The FRY case does not show that the phenomenon of socialization
had any impact on the decisions taken. However, it does reveal the
existence and impact of the positions taken up by different areas of the
administration on a state's position, and especially the impact of peer
group pressure. This concept is catered to in intergovernmentalist
theory. 'Peer group pressure' refers to the pressure put on one or more
state officials by the majority of state officials, who want to reach a
common position. This pressure is mostly effective if exercised over a
long period of time on the same official. It is not a sufficient factor for
the reaching of a common policy, but it can be a trigger for a state's
change in position.

The final lifting of the EU flight ban was facilitated by internal administrative divisions within the British government, and triggered by the pressure exercised by the other EU states on the United Kingdom. This internal division was apparently not solved when the United Kingdom came to the negotiation table in mid-February 2000.

State representatives used the division in order to put pressure on British Secretary of State for Foreign and Commonwealth Affairs Robin Cook. An interviewee observed:

> On Sunday and Monday morning, Fischer, Gama and Solana spoke to Cook. The Commission and the member states also told Cook a common position was needed in order to boost the Serb Opposition, and Cook agreed to lift the flight ban on Monday.

According to another interviewee, at the GAC in February 2000, 'Cook agreed to lift the flight ban for all carriers at the GAC, knowing Blair and his private office were against it.' Cook might have calculated his position and estimated first, that by giving today, the United Kingdom would be able to gain tomorrow in another field, and secondly, that by lifting the flight ban, some reinforcement of the financial sanctions would be made, to the advantage of the United Kingdom. An interviewee argued that 'Cook was very cunning, as this was a way to obtain something on the financial sanctions. Indeed, no one ever spoke of reinforcing the sanctions before Cook's intervention. The United Kingdom took its responsibility but set its conditions.'

In the end, some interviewees indeed perceived the British position as a bluff; interviewees believed 'the United Kingdom was very well served.' A British official confirmed their belief, as he stated that 'the decision did what we wanted it to do.' If this is true, then intergovernmentalism can explain this strategy. However, the disagreements within the British government seem to have been genuine.

The main reason given by interviewees for the United Kingdom's acceptance of a lifting of the flight ban was Robin Cook's unwillingness to stay in an isolated position. He was isolated for five months, from July until the end of December 1999, at the General Affairs Council, with the other thirteen state representatives pushing for the flight ban to be lifted. He agreed to give in under the pressure of his EU colleagues. In return, he succeeded in achieving a bargaining process, and obtaining a good deal for the United Kingdom. Here again, intergovernmentalism provides the appropriate terms for the process: peer group pressure triggered discussion and a package deal characterized by issue-linkage was negotiated.

First Pillar Phase: Commission in Charge

The states' freedom of decision with regard to the sanctions against FRY was also curtailed by the influence of the European Commission itself. When the institutional rules give a formal power to the Commission, that is, when the first pillar is involved in CFSP issues, the Commission will always be able to inflect the CFSP decision-making process and policy outcomes. In this case study, under the first pillar phase, the Commission played more than a managerial role; it shaped the EU's common policy on the reinforcement of financial sanctions. The final outcome was brought about by the constraining effects of the EU rules.

The Commission's aim was to have an effective financial sanctions policy, in the sense that the sanctions against the FRY should actually be implemented. This was not usually the case either in the member states or in the United States. For instance, when there were sanctions set against Iraq, EU states did not implement them: according to one EU official, 'although there were sanctions against Iraq, France decided to go to the Baghdad fair [similar to the Hanover 2000 fair]. Within two years, all EU states went to Iraq. The Commission would like to prevent this kind of situation from happening again.' The Commission made use of its expertise, the legislative procedure, and the divisions among the member states, in order to widen its prerogatives. It succeeded, as interviewees criticized the Commission for having a 'very political attitude'; it was 'getting what it wants,' and it opposed Belgium, Finland, France, and Germany 'until the end.'

The Commission made use of the management committee, which was responsible for implementing the EU's sanctions policy. The mere existence of this management committee showed a blurring of the competences between the first and the second pillar. In 1999, some big states, mainly France and Germany, had wanted to create just such a committee that would have operated exclusively under the CFSP pillar. These states could not, however, justify this, as the Treaty on European Union stipulated that implementation of the sanctions policy should come under the first pillar. The CFSP decision-making process on FRY sanctions was therefore completely dependent on a purely first pillar mechanism. The existence of the management committee and of the comitology procedure reinforced the Commission's capacity for action within the CFSP framework, and reduced member states' room to manoeuvre.[46]

In spring 2000, a management committee meeting was organized for the reinforcement of the financial sanctions. On 10 March 2000, it met for the second time since its creation.[47] The Commission played a dominant role within this committee, in every sense. Unlike meetings at the Council where seating arrangements are such that all officials feel they are on an equal footing, the layout of seats at the meetings of the management committee placed the Commission physically in a dominant position. This can be seen clearly in figure 4.1.

According to a Commission official, this physical disposition was not specifically wanted by the Commission. However, whatever the intention, management committee meetings would seem like a classroom meeting, where the teacher sits alone facing the pupils. As regards the discussion, there were apparently rarely interactions between member states. The interaction followed the pattern: Commission/state A/Commission, Commission/state B/Commission. State representatives were therefore not encouraged to engage in discussion with one another, and more importantly, states seemed to be individually responsible towards the Commission.

As regards the substance of matters discussed, European Commission officials seemed to be much more informed, and in control of the issues, than the member states. The whole discussion was led by the Commission's official, who clearly had greater expertise. For instance, an interviewee reported that one of the EU state representatives, who had no answer to the Commission's question, complained that the item discussed was not on the agenda. However, it was. The Commission was extremely surprised that state representatives did not complain about the white list, as that was supposed to be the main discussion item. State representatives did not succeed in explaining their positions, and did not manage to show the advantages of a black list to the Commission, which was in favour of a white list for FRY companies. The outcome of the management committee was therefore – inevitably – agreement that the Commission had adopted the right approach as regards its strict proposal, that is, a white list, and not a black list, for the reinforcement of financial sanctions against the FRY, and that it could propose this approach to the state representatives within the CFSP framework.

Figure 4.1: Meetings when Portugal Held the Presidency
(January–June 2000)

1. Council meetings:

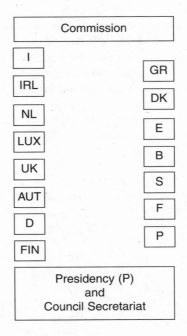

2. Management committee meetings:[48]

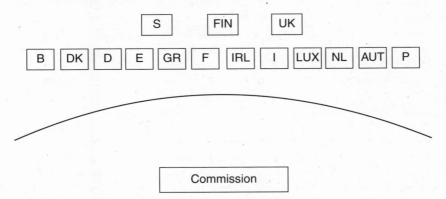

As regards the decision-making procedure, the fact that the result of the management committee meeting was waited for before a decision was taken at the CFSP counsellors group shows how involved the first pillar had become in decisions to be taken under the CFSP pillar. This was a new situation. Before 1999, when implementation of the sanctions policy was being decided, the issue was discussed exclusively within the CFSP framework at the Council of the European Union. A parallel can be drawn between the opinion of the first pillar committee, which must be considered before taking a CFSP decision, and the opinion of the European Parliament required when a Council decision, in the commercial sphere for instance, is taken. One would think that a mere opinion could be ignored by the Council. But it is difficult to do so. In addition, as has been the case with the European Parliament and its rise in power, if the Commission succeeds in forcing member states to create sanctions committees within the first pillar framework every time the states decide to sanction a third party, then management committees for EU sanctions policies could become the norm, and the Commission will be able to give its opinion on a regular basis. This is still the case under the Treaty of Lisbon.

In this instance, then, the discussion that took place at the management committee was used by the European Commission in the CFSP counsellors group. The Commission emphasized that, as states had failed materially to create a black list, a white list was the only solution for effective implementation of the reinforcement of financial sanctions. The Commission played more than a managerial role here. Its initial proposal of a white list was not accepted as such by all the states: many modifications were made. However, in the end, the creation of a white list, and not that of a black list, was accepted. This was facilitated by the nature of treaty provisions, by the role of the presidency, by the lack of expertise among state officials, and finally by some state representatives' will to reach a common policy, as they were pressured by their peers.

Treaty provisions were important. States could only change the Commission's proposal by unanimity. Initially, the majority of states were opposed to it; but then they progressively accepted the proposal made by the Commission. Italy and Greece, for instance, accepted the Commission's proposal in principle, as both countries are in favour of respecting the Commission's prerogatives in the EU decision-making process. The last states resisting the Commission's proposal, namely Belgium, Finland, France, and Germany, soon realized that they could not stay isolated, especially as these same states had officially agreed upon the reinforcement of the financial sanctions in the second pillar framework in February 2000, and did not want to go against their own decision. The February decision had constrained the positions of states.

The absence of a deadline in the second pillar decision for implementing both the suspension of the flight ban and a reinforcement of the financial sanctions was used by the presidency, which appeared to be in favour of the Commission's proposal. The presidency proposed a deadline in the framework of the implementation of the second pillar decision. It also proposed that suspension of the flight ban and reinforcement of the financial sanctions be put into effect simultaneously. Member states were compelled to agree with this proposal. They had not expected the presidency to make the second pillar decision more specific, and to propose a deadline. They had envisaged simply dealing first with the implementation of the suspension of the flight ban, and secondly with the implementation of the reinforcement of financial sanctions.

It seems the presidency was playing with the rules. It proposed at the 20 March 2000 General Affairs Council that the necessary adoption of the regulation on the reinforcement of the financial sanctions should be completed before the end of the month, although there was no need to have a text with a deadline. The presidency could simply have proposed a text on the flight ban, and not on the financial sanctions, and, especially, need not have fixed a deadline for conclusion by the Council. In that case, only the proposal on the flight ban might have got through, as only a qualified majority was required for its approval. The United Kingdom and the Netherlands were the only countries against deferred adoption of the regulation on the flight ban and the regulation on financial sanctions, and these two states wanted to be sure the financial sanctions would be implemented as early as possible. Once the presidency had proposed the inclusion of a deadline in the Council conclusions, the majority of the member states could not refuse it, as they had accepted the package 'lifting of the flight ban and reinforcement of the financial sanctions' at second pillar level.

One can conclude from this event that the presidency, held at that time by Portugal, did not act according to the rules written in the presidency handbook (1996, 5) according to which 'the Presidency must, by definition, be neutral and impartial.' The Portuguese presidency had an informal alliance with the Commission, and it managed to pass a decision that the majority of states did not want. In the CFSP field, the presidency can have an agenda-shaping power. Taking into consideration that the agenda-setting powers of the presidency seem to be limited in the first pillar framework, as according to Hayes-Renshaw and Wallace (1996, 146), 'the real opportunity to promote initiatives ... is heavily constrained,' the presidency's role in the CFSP field on this occasion is remarkable. Dinan (1999, 524) would expect the presidency to be influential in the CFSP field, as he underlines that 'clearly, the Presidency remains central to CFSP representation and to other aspects of the CFSP's operations.' This situation is not anticipated in intergovernmentalist theory.

The majority of state representatives were clearly taken by surprise. One delegate stated that she or he did not think that the negotiation would advance as quickly as it did: 'The United Kingdom acted with a Damocles sword, it is going much quicker than I would have thought, there is going to be a result at next week's Coreper, it is absolutely amazing.' Other interviewees said that 'as regards the financial sanctions, the member states were not aware of what they signed,' and 'this measure is equivalent to a trade embargo. We had never expected that.' There were unanticipated consequences. The majority of the states were so much involved in the lifting of the flight ban, which they regarded as very important in order to show their will to support the Serbian opposition, that they had not evaluated the consequences of their agreement to reinforce the financial sanctions. They had not foreseen the possibility that the Commission could propose a text which for many of them was equivalent to a trade embargo, and that the presidency could set its deadline. But they could not at this point refuse to do something they had accepted two weeks before; and they had very little time to establish a strategy to reach a final outcome different from the Commission's proposal.

In addition to this lack of foresight, there was a lack of expertise. During the negotiations, some state representatives admitted that they were 'losing track of what was going on,' that 'the decision during the first phase was very badly made,' and that 'no one had thought of its consequences.' The issue of the implementation of the financial sanctions was extremely technical and difficult to understand. The Commission's superior expertise would not be expected by theorists of intergovernmentalism, who assume that supranational actors do not have more technical expertise than states. According to Moravcsik (1998, 480), they can even have less: 'sometimes, the Commission simply could not follow technical negotiations.' This was clearly not the case on this occasion.

State representatives, who were facing particular difficulties towards the end of the negotiation, played an interesting game when deciding on the extent of the white list in order to reinforce the financial sanctions, which does not correspond to the intergovernmentalist vision of the negotiation process. A double negotiation went on for some state representatives during the negotiation process: one with colleagues from other states and from the Commission in Brussels, and another with their own governments.

This negotiation proceeded as follows: a state representative in Brussels would present his or her state's position at the beginning of the EU negotiation process. Then, this representative would realize, under the pressure of the Commission and other state representatives, that his or her state had to adapt its position to the Commission's proposal in order to reach a common policy. At this point, the capitals were also involved: representatives were constantly in contact with their capitals over the phone during the meetings. They spent more time talking to and negotiating with their capitals (intrastate negotiation), than negotiating with their respective EU colleagues (intra-EU negotiation). An EU official stated that: 'A colleague had to lobby his government to find an agreement. In general, representatives spend a lot of time lobbying their own state, even a big state.'

As a result of this intrastate negotiation, interviewees reported what some representatives had said during the EU negotiation process: 'As we are among friends, I can tell you that I am here at the limit of my instructions,' and 'You asked me to sell this proposal to my government ... this is what I did.' This attitude recalls the one described by Lewis (1998, 11) in his study of Coreper. State representatives feel they have a 'dual personality or a Janus face': they act on behalf of their governments in Brussels, and they act on behalf of their EU colleagues in the capitals.

At the beginning of the negotiation process, many interviewees were extremely concerned with the outcome of the negotiation. They were worried that there would be no agreement, because the positions of the various states were so divergent. The blocking of agreement by one or another state seemed very likely. The atmosphere was extremely tense. The fact that CFSP counsellors negotiated more with their own state than with other CFSP counsellors meant as a consequence that their state did not block the proposal at a later stage. A common policy was facilitated by this exchange of information and negotiation between the representatives in Brussels and their home capitals during EU meetings. Some states finally accepted a common policy they had refused at the beginning of the EU process, because their representatives at EU level decided to negotiate a new national position with their own governments, and because their representatives were prepared to go to the extreme limit of their instructions. These representatives were not convinced by the arguments from the Commission, or from other states, that a white list was better than a black list. Instead, as intergovernmentalist theory suggests, they were convinced that reaching a common policy was better for their states than the absence of a common policy. The reputation of a state thus seems to be an important factor in reaching a common policy.

A Higher than LCD Policy Outcome

Not all intergovernmentalist assumptions seem to be validated by this case study. Member states are certainly the most important actors; they are the only ones who could legally decide on the issue of the sanctions policy towards the FRY. And, as predicted by intergovernmentalism, states did not look at the gains other states might make out of the EU position. They were only concerned about their own national gains ('absolute gains' in intergovernmentalist terminology).

There is, however, no evidence to support the intergovernmentalist assumption that states can always be considered to be acting as unitary states. The example of Robin Cook's taking a different position from Tony Blair shows that states can have internal divisions, and that these divisions can be made public at EU level. Nor is the intergovernmentalist assumption that state representatives act rationally validated here. Some officials, first the British, and then the French and the Germans, acted in a surprising way, accepting a final common policy which did not correspond to their initial interests. In addition, states were constrained by past decisions, both when the Commission proposed the creation of the management committee and reminded the states of its existence, and when the Portuguese presidency made the second pillar decision on the financial sanctions more precise and proposed a deadline that states could not refuse. Intergovernmentalist theory would not expect these past decisions to have an impact on positions of states – though historical institutionalism would. There could be new information here, to help predict future situations.

Under the Treaty of Lisbon, the High Representative takes the place of the rotating presidency at the Foreign Affairs Council. Given that the High Representative also is vice-president of the Commission, it is possible that she or he might adopt the same type of strategy as the Portuguese presidency did in this case. However, she or he might be more limited in his or her action than a rotating presidency, as his or her actions are accountable to states.

In this case study, EU decisions concerning the FRY had few consequences for the national economy of EU states. Some states did not benefit from the modification of sanctions policy. For instance, for the United Kingdom, the lifting of the flight ban was not beneficial per se, as British Airways could not benefit from it in the same way as the other EU companies. The British government had an air services agreement with the FRY government for air slots. It therefore had had legal difficulties in implementing the flight ban, as British Airways was afraid of a breach of contract, and it would have problems in re-establishing links with the FRY when the flight ban was lifted.

The external influence of the Serbian opposition was not a determinant factor for the reaching of a common policy. Had the Serbian opposition played a role, it seems that the United Kingdom would have agreed to reach a common policy before February 2000. A letter written by the Serbian opposition in January 2000 stating that 'the EU should lift the ban for all carriers, and not only the European carriers as the EU would then be accused of only taking care of EU matters' was presented at the Political Committee, but it apparently did not have an impact on the EU's decision-making process. Although one EU official stated that 'the letter from the opposition helped a bit,' another was persuaded that 'the letter did not count at all. In November and December, the opposition was already issuing declarations, and the United Kingdom did not give in at that time.'

The final common policy on the lifting of the flight ban and the reinforcement of the financial sanctions appears to satisfy all states. However, the lifting of the flight ban for all carriers was apparently not the preference of the United Kingdom at the beginning of the negotiation process, and the reinforcement of financial sanctions by implementing a white list, instead of a black list, was apparently not the preference of France and Germany at the beginning of the negotiation process. Big states thus accepted a final common policy which did not correspond to their initial policy strategies. It seems to have been a higher than LCD common policy.

The United States played an important role in the CFSP system, especially through the Quint. It apparently determined the absence of discussion at EU level on a possible lifting of an oil embargo, and it also contributed to the debate on intra-EU bargaining, as the deal 'lifting of the flight ban versus reinforcement of the financial sanctions' was struck at EU level after the United States gave its approval.

The Commission played an influential role in the reinforcement of financial sanctions. Its white list was passed, despite the opposition of mainly France and Germany, two big states. The reaction of some representatives showed that the outcome of the negotiation was far from what their initial position had been: 'One knew the orientation of the Commission but not the methodology. The Commission had a very strict interpretation of the texts. The Commission was ignoble.' The role of the Commission does not correspond here to the definition given by Moravcsik whereby, at its best, the Commission is at the service of the member states: 'The Commission increases the efficiency of bargaining by providing a set of passive, transaction-cost reducing rules' (Moravcsik 1993, 518). The Commission did not just 'correct' member states' texts.[49] Nor did it act as a mere secretariat, but in fact it led the discussion under the EC framework, by shaping the proposal, and outvoting France and Germany. It carried out 'autonomous action' (Pierson 1996, 132), and exploited treaty rules and past decisions in its favour. Intergovermentalists would not have expected this to happen. For intergovernmentalism, the most likely outcome would have been no agreement at all on the reinforcement of the financial sanctions, or at least an agreement which corresponded to French and German preferences, as these states should have been capable of changing the Commission's proposal.

To conclude: analysis of the EU decision not to modify the oil ban, to lift the flight ban, and to reinforce financial sanctions reveals understudied facets of the CFSP decision-making process. One could argue that the United Kingdom bargained with France and Germany. Big member states all had to make concessions. It was a higher than LCD decision, constrained by the United States and the Commission.

5 A CFSP–ESDP Case:
Institutional Relations with NATO (1998–2008)

This chapter concentrates on EU links with NATO since 1998. It seeks to understand the conditions under which member states accepted or refused certain links with NATO and succeeded in reaching EU common policies in the European Security and Defence Policy (ESDP) field. Intergovermentalism by this showing is insufficient to explain the making of CFSP–ESDP policies, as the United States and past decisions both influenced the reaching of common policies.

CFSP–ESDP issues are mainly decided by big EU states. The political directors of the three biggest EU states, Britain, France, and Germany, meet informally on a regular basis. However, according to an interviewee, 'The motors of the negotiation are France and the United Kingdom. Germany is in between the two to adjust. Then, the other member states look at the compromise decided by the three large states and accept it.' The focus here is on France and the United Kingdom, as they had major disagreements with one another and as both are major security actors. They possess nuclear weapons, are part of the UN Security Council, and are part of the world's top three biggest military powers, based on defence expenditure.[50]

External and Internal Constraints on the Foundations of ESDP

Both France and the United Kingdom started making concessions to one another at the beginning of the 1990s.[51] The United Kingdom made some efforts to accommodate the Europeanists, represented by France. For instance, the United Kingdom made a compromise in 1992, when it agreed with the 'Declaration on Western European Union,' a protocol attached to the Maastricht Treaty, which allowed the WEU to strengthen itself as the defence arm of the EU. At the same time, France satisfied the Atlanticists, especially the United Kingdom and the United States, as it accepted that 'the objective is to develop WEU as a means to strengthen the European pillar of the Atlantic Alliance,' and that 'the WEU will act in conformity with the positions adopted in the Atlantic Alliance' (K. Smith 2004, 182). The British Minister for Foreign Affairs, Douglas Hogg, made it clear that 'NATO is the core of our defence arrangements and that anything done within the WEU must be compatible with existing NATO arrangements' (House of Commons Document, 28/10/92).

Then, at the Birmingham WEU ministerial meeting in 1996, following the French rapprochement with NATO, the British government suggested that the Common Joint Task Forces be used without U.S. involvement, but with the logistical support of NATO. The United Kingdom also proposed that NATO's Deputy SACEUR (Supreme Allied Commander Europe), the deputy NATO commander, who is always a European, be commander of the WEU forces. NATO states agreed that the Deputy SACEUR could act as 'strategic commander' of the WEU, if the WEU required this. The EU was nevertheless 'practically paralysed over the issue of merging the WEU into the EU' (K. Smith 2004, 205) in the mid-1990s.

Unexpectedly, the United Kingdom committed itself in the late 1990s to the development of a European defence, whereas before it had constantly argued in favour of an exclusively NATO defence of Europe. Furthermore, interinstitutional consultation between the EU and NATO was recommended: France accepted in-depth contacts between NATO and the EU, whereas previously it had always wanted the EU to be autonomous vis-à-vis NATO.[52]

The Franco-British declaration at St Malo on 4 December 1998 represents a milestone in the history of the construction of a Common European Security and Defence Policy (CESDP, or, as referred to in this text, ESDP). It was described by one high-ranking French NATO official (House of Commons Debates, 1999–2000) as a 'Copernican Revolution.' Also, for Andreani, Bertram, and Grant (2001), it was 'Europe's military revolution.' It enabled the European Union to become competent in military and defence issues, as it gave the EU the possibility of developing European headquarters, and using intelligence and armaments. It stated bluntly: 'The European Union will also need to have recourse to suitable military means (European capabilities pre-designated within NATO's European pillar or *national or multinational European means outside the NATO framework*)' (St Malo Declaration, 04/12/98; my emphasis).

The Helsinki European Council in December 1999 acknowledged the Franco-British decision. EU states decided to create a European military capability which would cover the full range of Petersberg tasks. Then, in June 2000, at the Feira European Council, EU states focused on the conditions for implementing the Helsinki decisions. Finally, at Nice in December 2000, the European Council decided to develop ESDP institutions, and to make plans for the creation of the EU's strategic command, capabilities, and intelligence.

British and French Concessions

The relationship between the EU and NATO was the main point of contention between France and the United Kingdom when negotiating the creation of ESDP. The United Kingdom and France both agreed on EU positions towards NATO, which was perceived by academics and the media as unexpected and as going against their own interests. They gave the impression that they had changed both preference and position and they had been convinced by the arguments of their colleagues at EU level. This would correspond to a socialization process. However, in intergovernmentalist terms, these states only changed position, and not preference.

Before the St Malo agreement, the United Kingdom was opposed to the creation of ESDP for two reasons. The United Kingdom wanted to rely entirely on the existing NATO structure. Britain had long opposed the direct involvement of the EU in military matters, arguing that it could undermine NATO and annoy the Americans (Schake, Bloch-Laine, and Grant 1999, 27). Even in early 1998, at the NATO Amsterdam Summit, the British government prevented the merger of the WEU and the EU. In addition, the United Kingdom was reluctant to let the EU deal with a sovereign matter. The 1996 UK White Paper on the second intergovernmental conference stated plainly that decisions to send servicemen and women to risk their lives were for national governments, and not for decision in the European Union (Rees 1998, 62, 66).

The British U-turn of 1998, agreeing to confer upon the EU a genuine security remit (Howorth 1998, 274), shows a change in both preference and policy. For many, this was also a major change in position. Howorth (2000, 33) qualifies the United Kingdom turn as a revolution in military affairs. The United Kingdom is effectively 'at the pivot' (Heisbourg 2000, 9) of the European defence process. According to a prominent Labour Member of Parliament, St Malo was a surprise, and a schizophrenic policy. The former prime minister, Margaret Thatcher, and the Conservative Party were against the development of a common European security and defence policy, arguing that it would lead to the collapse of NATO (Howorth 2000, 47). Prime Minister Tony Blair therefore took a decision against the Conservative Party and against some members in his own party.

The Helsinki European Council text of December 1999 specified that the 'EU would intervene only where NATO *as a whole* was not engaged' (Helsinki European Council, 10–11/12/99; my emphasis).This was an ambiguous sentence, as the United Kingdom and France could give a different interpretation of the phrase 'as a whole.' The United Kingdom could say that the Helsinki declaration envisaged two organizations, and that there was no sequencing between the two. There would be no duplication, and NATO would remain the essential security and defence structure. However, France could argue that when NATO was not involved in a crisis, the EU could act alone and without NATO's authorization. France was especially afraid of giving NATO a right of first refusal. In the event of a crisis, NATO could decide that neither it nor the EU should act. NATO would be able to decide everything, which was exactly what the United States wanted.

There are three main reasons, given both in the textbooks and by my interviewees, for the British change in preference and acceptance of the creation of ESDP. The Prime Minister was dissatisfied with the way the United States behaved towards the United Kingdom during the Balkan crises. UK–US disagreements go back to 1995 when, according to an interviewee, the United States instructed the United Kingdom on how to conduct its policy. The United States was encouraging the EU to put an embargo on the Serbs and to bomb Serbia. British leaders were disturbed by this. Transatlantic relations were at a low point at that time. In 1998, the United Kingdom was in favour of an international military presence on the ground of approximately 36,000 to protect the Kosovar Albanians (Sharp 1999, 68), but the United States refused to contribute to ground troops. By early 2000, Prime Minister Tony Blair argued that Europeans should not expect the United States to play a role in every disorder in Europe. He made it clear that he wanted the EU to be able to act independently from the United States, in order to act, if need be, on the European continent.

In addition, the United Kingdom learned from pre-existing policy failures. The fact that the Europeans were incapable of dealing with the Balkan crises also influenced the UK decision to create ESDP. The Dayton agreements were reached through U.S., and not EU, mediation. Holbrooke (1999, 318) emphasized that 'Dayton shook the leadership elite of post Cold War Europe. The Europeans were grateful to the United States for leading the effort that finally ended the war in Bosnia, but some European officials were embarrassed that American involvement had been necessary.' Minister for Foreign Affairs Robin Cook himself explained on ITV on 1 April 2001 that Srebrenica was the reason for having a European defence policy. The British Prime Minister had already expressed his frustration over European inability to act in Kosovo at the summit of Poertschach in October 1998 (Ojanen, Herolf, and Lindahl 2000, 41).

Before the Helsinki summit of December 1999, the United Kingdom realized, having seen the events in Kosovo, that a European security and defence force was a necessity. An EU official commented that the EU lacked credibility because in Kosovo the EU could not put 40,000 soldiers together within six weeks and because the Russians were in Pristina before the United Kingdom. (This last instance was actually a question of strategy rather than impotence. British troops could have entered Pristina before the Russians, and were indeed ordered by General Clark to do so. The British commander General Jackson refused to follow NATO's supreme commander General Clark's order, as he did not wish 'to start World War Three' [Clark 2001, 398].) The NATO Allied Force air operation in spring 1999 would not have been possible without American combat planes. According to several writers (Quilès and Lamy 1999, 98; Missiroli 1999; Meiers 2000, 57), the weight of the United States was preponderant: 90 per cent of bombings were made by American aircrafts only, and the Europeans depended entirely on America's intelligence, its satellite information, and its transport capabilities.

Lastly, the United Kingdom wanted to be part of the European Union decision-making process and to take the lead in European security and defence policy, as it was excluded from the most important decisions taken at the EU level. It could not take part in the Euro-11 Council, and it could not take any decisions concerning the Schengen area. On 23 November 2001, Blair claimed that 'the argument is simple. We are part of Europe. It affects us directly and deeply. Therefore we should exercise leadership in order *to change Europe in the direc-*

tion we want' (Blair Speech, 12/11/01; my emphasis). The United Kingdom thus took the lead in creating an ESDP.[53] According to Anne Deighton (2002, 725), Blair was obsessed by the notion of leadership for Britain in Europe and on the global stage. The British change in position is related to British status, effectiveness, and credibility in the world arena. Britain realized it had to deal with the fact that the United States was not a fully reliable ally. At the same time, it was aware it could not completely trust France either. The Eighth Report of the Select Committee on Defence (House of Commons, 1999–2000, xxi) emphasized that 'differences between French and American perceptions of NATO's future are likely to remain for some time to come, and have the potential to cause the Alliance major problems.'

Throughout the 1998–2001 period, France also made several concessions in the field of EU–NATO relations under the ESDP framework. At the Helsinki European Council in December 1999, France made an important concession when it accepted that the EU would only intervene 'where NATO as a whole is not engaged.' According to an interviewee, 'ten days before the Helsinki agreement, this sentence was not in the draft. France was persuaded to revert to the American language.' An issue of linkage seems to have been one of the reasons for this French change in position: the agreement on the role of NATO in the EU, as noted above, was linked to policy on the BSE crisis, commonly known as 'mad cow disease.' In December 1999, France had agreed to lift the beef ban against the United Kingdom, and just before the Helsinki Council, it changed position and refused to do so. The United Kingdom did not put the issue of the beef ban on the table at Helsinki. An interviewee said: 'The Labour government had concluded it was better to use the long-term legal mechanisms of the EC and play it slowly, instead of taking unilateral decisions to attack France. By adopting this attitude, the United Kingdom could increase the pressure on France.'

At the Political Committee meeting on 7 March 2000, the negotiations were fierce. As one interviewee pointed out, 'France blocked all the discussions: the Political Committee was quite disappointing. France was totally isolated. France does not want any links with NATO and the non EU Allies whereas in the end, NATO will have to be used.' In addition, according to another interviewee, 'France is going to get very quickly to the end of its argument. France should stop being so stubborn; other member states are now having doubts about the French interests.'

France agreed to change its policy on three issues. It gave formal recognition to the informal links between NATO and the EU. France had always been happy with informal contacts between the High Representative and NATO's Secretary General. However, France was against any interinstitutional relations between EU and NATO staffs and state representatives during the interim phase. France argued that it wanted to establish equilibrium between the two organizations. For France, cross-participation should exist, but only 'as appropriate,' not on a permanent basis. In March 2000, France opposed the presence of an American officer in the EU building. However, France finally accepted interinstitutional relations, when EU states decided at Feira that the Deputy SACEUR would take part, during the interim period, in the ad hoc working groups for determining the conditions on EU access to NATO capabilities.

Also, France was against using NATO instruments in order to set up common capabilities. An interviewee stated that France 'does not want a relation EU–NATO similar to the WEU–NATO relation where NATO acts as a big brother, as the EU is different from the WEU.' However, at Feira, France agreed to make use of NATO expertise to set up a military capability target known as the headline goal by 2010. Finally, although France was both formally and informally against a differentiated relationship for the non-EU NATO members, it accepted an ambiguous agreement at Feira. The EU agreed to host an EU–NATO dialogue within its institutions.

The French government had to change its position in order to agree with these three points. However, it never changed its preference. For France, the EU should have an autonomous decision-making structure and process vis-à-vis NATO. William Wallace has told me (personal communication) that preferences within the French military differed from those within the Elysée throughout the 1990s and the early 2000s. However, the French position was presented as unitary at the EU. The long-term objective was stated by President Chirac at NATO's General Assembly on 19 October 1999:

> The Europeans now wish to be fully present on the international scene. The European countries have four out of five ground contingents deployed in Kosovo and are responsible for four KFOR [NATO Kosovo Force] sectors out of four. However, they do not have access to intelligence nor to command structures to carry out such a mission. We have to remedy this quickly. A reinforced NATO with the emergence of a real

European pillar should give impetus to an adult dialogue between the two sides of the Atlantic, based on mutual trust. (Chirac Speech, 12/11/01)

At the Feira European Council in June 2000, France shifted position but not preference. According to an interviewee:

> France had not foreseen it would have to give in so early, that is during the interim phase, at Feira: the French political director said that there would be no relations with NATO and non-EU NATO countries until the permanent structures were settled. France wanted to deal with these matters under the French presidency, but soon realized it would be impossible.

France changed position for three reasons. It had signed the Helsinki agreement, and it could not go back on that text, or interpret it differently from the other EU states. In addition, France could not resist pressures coming from other states. The United Kingdom and Germany were particularly active, at all levels, in pressing France to change its attitude. Blair and Schroeder spoke to Chirac. The French political director was pressurized by his fourteen colleagues. France was very isolated, and agreed to change its policy because there was no way out. As EU officials told me, long-term pressure on and isolation of a state representative can have an impact on the state's position. France, with its limited capacities, could hardly continue to ask its partners, all NATO members at the time, except for Austria, Finland, Sweden, and Ireland, for an autonomous ESDP: 'Unwilling to follow the American lead, France finds itself in a somewhat restricted situation because of its own limited capacity and because it cannot expect automatic support from its EU partners' (Mahncke 1999, 362). The credibility of France was at stake. France, while asking for a European defence system for Europe, had to reassure its partners that it was willing to maintain transatlantic relations (Andreani 1998, 92). This credibility was all the more necessary as France was holding the presidency from July until December 2000. Reputations are strengthened or damaged by the conduct of the presidency. William Wallace, in a personal communication to me, noted that if France had blocked the development of the links between the EU and NATO, it would have been at the cost of sharp resentment from its partners.

Finally, by accepting formal EU–NATO links, France could tell itself that it was merely acknowledging the existence of informal links between the EU and NATO. It was well known that there were contacts between the two bodies: 'Council and NATO civil servants meet one another irregularly ... their aim is to exchange information between the EU and NATO, which have not established official links. Their fear is to be caught by a French official' (*Le Figaro*, 29/02/00). Effectively, informal links between the EU and NATO, which were non-existent before 1998, had grown rapidly from 1998 to 2000. France could not prevent these informal relations from happening. Past decisions, peer group pressure, and isolation, especially for a state holding the presidency, have been determining factors for the French change in position.

At the Nice summit in December 2000, the United Kingdom failed to modify the EU policy in order to make it acceptable to the United States. Closer links between NATO and the EU were not established. Although France did not obtain all its initial demands, its representatives succeeded in loosening the EU connection with NATO. The conditions for the review mechanism of the Rapid Reaction Force (RRF) and ESDP planning were close to the French position. Table 5.1 shows the issues of contention between the United Kingdom and France.

The Nice formulation puts NATO and the EU on a same level, allowing the EU to intervene independently of NATO. The British prime minister thought that the Foreign Office had gone too far. According to one interviewee, 'the United Kingdom has had to swallow the fact that a European force, such as Eurocorps, could be used without referring to NATO at all.' The British position was conditioned by the French presidency. One interviewee believed that 'it was better to have a deal with France than not to have any deal at all.'

In the aftermath of Nice, and following the change of administration in the United States, the United Kingdom tried to tighten EU–NATO relations. This revealed the dependence of the United Kingdom on the United States. According to an interviewee, 'when the United States read the Nice conclusions, they were angry and said that the French had led the United Kingdom astray. The United Kingdom was rebuked by the United States. Blair had to satisfy the United States on ESDP.' For the Italian daily *Il Sole-24 Ore* (28/02/01), 'it [was] clear that this administration [the Bush administration] look[ed] with suspicion on EU defence policy.'

As early as December 2000, Richard Perle, a former U.S. assistant

Table 5.1
Issues of Contention between the United Kingdom and France

Issues of contention	United Kingdom	France
The role of NATO in the RRF review process	In favour of transparency	Reduced to a minimum
EU planning	With the use of NATO's planning procedures	Development of its own autonomous defence and force planning procedures: – Reinforcement of the planning cell and of the situation centre for evaluation – Strategic command should be created on the basis of national capabilities – Intelligence
First refusal	Only if NATO as a whole does not wish to engage in an operation	No hierarchy of decision-making with NATO taking precedence over the EU

defence secretary, and former adviser to President George W. Bush, said:

> This is a catastrophe for NATO. This is going to be a force that is not integrated within NATO. It is what the French have always wanted, but I am not sure why the others have gone along. Blair is either naive or embarrassed and is trying to claim victory. I think it is a British defeat. (*Telegraph*, 09/12/00)

The first critical comment by a senior member of the new Bush administration was made in February 2001. Donald Rumsfeld, U.S. Defence Secretary, told delegates attending a conference in Munich that he was a little worried by proposals for a 60,000-strong European Rapid Reaction Force, and that actions which could reduce NATO's effectiveness by introducing confusing duplication or perturbing the transatlantic link would not be positive. In contrast, Secretary of State Colin Powell (Department of State, 06/02/01) said the Bush administration had a very good understanding of what the European Security and Defence Identity (ESDI) was all about, and that if it was firmly embedded in NATO, with no duplication, there was no reason to see this as destabilizing NATO.

In February 2001, the United Kingdom tabled a paper on capabilities, which had not been discussed in the EU. Paris diplomats resented this. One interviewee stated: '*C'est la guerre*' (We are at war).' There were two reasons for their annoyance: the substance of the paper, on the type of relation the EU should have with NATO, and the fact that the United Kingdom had not worked on the paper with France. According to this interviewee, the British document stated: 'A new NATO/EU capabilities group involving representatives of all member states of both organisations (paragraph 9 of Nice text) should meet – inter alia – before agreement of new/revised national commitments/targets in either organisation (e.g., prior to an EU commitments conference).'

It also underlined the 'importance of shared databases on relevant capability goals and actual capability (including aspects such as readiness, training) from both organisations.' Then, on 23 February 2001, Blair assured Bush that a European defence policy would not undermine NATO. There would be a joint EU–NATO command and military planning would take place within NATO. In addition, NATO was given the right of first refusal: Blair stated that the EU would only act when NATO decided not to act. In exchange, the United States should satisfy the United Kingdom on missile defence policy (NATO Notes, 2001, 2). However, according to an EU official, France would not let the United Kingdom reverse the work carried out since 1999 at EU level. The ESDP *acquis* could not be modified.

The disagreements on the relationship between the EU and NATO were not resolved in the summer of 2001. The first ministerial meeting between NATO and the EU, held in Budapest on 29 May 2001, did not even look at the NATO–EU security relationship.

U.S. Authority and Path-Dependency

The inconsiderate conduct of the United States in the Balkans seems to have been the trigger for the creation of ESDP. Both France and the United Kingdom lost trust in U.S. foreign policy, and did not always agree with the United States on how to respond to the Balkan crisis. EU states did not like the division of labour between the EU and the United States. Europe took responsibility for soft power issues such as foreign aid, while the United States took responsibility for hard power issues involving the use of force. For Schake, Bloch-Laine, and Grant (1999, 21, 37), 'as a result, Americans and Europeans are growing resentful of each other in ways and at pace that will become difficult to reverse.' The conflict had come to a head when Clinton was in power:

> The transatlantic rift became particularly apparent when, in March 1993, the Clinton administration proposed air strikes against Bosnian Serb positions and lifting the arms embargo against the Bosnian government. Both were strictly opposed by Europe which emphasised humanitarian measures and negotiations; Europe was confronted for the first time since the Second World War with an American administration which was everything but consistent in its policies. Thus Europeans had to learn that nowadays U.S. policies will be less predictable. (Jopp 1994, 36)

France and the United Kingdom were in favour of sending ground troops, but they were not able to do so because the United States disagreed. In the end, the United States acted without consulting the United Kingdom and France: 'some flights were organised with no information to the Allies' (Quilès and Lamy 1999, 98). After the Balkan experience, the United Kingdom and France had doubts about the future support of the United States in any potential conflict, as the United States might decide either not to act at all, or to act in a different way from what the EU would like. A French interviewee concluded that 'there may be cases where Washington will not want to intervene.'

EU states realized they did not want to rely permanently on the United States. Quilès noted:

> The weaknesses, both political and military, revealed by the Gulf war in 1990–1991 and by the Yugoslav crisis since 1991, have set a dilemma for the Europeans: to be able to be responsible for peace-keeping and peace-making operations, or to align themselves *systematically* with the American positions. (1999, 26; my emphasis)

Given the negative perceptions Europeans had of their limited military capabilities, and given the EU states' dependence on the United States, the St Malo decision of 1998 was inevitable. William Wallace, in a personal communication, told me that the French and the British developed their relationship in the European security field after 1997, especially in order to accommodate the development of CFSP and the arrival of the High Representative.

The creation of ESDP seems to have been possible only because the United States, at the highest level, did not oppose it. At the time of the St Malo agreement, U.S. Secretary of State Madeleine Albright argued at NATO on 8 December 1998:

> I think it's very important for the Europeans to carry a fair share and have a sense of their own defence identity ... I think that what happened there was very important. There is a reason for the Europeans to find an identity in their own defence, but this is a thing that cannot be a duplication or discrimination. It is a manner by which the Europeans can share in the work of NATO. It is something that cannot hurt NATO because this is the most important alliance. But we think it is very important that the Europeans work in this manner because it is something that helps us in burden sharing.

And in 1999, after the Helsinki summit of the European Union, President Clinton praised the decisions to proceed with EU enlargement and with strengthening EU defence and security capabilities. These two statements are in sharp contrast to the Bartholomew letter, sent to a WEU ministerial meeting in February 1991. In that letter, George Bush warned the Europeans that the United States might review its commitment to NATO, if the EU created a security policy separate from NATO.[54] And in the event, the Maastricht Treaty did not do so.

The United States was concerned about the development of the EU in the defence sphere. The U.S. made its presence felt in the EU's decision-making process through NATO and through bilateral relations with EU institutions and EU states. The United States was indirectly present at the EU through its seat in NATO. An EU official stated: 'At the NAC [North Atlantic Council] last week that took place before the EU defence ministers meeting, the United States, Turkey and Norway initiated a clear discussion on the EU–NATO relationship and required a more visible framework.'

Informal links between NATO and the EU were also used by the United States. The EU High Representative Javier Solana and NATO's Secretary General George Robertson met on a weekly basis. The unofficial links between Solana and Robertson were accepted by all the member states, including France. It is worth remembering that Solana used to be Secretary General of NATO, so he had strong personal links with the organization. In addition, EU officials sitting in the Interim Political and Security Committee and the Interim Military Body were mostly double- or triple-hatted. They were therefore immediately aware of what happened in both organizations. At the same time, NATO was already contacting the Permanent Representations of EU states, in order to find out about the nature of the discussion being conducted at EU level.

The United States was in direct contact with all levels of the EU's decision-making process: the European Council which makes the decisions, the political committee where the negotiations essentially take place, the Secretariat General of the Council, and the presidency. The contacts were made by the U.S. Ambassador to the EU, Richard Morningstar. As he affirmed at the American Chamber of Commerce in Brussels on 23 January 2001:

> The nature of our relationship and the nature of my job has changed dramatically. Before I took this job, the U.S. Ambassador to the EU dealt almost exclusively with trade issues. But that has changed – I now spend half of my time on political and security issues. The U.S.–EU mission now works with our NATO mission on a daily basis. (Morningstar Speech, 23/01/01)

He also said in a speech at the Salzburg seminar in March 2001 that 'a year ago, we seemed to want to micromanage the process, now we are not doing it any more as it did not work.' Additional contacts between the United States and the EU were made by the Head of State and the Secretary of State; and the U.S. was in regular touch with individual European capitals.

The U.S. presence in this discussion, and its lobbying activity, is not in itself surprising. Given that the issue directly concerned the United States – as the development of ESDP has consequences for the future of NATO – frequent contacts between the EU and the United States would seem inevitable. There were active negotiations taking place in parallel within NATO and the EU about the acceptable terms of EU autonomy.[55] Through its presence in NATO and its negotiations with EU states, the United States succeeded in making its position known; and my interviewees all considered the U.S. position on the EU–NATO relation as being the most important element in the discussion. EU state officials were fully aware of it. British Secretary of State for Defence Geoffrey Hoon knew exactly what that position was; at Helsinki, he stated that 'clearly, there are concerns in the United States' (House of Commons Debates, 13/12/99).

But even though the United States was informally and indirectly present in the EU's decision-making process, it apparently never opposed, at the highest level, the wording of the St Malo agreement and the Helsinki summit, and it never commented on the negotiations before and during the Feira and Nice summits, though it was aware of them. It seems to be this absence of opposition that made EU common policies in the ESDP field possible. According to Heisbourg (2000, 66), British officials knew that the United States would not act against the United Kingdom as a consequence of the creation of the ESDP.

EU officials believed the Feira conclusions were close to the U.S. position. An interviewee told me that the United States was one of the reasons for the French change in position: 'France agreed to give in to the United States because as regards the U.S. Congress, it is good to look good.' The member states could have accepted a final common policy which would have been even closer to the U.S. position. In February 2000, an unpublished document stated the possibility of having

... cross-participation by Secretaries General at routine Ministerial and Summit meetings, joint meetings between the NAC and the EU PSC, a

NATO/EU Military Liaison meeting, the latter facilitated by SHAPE and
EU offices in each others' HQs and between the two Military Committees.

The United States apparently did not seek to impose its position at the
highest level; but the Feira conclusions would have suited it very well.

After Nice, and with the arrival of the Bush government, the United
States no longer agreed with EU policy towards NATO in the ESDP
field (see Posen 2004; Layne 2006). The position of the United
Kingdom after Nice was totally linked to the U.S. position, as can be
seen when the United Kingdom tried to reverse the decisions taken at
Nice in order to please its American friends. In general, it is possible to
speak of U.S. influence on the EU's decision-making process; and
indeed, I would agree with Gourlay and Remacle (1998, 90) that the
EU is subject to strong American influence.

Big member states seem bound to take the U.S. position into
account, and to accept it, if the demand for this comes from the highest
level. An interviewee related that a political director had complained
about this situation at the political committee; and had asked the other
states at least to try to behave as though they were not totally subordinate to the United States.

The U.S. Shadow over ESDP Military Missions

Chilton has pointed out that (1997, 245) 'whatever new political institutions come out of the Intergovernmental Conference, Europe's common
defence aspirations will only ever be as good as their operationalisation.' Once ESDP institutions are in place, it is more important that they
work than how they have been created. In this 'operationalisation'
phase, there is continuing tension between Atlanticists and Europeanists
on the exact role of NATO in the deployment of EU missions.

This section analyses the positions of EU states in relation to the
United States in the context of particular military operations and in the
light of intergovernmentalist theory, with special reference to the
concept of bandwagoning. It will first study the constraints on state
positions regarding the Concordia and the Artemis missions in 2003. It
will then analyse relations with NATO in the decisions to launch the
EU military operation in Bosnia and Herzegovina in 2004 (code-
named Althea) and to support AMIS (the African Union Mission in
Sudan) in Darfur from 2005 until 2007.

Impressing the United States

ESDP changes the balance in the EU–NATO relation.[56] NATO is no longer the only organization in which the future of the defence and security of Europe is discussed. However, NATO capabilities are much more substantial than EU capabilities. This can make the EU dependent on NATO for missions, which require effective strategic lift capabilities, intelligence, and strategic command.

The Berlin Plus agreement of 2002 allowed the EU to rely on NATO for EU access to NATO planning, NATO European command options, and use of NATO assets and capabilities. Two operations have been conducted on the basis of this agreement: Concordia in 2003 and Althea from 2004 onwards.

The EU and NATO coordinated their efforts to help Macedonia as early as 2001, and the EU Concordia mission, with approximately 400 personnel, took over the NATO military mission in Macedonia in April 2003. However, the EU mission was conducted in close coordination with NATO in order to accommodate the United States (Gegout 2005). In effect, on the ground, NATO was in overall charge of the operation. According to the researcher Bono (Weltpolitik, 14/03/04), the U.S. government agreed to the Concordia operation because it estimated that it needed to redeploy its soldiers from the Balkans to Asia, Africa, and the Middle East.

As a reaction to Concordia, and to the divisions within the EU due to the war in Iraq, France was apparently desperate to follow a 'strategy of autonomy' (Macleod 2006, 128) and create a mission which would specifically not rely on NATO, in order to prove the EU could act independently of NATO. EU autonomy vis-à-vis NATO was made clear during the EU Artemis mission in the Democratic Republic of the Congo (DRC) in 2003. The Americans were apparently surprised by the EU deployment. Michel reports:

> French military officials reportedly informally asked U.S. officers if U.S. transports would be available to airlift European troops to Bunia. The U.S. side advised that such requests appropriately should come under Berlin Plus. The French soon dropped the matter and opted to lease Ukrainian transports. The incident reinforced perceptions in Washington and elsewhere that Paris was determined, for political reasons, to conduct an autonomous EU mission. (2004, 90)

These two EU missions in 2003 were small-scale operations in terms of troops deployed and time (400 troops over nine months for Concordia, and 2,000 troops over ten weeks for Artemis). The first EU mission was conducted with NATO. France made this concession in early 2003. With Artemis, the United Kingdom conceded an EU mission without NATO. However, it only took part symbolically in this mission, as the total of UK military personnel in Africa on the operation amounted to eighty-five, seventy of whom were Royal Engineers, who upgraded the airfield at Bunia.

The two missions illustrate the relevance of intergovernmental bargaining. France agreed to launch the first EU mission Concordia in March 2003, aided by NATO, as it was in favour of the development of ESDP. By agreeing to this mission, it hoped that a future one could be created without NATO. At the first opportunity, in June 2003, France took the initiative to create Artemis. The United Kingdom agreed to launch this EU mission, as it had signed up to the possibility of the EU carrying out missions without NATO. This negotiation corresponds to the intergovernmentalist scenario of how decisions are reached: a bargaining process over time, conducted between two major EU states.

These missions also show the dependency of EU states on U.S. officials' opinion on EU military missions. In the case of Concordia, EU states reassured the United States that ESDP was not synonymous with an independent EU military institution. In the case of Artemis, the United States was informed of the mission, and did not oppose it. The EU made sure it was compatible with U.S. interests. Once again, the United States appeared here as an ad hoc veto player: the EU states agreed on a common EU position after establishing the U.S. position. The EU seems to comply in its decision-making with U.S. demands.

Depending on U.S. Assent

The Althea mission was decided in 2004 (see Van Ham 2006; Whitman 2004). This largest-ever EU mission, made up of 7,000 troops, replaced NATO forces in Bosnia (the SFOR), but NATO remained engaged with Bosnia. European leaders did not want to share tasks with NATO, but they had to accept the ongoing presence of NATO in Bosnia and its role in defence reform, anti-terrorism issues, and the search for war criminals. NATO was still responsible for high security issues. The EU mission satisfied American officials, who wanted to concentrate their military forces in the Middle East and Asia.

Since the Darfur crisis began in 2003, EU states have discussed ways of negotiating an end to it. In February 2005, Secretary General Kofi Annan called upon the EU and NATO to help the African Union. In May 2005, NATO was the first to offer logistical help to the African Union with planning, coordination, communications, and training. The EU did not have sufficient airlift capacity to transport African Union troops from their countries of origin, such as Rwanda, Nigeria, Kenya, South Africa, Senegal, Ghana, Botswana, Egypt, and Mali, to Darfur. But from mid-2005 until the end of 2007, at which point the African Union/United Nations hybrid operation (UNAMID) took over the African Union Mission in Darfur, the EU provided military, technical, and police advice to the African Mission in Sudan.

In June 2005, there was open disagreement between NATO and the EU on which organization should respond to the African Union. The United States favoured NATO, France wanted an EU action, and Germany and the United Kingdom were undecided (Reichard 2006, 272). Eventually, both NATO and the EU worked with the African Union on military issues in Darfur. In terms of EU decision-making, France took the lead in promoting an EU policy, and the other EU states agreed to what turned out to be a very low-scale mission to help the African Union. The decision was taken with the agreement of U.S. policy leaders, in parallel with the decision to use NATO capabilities. NATO undertook the transportation of AMIS troops to Darfur.

These two missions show that EU state representatives recognized the limits of ESDP missions. The British Defence Secretary Geoff Hoon stated that 'it is highly unlikely that the United Kingdom would be engaged in large-scale combat operations without the United States, a judgment born of past experience, shared interest and our assessment of strategic trends' (Hoon, quoted in Michel 2004). French officials acknowledged the importance of NATO for high-scale operations. The French General Neveux wrote in May 2004: 'Would the real political unanimity expressed during Artemis have been the same, if the risks had been greater, the stakes more sensitive, the contributions more numerous, and the engagement on the ground more important?' (quoted in Michel 2004, 90). This echoes the view of Zielonka (2006, 159), who argues that 'even the French political elite seem to believe that American military engagement in Europe offers a more sound security base than a nascent ESDP.'

Bargaining, Path-dependency, and External Approval

Intergovernmentalism, path-dependency, and the concept of band-wagoning are particularly relevant to explain state positions on the creation of ESDP institutions and ESDP missions.

As expected by intergovernmentalist theory, member states were the most important actors, as they were the only ones who could decide the issue of relations with NATO in the ESDP framework. The Commission played no role in the CFSP–ESDP decision-making process. When CFSP–ESDP issues were discussed, the Commission generally sat at the table, but made no proposal. EU states acted as unitary states, presenting a unitary position at EU meetings even when there were disagreements among ministries within the same state. For instance, a British high official said she or he had been working for the EU for many years and was a convinced European, but her or his personal position had had no influence on the United Kingdom's foreign policy in the EU security and defence field.

The intergovernmentalist assumption that state representatives act rationally might not, at first sight, seem validated here. Some officials, the French at Feira and then the British at Nice, acted in a surprising way; they accepted a final common policy, which did not correspond to their state's interests. However, representatives who changed position during the negotiation process did not change their preferences. They all maintained the same preferences at the beginning and end of the negotiation process.

As described earlier, British officials changed their state's preferences before, and not during, the negotiations with the other EU states. The United Kingdom, like the majority of the other member states, changed its position on the necessity of developing capabilities which could be used independently of the United States. This British change in position was possible because the United States did not oppose such development on this occasion, whereas it had done so in the past through the Bartholomew letter. French officials did not change France's preferences at all, always pursuing the same aim: an autonomous EU decision-making process in the ESDP field, or a European security force and a European defence of Europe. The reintegration of France in NATO's military command decided by President

Sarkozy in March 2009 does not change this analysis. French leaders were and still are in favour of promoting EU missions with effective capabilities (*Financial Times*, 12/11/07; Document of the French Government, 13/03/09). In order to achieve this aim, France needed the agreement of the United Kingdom, and therefore of the United States. This is why President Sarkozy was at a joint session of Congress in Washington as early as autumn 2007. Intergovernmentalist assumptions about states' behaviour are shown here to be correct.

States did not look at the gains other states might make out of the EU position. They were only concerned with their absolute gains. All the EU states, apparently even France, were concerned about the consequences of the EU common policy for their bilateral relations with the United States.

However, contrary to the expectations of intergovernmentalism, path-dependency came into play in these negotiations. When creating ESDP institutions, the United Kingdom and France were constrained by past decisions: France by the Helsinki agreement, and the United Kingdom by the Nice agreement.

The intergovernmentalist claim that it is difficult for states to reach higher than LCD agreements, and that non-state actors do not play any role in CFSP outcomes, does not seem valid in this case study. By agreeing to sign a deliberately ambiguous text at Helsinki, both the United Kingdom and France gave the impression their own interests had prevailed. However, if we look at the substance of their policies, a different story is revealed. Higher than LCD outcomes were reached at Feira and at Nice, where France and the United Kingdom had to make concessions, constrained by the implied decisions at Helsinki. Recent agreements on the type of EU military operations that should be conducted do, in contrast, seem to have been LCD agreements. When France and the United Kingdom agreed to launch Concordia and Artemis, they engaged in bargaining with one another over time.

A non-EU state actor, the United States, clearly played a role in the making of ESDP institutional structures and in the creation of ESDP missions and could hardly have done otherwise, since the debate on the·future of ESDP is so closely linked to the role of NATO in the world. If the United States had disagreed with the creation of ESDP, between St Malo and the Nice summits, and had opposed autonomous EU military operations, none of these agreements would have existed, at least in their present form. Small-scale ESDP missions are promoted by both France and the United Kingdom, but the United Kingdom is generally reluctant to encourage missions independent of NATO (that is, without a U.S. component), and rarely takes a military part in such missions.

Seth (2003, 115) argues that 'the lower the American military presence in Europe, the greater the impetus for EU security cooperation to ameliorate a potential security dilemma.' But EU security cooperation and ESDP common positions are always constrained by the view of U.S. officials on the conduct of ESDP missions. EU states want U.S. approval of their decisions, or at least U.S. indifference, whether the United States is present militarily in Europe or not. When the EU takes decisions to launch military missions, it wants to bandwagon with the United States.

The next part of this book evaluates the extent to which the findings of these three case studies on EU policy-making towards China, the Balkans, and NATO can be generalized to all CFSP decisions taken both before and after the drawing-up of the Lisbon Treaty.

PART THREE

The Unexpected Actors in the CFSP System

6 The United States: Partial Bandwagoning

Zielonka (2000) wrote that CFSP has a marginal impact on transatlantic relations. What can we say, though, about the impact of transatlantic relations on CFSP outcomes? This chapter evaluates how and under what conditions the presence or absence of a CFSP decision is influenced by the United States, when an issue considered vital for EU states is at stake; and more generally, it observes the role of the United States in the CFSP system. The importance of the United States is never (see Carlsnaes and Smith 1994) or rarely discussed in the literature on the CFSP (Wallace 1983; Peterson 1997). In such cases, only particular examples are given, without drawing conclusions about the general role of the United States in the EU's decision-making process, and without looking at the conditions under which this actor might have an impact. Instead, academics concentrate on describing the differences and relations between the United States and the EU (see, for instance, Peterson 1996; Featherstone and Ginsberg 1996; Peterson and Pollack 2003; Gordon and Shapiro 2004; Jones 2004; M. Smith 2004).

This chapter is divided into two parts. The first part looks at the influence of the United States on the CFSP system. The second part focuses mainly on the workings of the Quint and the Quad, to bring out the special informal links between the EU and the United States.

A Significant U.S. Constraint on CFSP Outcomes

The United States has a significant impact on the CFSP system. It can play four roles in the CFSP decision-making process. It can be an indirect observer. It is both an official and an invisible actor. It can be a stimulus, either through its own lobbying, or through the EU copying, or learning from, its foreign policy and strategies. EU representatives can observe the assertive foreign policy conducted by the United States, and develop policies they might otherwise have overlooked. Finally, the United States is an authority. EU states ask for U.S. authorization before issuing an EU foreign policy towards other states, when the United States is considered a main actor by those other states. The United States can be considered a de facto veto player, as it seems to influence CFSP outcomes on major issues. Apparently, there cannot be a CFSP common policy on any highly sensitive issue, if the policy goes against the will of the United States. This is particularly the case when U.S. opposition is expressed at the highest level, but may also be evident in more routine matters. The concept of qualified bandwagoning is pertinent to explain the constraints laid by the United States on the positions taken by EU states, and on CFSP outcomes.

An Indirect Observer

The United States has privileged access to CFSP topics of discussion and negotiation through extensive unofficial and official institutional links between itself and the EU. U.S. lobbying is directed towards both states and EU institutions.

The indirect presence of the U.S. in the European foreign policy system is not a new phenomenon. The United States has always been eager to take part in the EU's institutional structures, and there have been close links between the United States and European institutions ever since the latter were created. Consultations with the U.S. were part of the European integration process from the early 1950s (Grosser 1980, 97–128; Lundestad 1998, 29–57). The U.S. administration was the sponsor of the European Coal and Steel Community. It was the first country to accredit a diplomatic representation to the ECSC in 1952, and the European Economic Community and European Atomic Energy Community in 1958. According to Hoffmann (1980, vii), 'the United States has played – sometimes as a goad, sometimes as a foil – a major role in the slow but constant progress of West European unification.' Milward (1984, 502) also believes that 'without the drive of the United States to impose integration to suit its own strategic goals, Western Europe would perhaps not have discovered its own different route to a settlement.'

In foreign policy issues, since the creation of European Political Cooperation, the objective of U.S. lobbying has been to secure participation in the EU's institutional set-up by sitting in on EU foreign policy meetings. On 23 April 1973 in New York, Secretary of State Henry Kissinger announced: 'The United States proposes to its Atlantic partners that by the time the President travels to Europe towards the end of the year, we will have worked out a new Transatlantic Charter setting the goals for the future of the Transatlantic relation' (Kissinger, quoted in Wallace 1983, 380). Kissinger wanted U.S. officials to be allowed to sit in on EPC meetings; but Christopher Hill pointed out in a lecture given at the London School of Economics in early 2001 that in 1974, when the Gymnich meeting (an informal meeting of European ministers for foreign affairs) was set, the United States was not granted a tenth seat at the table (Hill 2001). The NATO Council Ottawa agreement of June 1974 dealt with the U.S. demand by agreeing that the EC presidency would brief U.S. officials after each EPC meeting, and that foreign ministers would consult regularly with 'allied or friendly' countries on EPC issues (Grosser 1980, 283; Regelsberger 1988, 15). In the year 2000, the United States was still trying to attend EU meetings. It asked, for instance, to attend the EU management committee relating to the sanctions towards the FRY.

The EU has set up official meetings with the United States. These meetings do not necessarily mean that the relations between the United States and the EU, or the relation between the United States and some member states, are stronger than they were before. According to Gardner (2001, 86n4), 'the meetings [of the U.S. Secretary of State with all EU Foreign Ministers on the margins of the UN General Assembly] began and have continued because they provide the Secretary of State with a useful opportunity to pay courtesy to the Foreign Ministers and an excuse not to spend time seeing many of them again during the course of the following twelve months.' In 1990, the EU and the United States adopted a Transatlantic declaration laying down the principles for greater EU–U.S. consultation and cooperation. In 1995, they agreed on a New Transatlantic Agenda (NTA) and an action plan to promote cooperation, partnership, and joint action in areas ranging from trade liberalization to security. The presidents of the European Commission and the European Council and the president of the United States meet on a yearly basis. There have been increasingly frequent CFSP–U.S. consultations; for example, five special joint Council working groups have existed since 1995. The EU and the U.S. work together in the field of both civilian and military crisis management and conflict prevention. In March 2008, they concluded a work plan on crisis management and conflict prevention, with a special emphasis on conflict prevention and early warning. They also cooperate on policies towards the Balkans, in particular concerning the EULEX Kosovo rule of law mission.

The U.S. mission to the EU, which has followed foreign policy matters since 1985, increased its staff after the creation of the CFSP (Bretherton and Vogler 1999, 187). In terms of unofficial links between the United States and EU states, daily traffic takes place between different agencies of the U.S. government, Brussels institutions, and EU national governments. Officials, parliamentarians, advisers, and business representatives are constantly in touch. Already in 1976, Wallace (1976, 168) underlined that 'the development of transgovernmental contacts ... has been a marked feature of Atlantic intergovernmental relations in the last fifteen or twenty years.' These contacts can have long-term impact on U.S.–EU relations in the foreign policy field. Furthermore, the United States holds regular informal meetings with some EU states. The United States and big EU states participate in the Quint or Quad, the informal structures to be discussed below, whose operations are very discreet.

A Stimulus

U.S. pressure does not automatically lead to the reaching of an EU common policy, but it can act as a stimulus, or provide the motivation for European foreign policy-making. In the EPC days, member states took into account U.S. foreign policies and lobbying to the point of accepting European policies they did not favour initially. Throughout the winter of 1979–80, the EU states' ambassadors in Teheran had operated as a group, going together to make representations to the new Iranian government on European interests. The decision to impose sanctions on Iran was, strictly speaking, the first non-declaratory action taken within the framework of political cooperation. According to William Wallace (1983, 393), this step was taken 'as a necessary response to intense and sustained American pressure, and it was taken reluctantly!' In 1982, according to Nuttall (1997, 32), following the Afghanistan crisis, it was under rising pressure from the United States to impose economic sanctions that the EC finally acted against Russia. For Hill (1988, 180), 'in practice, the Community states could not avoid – especially when under American pressure – facing the issue of what practical response to make to perceived provocations by third countries.' During the Gulf War, according to Pfetsch (1994, 126), 'the EC had not developed a standpoint of its own, but more or less consistently followed the line of the U.S. government and the Security Council.' Burdett (1997, 311) wrote that in general, 'the major EC countries made sure that U.S. wishes were taken into account during the formulation of EPC proposals, because U.S. support was seen as vital.' After the creation of CFSP, Peterson (EUI conference, 09/02/02) argued that in the Balkans in the 1990s 'an important force for European unity in Foreign Policy – perhaps even a precondition – is American prodding.'

The United States acts as a stimulus for EU foreign policy either with or without U.S. lobbying. It gives its opinion on EU issues it considers belonging to its domain, and is involved in such issues from an early stage in the decision-making process. This does not necessarily entail that this opinion is followed, but it shows the United States is aware of all CFSP discussions taking place at the Council. The United States lobbies at both EU and national levels.

At the EU level, Cameron (1998, 148) emphasizes that 'few in Brussels will forget the U.S. lobbying against the idea of a common European defence in the run up to Maastricht in 1991.' At the national level, the United States makes its own position known to all EU states' representatives on EU policies in the making. On Middle East issues, the United States lobbies the department responsible for the Middle East in the foreign affairs ministries. In 2000, the United States cautioned the EU and its member states to go slow on reintegrating Libya into the international community. The United States was also constantly asking EU officials about the evolution of the negotiations on reinforcement of financial sanctions towards the FRY in 2000. More recently, U.S. representatives lobbied EU states to ensure a quick recognition of Kosovo as an independent state after the elections in early 2008. A senior EU official (*International Herald Tribune*, 10/01/08) said: 'Washington was aggressively pressing the EU … The cake has been baked because the Americans have promised Kosovo independence. And if Washington recognizes Kosovo and European nations do not follow, it will be a disaster.'

Even without direct lobbying, the United States can be a stimulus. For instance, the 2003 European Security Strategy was a response to the U.S. National Security Strategy. The U.S. presence in EU foreign policy-making is both disliked and approved of within EU diplomatic circles. Some EU officials believe that without this involvement, there would be fewer foreign policy decisions.

An Authority

EU states seem to consider the United States as an authority; they inform and consult the United States, and make sure that it is not opposed to EU decisions. For instance, EU states are dependent on the United States when dealing with the Middle East Peace Process. The EU recognition of the 'unqualified Palestinian right to self-determination including the option of a state' at the 1999 Berlin European Council was not expected. Germany apparently only agreed to recognize the Palestinian entity because the United States had accepted it, and only after negotiations with U.S. representatives, to avoid irritating them. Peters (2001, 157) explains that 'the wording of the Berlin Declaration was crafted in close coordination with the U.S.' France also knows the EU has to rely on the United States when deciding on its policy towards the Middle East, as the United States has the most means to intervene in the conflict. According to a Quai d'Orsay official, 'Europe, and it is not new, does not have the means to bring its weight to bear on Israel' (*Libération*, 04/04/02).

EU states consistently discuss ESDP military missions with the United States before a decision is taken at EU level. Even when EU states discuss the creation of an independent military mission, they make sure that the United States is informed, and is not vehemently opposed to the deployment of such a mission. This was the case for the Artemis mission in 2003.

A Veto Player

The United States cannot influence all CFSP outcomes, but it can act as a veto player in the CFSP system. Before the existence of the EPC, NATO was the framework for discussing European security and defence issues. Within NATO, the United States was used to having a right of veto. So, when EPC and CFSP were created, U.S. leaders expected to have the same right in those arenas.

In the case study on EU relations with China on human rights issues, the United States was shown to have had an indirect de facto veto. The EU never decided to put forward a policy condemning China unless the United States had also done so. EU states could not afford to lose Chinese markets to the advantage of the U.S. economy. In the case study on the sanctions towards the FRY, there was more evidence of a U.S. de facto veto; the United States seems to have prevented the EU from discussing the possible lifting of the oil embargo. The U.S. de facto veto was also seen in the case study on EU relations with NATO in the security field. In February 1991, the Bartholomew letter sent by President George Bush prevented European states from developing a security and defence policy. At the time, this letter was perceived as a peremptory intervention in the European debate by some European officials, who were evidently embarrassed (Menon, Forster, and Wallace 1992, 105). The fact that the U.S. reaction in 1998 was weak, compared to its reaction in 1991, seems to be one of the reasons why the United Kingdom accepted the creation of ESDP.

The U.S. de facto power of veto is limited. The United States seems to have no impact when an EU common policy implements pre-existing EU policies in the same area. For instance, once the member states had decided on the reinforcement of the financial sanctions against the FRY in spring 2000, the United States could lobby the Commission for the latter to present a white list, but it could not impose its wishes on the Commission. In the case study on EU relations with NATO, Tony Blair was unable to renegotiate the Nice agreement, even though U.S. officials were critical of it. Once the EU process is launched, the CFSP *acquis* is stronger than U.S. influence.

The Power of Hegemonic Leadership

The United States can play the various roles described above because it is a unipolar power, or a 'hyperpower,' in virtually all fields (Kraut-hammer 1990–1; Huntington 1999; Brooks and Wohlforth 2002). It does share power in the world with the EU in economic terms, but it is more powerful than the EU in the military and diplomatic fields. As a result, EU states partially bandwagon with the United States.

The EU and the United States is a partnership of equals in economic terms (Smith and Steffenson 2005, 345). The EU's GDP was higher than the United States' GDP in 2006: approximately $14,600 billion for the EU and $13,200 billion for the United States. The EU gives twice as much as the United States to the developing countries in terms of financial assistance, and three times as much in terms of public aid for development. EU trade with developing countries is twice that of the

United States'. The United States is the most powerful state in military terms. The U.S. military budget represented 47 per cent of the world's total spending on weapons and troops in 2006 (SIPRI 2007, 12). The EU's annual military budget in 2007 was less than half the U.S. military budget. The EU and the United States respectively spent 204 billion and 454 billion on defence in 2007, that is, 1.69 and 4.5 per cent of their GDP, and 417 and 1,504 per capita (EDA Data, December 2008, accessed 20/01/09).

The EU is dependent on the United States for high-scale military operations. When ESDP relies on NATO, in reality it relies on U.S. capabilities. The war in the Balkans and the war in Afghanistan showed this dependence. For Javier Solana (2000, 589), 'politically and technically, transparency and concerted action with NATO is a necessity.' EU states know they must maintain strong links with the United States if they are to preserve positive relations with NATO.

The three big EU states all make clear their desire to be in close cooperation with the United States. In the United Kingdom, the United States is still mentioned, prior to the EU, in foreign policy speeches. The Germans still have strong ties with the United States. Germany is 'a keen proponent of the idea of the Euro-Atlantic Union, which extends cooperation beyond security policy to include economics and culture' (Aggestam 2000, 79). In France, there is a gap between French rhetoric and the reality of Franco-American relations. Even on the war with Iraq, France was reluctant to go against the United States, and it did not exclude military intervention until February 2003.

EU policy towards Iran is another example of bandwagoning. The EU negotiated with Iran on the basis of an informal agreement with the United States on the policy to be adopted. In December 2003, the United States agreed with the Big Three to postpone bringing the matter to the UN. EU governments seemed to have succeeded, at least temporarily, in bringing the United States on board. However, a different argument could be made: the United States, at the highest level, preferred to let the Europeans deal with Iran, rather than commit themselves to a unilateral policy. This was because the United States was already involved militarily in Iraq, and because the Europeans, in accordance with U.S. policy, had agreed to take Iran to the Security Council should negotiations fail.

EU states bandwagon with the United States for profit. Profit in this context is enhanced European security, or recognition of the EU by the United States as an equal partner. This search for profit corresponds to one of the three main aims of EU foreign policy, namely: 'to work closely with EU neighbours, to apply the experience of multilateral cooperation to a wider stage, and to become a serious counterpart to the United States' (Patten 2000).

EU governments want to influence the United States. The United States is an ally, and it protects through NATO most Western and Eastern European states. In the future, some states, such as the United Kingdom, could decide to disagree with the United States, but the EU needs unanimity to reach a common position. Today, EU states rely both on the EU and the United States for their security. It is unlikely that all EU states would give up having a double security guarantee, in order to enable the EU to be considered an entity which can speak with one voice, independently from the United States. A recent illustration of this point is the following. When EU states considered lifting their arms embargo towards China in 2005, Germany, and not the United Kingdom, the traditional U.S. 'Trojan horse,' refused to countenance the suggestion. At the time, the German Chancellor, Angela Merkel, demonstrated her disagreement with China's human rights policy and her agreement with U.S. foreign policy towards China.

The EU does not blindly follow most U.S. foreign policies. It only partly bandwagons with the United States, and it can and does take decisions on issues which go against U.S. interests. For instance, at the EU–U.S. Goeteborg summit in 2001, EU governments announced that 'we [the EU and the United States] disagree on the Kyoto Protocol on global warming and its ratification.' The EU also disagrees with the United States on issues such as the International Criminal Court, the Ottawa Convention on land mines, the protocols for Chemical and Biological Conventions, the U.S. retention of the death penalty, and the U.S. plan to develop a national missile defence shield. These issues are discussed, but both sides of the Atlantic agree to disagree. Additionally, the EU has developed autonomous foreign policies towards Eastern Europe, the Palestinian entity, and the Mediterranean area, and has concentrated on peace-making in Aceh, Indonesia.

However, the United States did not express a strong position on any of these EU policies, and the EU does not adopt policies with which the United States, at the highest level, disagrees. In the case, for example, of the discussions on the war on Iraq, as states did not reach a position of agreement with U.S. policy, it was impossible for them to reach any EU common policy. EU states want to avoid irritating the United States. The French foreign minister explained in April 2002 that 'the EU is divided on the crisis in the Middle East, because certain member states think nothing can be done that would annoy the United States.'

The EU, where possible, tries to accommodate the United States, even if it is not sure of the reward it will receive for its cooperation. When EU foreign policy is addressed to a third state, it seems that the Europeans systematically consider the impact of this policy on the United States. The British and Danish representatives at the European Convention, Peter Hain and Henning Christophersen, acknowledged in *Le Monde* on 12 July 2002 that each member state wanted to act on the international scene, and in relation to the United States. Big EU states want to be in constant contact with the United States. Even in times of crisis between an EU state and the United States, links are never broken. For instance, French Minister for Foreign Affairs Dominique de Villepin and U.S. Secretary of State Colin Powell met on 6 March 2003 before the beginning of the war against Iraq and again in early April 2003. Despite the impression the public had of a complete break-up of the Franco-American links between these two dates, they had in effect spoken frequently to one another. After the disagreement between some EU governments and the United States on the U.S. military operation in spring 2003, EU states tried to restore their relations with the United States. The reconciliation was made public in December 2003 with the arrest of Saddam Hussein.

My first conclusion relating to the concept of partial bandwagoning is the following: CFSP decisions can go against U.S. interests only when the United States does not have a strong interest, which is expressed at presidential level, in opposing these CFSP decisions. The United States thus has a de facto power of veto on CFSP decisions.

My second conclusion is that the United States can exercise constraints on the positions taken by EU states towards other states in the international arena that consider the United States to be a major actor. This is, as was shown, the case for policies towards the Middle East. The EU apparently does not issue a foreign policy decision without first discussing it and agreeing on it with the United States. This analysis would imply that EU–U.S. relations are often quite strained, as argued by Kagan (2003).

This does not mean that the EU is unlikely to act collectively 'when it comes to the management of international conflicts,' or that it is always 'severely constrained by the dominance' of the United States, when the questions are those of crisis and conflict (Smith and Steffenson 2005, 350, 353). Although the EU can be constrained by the United

States in the sense that it will refuse to take an EU position contrary to U.S. interests, it can act collectively and independently in the management of a conflict as long as the United States is not involved, as, for example in 2003 and in 2006 in the Democratic Republic of the Congo, and in 2005 in Aceh, Indonesia.

In order to illustrate the way CFSP outcomes are influenced by the United States, and to understand the general role of the United States in the CFSP system, the following section focuses on the analysis of a particular group which worked mostly on the crises in the Balkans, namely, the Quint. This informal structure, which led in its turn to the creation of a Quad for general foreign policy issues, shows clearly the extent to which EU CFSP decisions can be influenced by U.S. foreign policy and the preferences of big states.

The Quint and the Quad:
The Informal Influence of the United States

On some occasions, final EU decisions reflect the outcome of the discussions within the Quint, which includes only five states: France, the United Kingdom, Germany and Italy, named hereafter the Big Four, and an important outsider – the United States. The Quint had an impact on the EU foreign policy decision-making process in relation to the Balkans from the early 1990s onwards. The Quint is considered here a *directoire*.[57] A *directoire* is a leadership group in the EU decision-making process that makes decisions affecting the interests of the other EU states without their participation.

The Quint appears to be more than a mere consultative group that pools ideas. It is a group that discusses EU foreign policy towards the Balkans and then takes initiatives, and small EU countries have to accept its authority. It seems now to have been replaced by the Quad, which includes the same members minus Italy.

This section underlines the importance of *directoires* in making EU foreign policy a reality. What follows is an overview of the Quint's structure and mechanisms, and then an analysis of the Quint's apparent field of interest and its influence on the creation of an EU common policy.[58]

Great Powers in the Balkans

The Quint seems to have begun within the NATO framework, during discussions about Greece and Turkey. But the Quint's direct parent was the Contact Group on Bosnia, which was created to overcome disagreements between the Europeans and the United States, to prevent the then president of Yugoslavia, Slobodan Milosevic, from playing on those disagreements, and to discuss policy on the Bosnian crisis with Russia. The Quint enabled the Europeans and the United States to go on with discussions, separately from the Russians. After the Rambouillet agreement on Kosovo in March 1999, the Contact Group and the Quint continued to meet to discuss issues pertaining to the Balkans in general.

Unlike the Contact Group, the Quint does not include Russia, it is not acknowledged by the EU states, and its discussions are not restricted to policy towards the Balkans. The Quint does not look like a 'coalition of the willing,' as all those who might be willing cannot join. It is a coalition of self-selecting states, possessing considerable economic and military power, which reaches agreement outside the official CFSP decision-making process. The Council Secretariat is seldom associated with it, although during spring and summer 2001, the Secretariat was present at the Quint because of the role played by the then High Representative Javier Solana in Macedonia. Finally, it rarely involves the Commission, and it seems to exclude the presidency of the EU. The Commission takes part in the Quint from time to time, and officials from the Council Secretariat have been present at some of its meetings. The involvement of EU institutions in the Quint is therefore different from that in the Contact Group, where they were automatically present. The Quint meets whenever it is necessary on an ad hoc basis, and quite frequently. During the Kosovo crisis, for instance, 'the five would speak by telephone conference every evening' (Lockwood 1999). Since the ending of the crisis, Quint conference calls take place only once every two weeks. The Quint meets at ministerial level, at the political committee level, and at experts' level. It has adopted the EU framework for its own meetings. Quint members meet one another in various forums, such as NATO, the OSCE, and the UN.

The Quint is a very discreet institution. As there is no secretariat, there are no reports or summaries and no record of the meetings, except for rare reports from the Big Four. The Quint does not divulge the outcome of its meetings to the representatives of the EU states. It is not as transparent as the Contact Group, which does inform EU states of its discussions. As some of the Big Four share their diplomatic reporting with the Council Secretariat, some reports of Quint meetings appear to have found their way there. Since the former High Representative was in regular contact with foreign ministers of member states actively participating in Quint discussions, it can be assumed that he was informed about the operational results of Quint meetings. Likewise, as the political directors are in permanent contact with one another, it is conceivable that some information is passed on tacitly to the presidency. The press has reported on the Quint only on very rare occasions between 1999 and 2001. Since 2001, the Quint has been mentioned in the local press in the Balkans. Although all diplomats know about its existence, they either know little about its functions, or are reluctant to divulge any detailed information about it. Indeed, one of my interviewees said that the High Representative did not want to 'hear that name within the walls of the Council of the European Union.' The Quint has a strategy of non-communication.

The Quint is distinctly influential in the EU's foreign policy decision-making process on the Balkans. It has held regular meetings to discuss EU matters related to the Balkans. It seems to have determined the absence of discussion at EU level on the possible lifting of the oil embargo and the discussion of a lifting of the flight ban. It could be surmised that within the Quint the United States vetoed an EU decision on the lifting of the oil embargo and accepted EU discussion on the lifting of the flight ban.

The Quint met to discuss the Macedonian question (Strauss and Smith 2001), and more specifically to discuss plans to put troops into Macedonia. In 2002, official Quint meetings started to take place on the situation in Kosovo. Currently, the Quint still meets up as a separate entity before Contact Group meetings, which deal with matters related to the Balkans, mainly the situation in Kosovo, but also in Bosnia-Herzegovina and Macedonia. The Contact Group is still effectively the most important international mediator in these three areas.

The evolution of the Quint since the war in Bosnia shows a reinforcement of the links between the Big Four within the EU and the United States, despite the divisions among these two entities on the war on Afghanistan and Iraq. The Balkan states are the laboratory for the big EU states in terms of foreign policy-making in coordination with the United States and Russia.

The Quint deals with other foreign policy issues. One EU official commented that 'with Rambouillet, the Contact Group ceased its effective existence. However, the Quint continued its meetings on different issues: Turkey, the enlargement process and Russia.' As regards policy towards Russia, Lockwood (25/11/99) points out: 'During the Istanbul summit of the OSCE, the night before the summit opened, the five dined together to coordinate their stance toward Russia. They agreed that Russia would not be directly condemned for its excesses in Chechnya.'

Since the events of 9/11, it seems that it is no longer the Quint that is used as a framework to discuss major foreign policy issues. Instead, the Quad has become the informal institution for discussions between the Big Three in the EU and the United States. Through the Quad, the conduct of EU foreign policy on highly sensitive matters resembles that of the period of European Political Cooperation. As Lord Owen reminded the House of Commons on 5 December 2007:

> One has to remember that in those days of [EPC] there was very good structured co-operation in relation to Berlin among what were then called the Quadripartite countries – the United States, the United Kingdom, France and Germany – and so there was a constant dialogue going on. It did not always refer to Berlin, but that was why it came into existence, and it was a very effective mechanism. (House of Commons, 05/12/07)

To summarize: the Quint and now the Quad appear to be more than mere consultative groups. When big member states discuss an issue within them, and take a decision with the United States, this decision is accepted later as an EU common policy.

The Real Actors of EU Foreign and Security Policy-Making

The existence of the Quint or of the Quad is in itself not a surprise, but the existence of this type of *directoire* in the CFSP system is a useful indicator of both the major role played by big states and the involvement of the United States in CFSP decisions. It shows the validity of intergovernmentalist propositions concerning the role of big states in the reaching of a CFSP agreement, and the way in which unilateral national policies can prevail in the process; and it also substantiates the realist account of how states bandwagon with a superpower.

A *directoire* comprising big EU states and the United States can be seen as a negation of the spirit of CFSP, and the principle of EU solidarity. First, although totally external to the CFSP decision-making process, the *directoire* seems to discuss all CFSP issues on a regular basis. One interviewee even stated that 'it has an obvious direct impact on EU decisions.' The EU's foreign policy decision-making process can be regarded as discredited if its agenda is set outside the EU framework, whether because the agency setting the agenda includes the United States, or because it only comprises three or four big EU states. As Zielonka (2000) says, this means that 'the CFSP proper does not deal with the most crucial problems on the Transatlantic Agenda.'

Secondly, it is very dangerous institutionally for some of the EU states to be left out of shaping and making decisions. The Quint/Quad can be considered undemocratic; the majority of the member states do not take part in it, and CFSP decisions are therefore effectively taken by a minority. Sir David Hannay, UK Special Coordinator for Cyprus and former UK Permanent Representative to the European Community, has said that 'somehow, the EU will have to avoid restricted groupings as they are damaging for the solidarity of the EU ... but it will have to go on with them unofficially' (Hannay Speech, 23/03/01). Presumably they must continue unofficially because no big EU state will agree to lose its decision-making power to small member states which do not have the military power to act abroad. Former European commissioner for external relations Van den Broek, when talking about the proliferation of formations for coordinating foreign policies, noted that these formations are 'harmful to the image of CFSP as a unitary policy' (Van den Broek, quoted in Pappas and Vanhoonacker 1996, 28). Many academics also consider this kind of unofficial group as a competitor to the EU: Simon Nuttall (2000, 13) underlined the fact that the Contact Group was a kind of 'rival forum to the CFSP.' According to Helen Wallace (1986, 156), 'to the Community purist the notion that bilateral, let alone trilateral, relations are an intrinsic feature of the system smacks of heresy.' Pijpers (1990, 18) believes that 'whatever the possible merits of such "inner circles" or "directorates," they obviously do some harm to the pretences of a genuine European identity in the world.' Finally, Daniel Vernet (1995, 132–8) went as far as to see this kind of group as representing 'the return of the powerful nations in Europe.' The fact that sensitive issues are discussed outside EU institutions could imply that the EU is a mere framework and not an action organization, as it neither decides nor implements any policy (I am using Hill's terms here) (see Guido Lenzi, in Zielonka 1998, 115n19).

The fact that a small group of states appears to be more credible than the EU as a whole undermines the role of the EU as an actor on the international scene. For instance, as regards EU policy towards Iran, the EU Big Three appear more credible than the EU presidency. Similarly, the role played by the United States through the Quint/Quad formation undermines the standing of the EU. In 1974, the French minister for foreign affairs declared that 'the United States must on no account be allowed to become the 10th member of the EC' (*The Guardian,* 11/06/74, quoted in Kotsonis 1997, 131). At the beginning of the twenty-first century, the United States could be considered an unofficial external member of the EU or the fourth or fifth member of the unofficial leadership group in the CFSP system.

The Quint/Quad formation is, however, accepted by all the EU states because it does bring certain advantages to the way EU foreign policy is made and perceived. The final outcome is an EU decision, despite the non-EU character of the decision-making process. The Quint/Quad not only assists coordination between the United States and EU member states, but also apparently helps to resolve conflicting positions among EU members. When looking at the role of the Contact Group, Boidevaix (1997, 71) makes a similar analysis: 'The effective outcome of the Contact Group is to have succeeded in coordinating the policies not only between the Europeans, the Russians and the Americans, but also among the Europeans themselves.' For instance, when the United States wanted to lift the arms embargo on the Bosnian Muslims, this was resisted by the United Kingdom and France, which had UN peacekeeping contingents in Bosnia and did not want to endanger their troops. Germany was closer to the United States, as it wanted to isolate the Bosnian Serbs, but 'it did not want to break away from its European partners' (Leigh-Phippard 1998, 309). European solidarity prevailed. The Quint enabled the Big Four to coordinate their positions and reach agreements: an interviewee explained that 'when France, the United Kingdom, Germany and Italy agree, one can be almost sure that the Quint is behind that agreement.' Discussions between the United States and the Big Three have forced EU states to progressively define a common position on the policy to adopt towards Iran. In 2003, they entered the negotiations with Iran without a clear strategy or alternative outcomes (Roudsari 2007), but since then, the Big Three have apparently 'demonstrated a united approach and their interests – in acting on behalf of the EU and as a threesome – coincide' (interviews conducted by Kutchesfahani 2006, 18). The Quad therefore appears to be a trigger for cooperation among the Big Three, when highly sensitive issues are at stake. It can be considered a pluralistic security community, which, by definition, includes independent states, but which encourages social communication (see Adler and Barnett 1998, 438).

Through the Quint/Quad, European states can bring the United States on board. In 1993, France and Germany came to a common position on a peace plan for Bosnia, but the United States was needed to support and implement this plan. The French defence committee noted that the Contact Group needed NATO support in order to have an impact, in terms of foreign policy, on third states (Quilès and Lamy 1999, 18). The EU tries to use the Quint/Quad structures in order to bind the United States, that is, to influence its foreign policy. However, bandwagoning is the policy eventually adopted vis-à-vis U.S. power, as EU states do not usually succeed in convincing the United States to change its mind.

Over time, the EU seems to be supplanting the Quint/Quad, or at least gaining as much visibility and recovering a leadership role. Through the Quint, the EU has gained a de facto foreign affairs voice in the Balkans. The EU High Representative is perceived as a credible negotiator by the parties in Kosovo and Serbia. Through the Quad, and the growing involvement of the High Representative in negotiations with Iran, the EU is also increasingly considered a credible mediator. With its more active voice in crises in the world, the EU is playing a distinctive role, which is becoming more visible to the United States.

Finally, the Big Four, now the Big Three, can generally take a decision more effectively than when it is discussed by twenty-seven states. As shown in the FRY case study, the leadership of the big countries can be considered a major factor in achieving an EU policy. Moreover, the United States can listen more easily to a small group. As Helen Wallace noted as early as 1985, 'we can observe a concern that EPC with ten, and soon twelve, members may not be a sufficiently effective or a credible forum for dialogue with the Americans in particular' (49).

Also, a *directoire* type of group is more effective than twenty-seven states, when addressing crisis situations. UK Foreign Secretary Malcom Rifkind (quoted in Boidevaix 1997, 11), commenting on the Balkans crisis, claimed that 'fast-moving diplomacy required that a minority led diplomacy.' The FRY case study highlights the efficiency of the Quint, in comparison with the difficulty of reaching agreement on a common position in the Council. With the EU enlargement process, it is all the more difficult to reach a common position. *Directoires* are necessary for acting as a motor for the decision-making process.

To conclude: CFSP decisions and state preferences can be constrained by the United States, which is a multifaceted invisible actor in the CFSP system. The evidence collected here gives the lie to Zielonka's contention (1998a, 58) that 'France, Germany and the United Kingdom have a tendency to settle European matters by private bargains among themselves and maintain a largely independent policy towards the United States.'

A number of academic writers have noted that the influence of the United States is sometimes an important factor in the creation of EU policy. Hiester (1991, 46) said: 'One thing that does seem clear in 1990 is that even with the end of the Cold War, the role of the United States as a Power in Europe seems set to continue into the indefinite future.' Keens-Soper (1999) speaks of 'Mighty America in Europe,' and John Peterson (2002, EUI conference, 17) believes that '[h]owever more mature the EU is now than it was in the early 1990s, it often still needs the Americans to surmount its fissiparous tendencies. This role is emerging as one as the most important played by the United States as a European power.'

But the United States has not found the particular, and most important 'European role' which it has been searching for since the 1960s (see Von Geusau 1966, viii); and Kennedy's proclamation that 'the Atlantic Alliance should and will take the form of an equal partnership between a "strong and united Europe" and the United States' (van Cleveland 1966, 150) has not yet been realized. The EU is not always autonomous, and the United States does not currently consider it as an equal partner. EU foreign policy is dependent on U.S. foreign policy to the extent that for Hill (House of Commons Document, 20/01/08), the newly appointed High Representative 'must be somebody who the Americans are willing to take seriously.' European leaders appointed Baroness Cathy Ashton as High Representative in 2009, a British official who has yet to make her mark.

7 The European Commission: Modes of Intervention and Control in CFSP

The European Commission's role seems a priori extremely limited in the CFSP system, as legally it only has an indirect right of initiative through the High Representative, in effect equivalent to the shared right of initiative it enjoyed before the ratification of the Lisbon Treaty in the CFSP field. Intergovernmentalist theory argues that control of the CFSP decision-making process lies with the member states; decisions are taken by unanimity, and states, through their embassies and intelligence operations, have more information than the Commission on highly sensitive issues (Pollack 2003, 53). The Commission can be absent from CFSP negotiations, or it can have a presence in the CFSP decision-making process and even make proposals, but it is not expected to have any impact on the reaching of a CFSP common policy. In Nugent's book (2001) on the Commission, there is no separate chapter on the role of the Commission in CFSP issues; in these, he argues, it has only limited powers (2001, 328).

This chapter seeks to show that the Commission can have a major impact on the shape of CFSP outcomes, and that it can be an essential actor. It does not merely propose initiatives, mediate between governments, and tailor or revise proposals in order to fit national preferences, as Moravcsik (1993) suggests. Intergovernmentalism is incorrect in its assumptions about the role of the Commission in the CFSP field, and rational institutionalism provides a better explanation of its influence.

The Commission can promote its own preferences to the detriment of some states, including big states. According to Bulmer (1998, 376), 'the Commission has a pro-integrative mission which is partly inculcated by its rules and partly by its institutional structure.' Pollack

(2003, 39) posits that the preferences of Commission officials are to enhance the Commission's control of EU affairs, and to expand the political power of the EU. These assumptions seem valid in the CFSP field. The Commission's preferences are more integrationist than states' preferences. It wants to give a voice to the EU, and to make it an efficient foreign policy actor. In the sanctions field for instance, the Commission hates symbolic sanctions. It wants sanctions policies which have a tangible impact on a third party. State representatives frequently feel the Commission's influence, and they can be surprised by its scope of action.

There is only one field where the Commission does not seem to have any impact on the decision-making process and that is the ESDP field. Although the Commission has a seat at Council of the European Union meetings relative to ESDP issues, state representatives are reluctant to give powers to the Commission in this field. An interviewee justified this by emphasizing that 'power must be given to the one who has responsibilities. It is not up to the Commission to send troops abroad.'

The Commission plays unexpected roles in the CFSP decision-making process. It seems to have as much information on foreign policy issues as states. It can use its powers in European Community (EC) matters, and encroach on the potential role of states in the CFSP field. It can also exploit the lack of consultation between national foreign affairs officials. It can use the grey zones of EC law better than state representatives do, and can exercise control through the strict implementation of EC law.

Manipulating Information

Rational institutionalists do not support the idea that the Commission can play a role in the CFSP field. Pollack (2003, 154) asserts that the Commission has extremely restricted discretion in foreign affairs. However, this is inaccurate. Two methods observed by rational institutionalists in the EC system and used by the Commission to influence EC policy outcomes, that is, packaging and information asymmetry, deserve attention to understand the role of the Commission in the CFSP field.

The packaging process, whereby unpopular measures in the negotiation of one decision are linked to popular ones in another, is difficult to carry out in the CFSP field, because when the Commission implements a CFSP decision, there is usually only one decision to be dealt with. Information asymmetry, on the other hand, can certainly work in favour of the Commission, which has at least as much information as states on sensitive, non-military foreign policy issues. The Commission makes political reports and is an expert on many topics in the working groups. For instance, an official working on CFSP matters explained to me that on issues such as human rights, political dialogues with third countries, or the transatlantic relation with the United States and Canada, the Commission was always there – and not only for the exchange of ideas.

The Commission can be more knowledgeable than the states on some issues. It receives a mass of information due to the fact that, unlike states' representatives, it acts in both CFSP and Community matters. It receives information from many different sources: member states, EU delegations, and international organizations. EU delegations deliver political and economic analyses. Commission officials enjoy 'excellent access to political leaders as a result of their administration of development funds, trade expertise and knowledge about particular EU policies' (Cameron 1998, 64). As the Commission participates in the G8, and is an observer at the United Nations, it has expertise in areas such as human rights issues, small arms, and the death penalty.[59]

Commission officials can hold the same position for a long period of time, and become experts on a topic. As a result, their opinion is taken into account by state officials who are uncertain of their states' positions. For instance, the Commission led the discussions in the sanctions committee in the FRY case study. This is similar to the situation in pillar one observed by Pollack (1996, 450), who notes that a member of Delors' cabinet said: 'We knew what we wanted and [government representatives] were less clear.'

At the highest level of the decision-making process, the length of office of the commissioner (five years) means the Commission has a longer memory than heads of state and governments. The Commission can become more of an expert on CFSP issues than the states.[60] The Treaty of Lisbon changes this situation, as the president of the European Council has a mandate for two-and-a-half years, renewable once. But she or he will still not enjoy as much long-term institutional knowledge as the Commission and the High Representative.

Finally, the Commission does not share all its information with states. Its information, based on the management of first pillar policies, is kept possessively by the Commission as a *chasse gardée* (exclusive domain). There is no transparency; the Commission is not communicative. Its main aim is to make sure that CFSP does not deal with EC affairs. In general, the Commission tends to tell ministers that most first pillar foreign affairs issues do not concern them: it purposely never talks about pure EC issues at the Political and Security Committee. To sum up: in rational institutionalist terms, information asymmetry in favour of the Commission is a significant means of control in the CFSP field, because of the Commission's institutional knowledge of EC law and policies, the length in office of its civil servants and commissioners, and its determination not to share its knowledge with states.

Communautarising CFSP Issues

Information is not the only factor in the Commission's impact on CFSP outcomes. The Commission communautarises CFSP issues, that is, it makes CFSP issues become EC issues. It can do this in three ways. Decisions taken by states in the CFSP field are modified by the Commission according to its own preferences before being issued to the outside world as CFSP decisions. Also, decisions which could and/or should be taken in the second pillar, that is, which could and/or should be CFSP issues, are instead being developed exclusively in the first pillar by the Commission. The Commission acts diplomatically on the world stage.

Devising Sanctions and Aid Policy in Contradiction with CFSP Decisions

When a CFSP decision legally requires an EC decision in order to be implemented, the Commission can use its exclusive right of initiative to give its own interpretation of the member states' common decision. In this way, it can initiate a policy which can be contrary to the position of most member states, delay a policy, or not act at all and effectively veto the CFSP decision.

The role played by the Commission in the intergovernmental sphere of foreign policy decision-making is not something that has developed only recently. Twenty years ago, Nuttall (1988, 113) wrote that 'there are occasions on which the Commission is called on to play its part as a Community institution, although the dynamics of the operation lie entirely within political cooperation.' He (1993, 3) also described how at that time 'the Commission began to take on a substantial de facto role in EPC, as member states found themselves increasingly obliged to turn to EC instruments in order to implement EPC policies.' For instance, EPC ministers decided on sanctions, and the Commission acted to implement them, for instance, on Poland in 1982, Argentina during the Falklands crisis in 1982, and South Africa in 1986.

When a Council decision has to be implemented, the Commission plays a key role as the only institution that can make the proposal for implementation. A state official told me that this procedure was not wise, as the Commission could thereby obstruct the decision-making process. CFSP decisions often need the EC pillar in order to implement sanctions, and to finance CFSP decisions.

The Commission plays a major role when sanctions towards a third country are discussed. An interviewee realistically noted that, in CFSP matters, 'officially, the Commission does not exist. However, everyone knows about article 301.' Article 301 (now article 215) states:

> [W]here it is provided, in a common position or in a joint action adopted according to the provisions of the Treaty on European Union relating to the common foreign and security policy, for an action by the Community to interrupt or to reduce, in part or completely, economic relations with one or more third countries, the Council shall take the necessary urgent measures. The Council shall act by qualified majority *on a proposal from the Commission*. (my emphasis)

The procedure is the following. The ministers for foreign affairs decide within the CFSP framework that they want to impose sanctions on a third party. Then the Commission makes its proposal, and there is a vote. Unanimity is required to go against this proposal, and qualified majority is enough to have it adopted. The Commission can thus have a major role as agenda-setter, directing the kinds of sanctions the EU imposes on states.

The Commission can initiate a proposal for a form of sanction which is not wanted by some states. This was the case in my study on the FRY, where in 2000 the Commission made a proposal to states which established a white list and not a black list for the implementation of financial sanctions. Or it can simply refuse to implement a CFSP decision on sanctions. For instance, surprisingly, it never implemented the European Council's decision of December 1999 to impose sanctions on Russia, following the Chechnya crisis. As it did not agree with the sanctioning of Russia, it simply did not propose any measures to suspend the trade provisions of the Partnership and Cooperation Agreement.

Still in the field of sanctions, the Commission also succeeded in having member states agree with the creation of a sanctions committee at least on one occasion, that is, when imposing sanctions against the FRY. The creation and role of committees have been analysed by both intergovernmentalists and institutionalists. These studies show that committees, especially management committees, are instruments for states to control the activities of the Commission; and committees are usually created to guarantee that states stay the masters of the treaty. According to Aspinwall and Schneider (2000, 14), the Council gained considerable gate-keeping power on some supranational proposals, thanks to the creation of committees. Pollack (1997, 115) also sees management committees as police patrols. For Pollack (1996), a member state (in his terms, the principal) controls EU policy and EU institutions (the agent) through the use of monitoring and sanctioning. Institutions are 'the products of conscious member states' design' (Pollack 2001, 237). There are several reasons for creating an institution: to monitor states' compliance with their international treaty obligations and encourage cooperation among member states; to solve problems of incomplete contracting between states; to adopt complex regulations; or to act as an agenda-setter (Pollack 1997, 103–4).

In the instance I studied in the context of the FRY, the normal situation, as described by Pollack, was reversed. The Commission asked the member states to create a management committee, that is, the sanctions committee. This meant that the implementation of a decision to sanction a third country would be controlled by the Commission, and not just by states, as had been the case until then for sanctions towards the FRY. The sanctions committee was, in this case, not a way for states to control the Commission, but a way for the Commission to influence states. The Commission became the police patrol of the states.

Some big states opposed the proposal made to the management committee, but their position was not taken into account. Qualified majority was the rule, the committee was apparently created in a rush, and state representatives did not have time to understand fully the consequences of their act. A year after the creation of the sanctions committee, the sanctions regime needed to be reinforced. The Commission was responsible for the weakness in the policy, and the resentment of state officials could still be felt. Timing was relevant here. State representatives agreed to delegate the implementation of their sanctions policy to the Commission, because a sanctions committee was needed urgently to address the situation in the Balkans. But they later regretted it.

The fact that it was the Commission that asked for the creation of a management committee shows that it can use EC rules to enhance its power in the CFSP field, and to limit the power of states. It acted the same way as states do when they create management committees to limit the power of the Commission in the first pillar. All management committees are not then, as expected by institutionalists, instruments of control of the Commission by states.

Most CFSP decisions requiring financing have to go through the first pillar in order to be implemented. As with sanctions policies, the outcome of a policy decision corresponds to the Commission's interests, and not those of the states. For instance, the Commission took nine months to implement and finance the Stability Pact for South Eastern Europe, which was signed by EU states in June 1999. By stalling, the Commission was making a political statement. It did not believe the states in south-eastern Europe fulfilled the conditions for receiving this funding. Following the same scenario, the Commission waited seven months before implementing the decision, taken by the Council in November 1999, to fund the reconstruction of Montenegro.

In all the cases discussed above on sanctioning and financing, the Commission manipulated the CFSP process. The final common policy corresponded to the Commission's and not the states' interests. The Commission can, then, act against the member states. It need not seek to change the position of member states before an EU common policy is decided on; it can simply either refuse to implement the second pillar decision, or give its own interpretation of the decision when making the proposal for its implementation. It is helped by the fact that it can control the timing of an action. It can defer implementation, and thereby change or nullify the impact of member states' decisions; in the field of foreign policy, it is often only quick decisions that will have the required effect.

The Treaty of Lisbon might change the role of the Commission in the financing of CFSP missions. According to article 28: 'The Council shall adopt a decision establishing the specific procedures for guaranteeing rapid access to appropriations in the Union budget for urgent financing of initiatives in the framework of the common foreign and security policy.' This provision could mean that the Commission is no longer responsible for the budget when rapid access to funding is required. If this is the case, the treaty sets a clear limit to the Commission's ability within CFSP to use its powers in relation to the budget to make a foreign policy different from that intended by member states.

Past experience, however, precludes any certainty that the Lisbon Treaty will help constrain the powers the Commission derives from its control of the EU's finances. The fate of the European Community Monitoring Mission (ECMM) is a salutary tale. The ECMM was a unit created by the member states in 1991, in order to monitor conflict prevention. Its creation rested on a strictly intergovernmental decision, and it was funded by member states. In 1999, EU states wished to transfer the ECMM to the CFSP framework, but the Commission did not wish to take on the responsibility of financing it, as a large amount of funding was involved. Eventually, the Commission was forced to agree with the integration of ECMM financing into its budget, but it reviewed and restricted the amounts allocated. The Commission's attitude surprised many of the people I interviewed, who now realized that the Commission had a powerful say in the CFSP sphere. In the future, and despite Lisbon, the Commission could adopt the same position again, and delay or restrict transfers from the start-up fund to the Community or Union budget, after states had voted for them within the CFSP framework.

Working the EC Rules

The Commission uses EC prerogatives to preserve and expand the influence of the EC in highly sensitive matters, which could and even sometimes should be discussed and decided upon in the second pillar. It can do this in three ways: by initiating EC policies which would seem to be CFSP issues because of their emphasis on security-related and highly sensitive issues; by preventing member states from transferring first pillar measures to second pillar prerogatives; and by creating policies in the EC field before these are created in the CFSP framework, thereby obliging states to conduct negotiations on all subsequent related policies within the EC framework.

The Commission can make proposals under the first pillar relating to issues which should legally be discussed under the first pillar, but which in substance are more obviously CFSP issues. For example, in the late 1990s, the External Relations Commissioner, Chris Patten, initiated the creation of a Rapid Reaction Fund charged with financing prevention and crisis management operations, such as the deployment of police forces, as well as the monitoring of elections and respect of human rights, humanitarian aid, and support to the media. All these actions can be viewed as a communautarisation of CFSP issues. They reinforce the political role of the Commission.

Member states often agree with this communautarisation. They themselves have deliberately decided to delegate CFSP issues to the first pillar, such as demining actions, electoral assistance missions, and the promotion and defence of human rights. The Commission, for instance, monitored the Palestinian elections, and its action was considered successful by both the Council and the Commission itself.

However, states can also disagree with the role of the Commission in the EC field. We might look at the field of dual-use export controls. Dual-use items are goods and technology developed for civilian uses, but which can be used for military applications, or to produce weapons. Originally, initiating EU foreign policy in this area was the joint responsibility of second and first pillars, but now responsibility rests on the Commission alone. The transfer was supported by the European Court of Justice, which, according to the Commission (October 2002), cast very·serious doubts on the legality of such a two-pillar regime for this area of export controls under the treaties.[61] States' officials would much rather have kept this issue under the second pillar. Some states now have to change position in order to reach a common policy on dual-use export controls, as qualified majority is now the rule, whereas they did not have to do so in the past when unanimity was the rule. In this instance, the Commission succeeded in making use of treaty provisions to draw a second pillar–first pillar issue into the first pillar.

The Commission can protect its prerogatives in the first pillar by stopping states from adopting CFSP decisions which would block or replace foreign policies already established in it. Foreign ministers have tried to take a second pillar decision in a field that belonged to the first pillar, but they have not generally succeeded. Nuttall (2002, 3) describes how the member states tried and failed to stop the Commission from giving aid to schemes of agricultural restructuring in Marxist Ethiopia. In another instance, state representatives meeting in New York decided to break off cooperation with Haiti, unaware that such an action was illegal under the Lomé Convention, which had been signed in 1975 between the EEC and the African, Caribbean, and Pacific (ACP) area. The Commission delayed the proposal for action in the EC context, and it succeeded in building a blocking minority. As a result, the Lomé Convention was not suspended for Haiti (Monar 2000). CFSP decisions on Bosnia and Russia were limited by the action already taken under the first pillar. Bosnia benefits from autonomous trade preferences, and since 1996, has benefited from assistance under both the EC Phare and Obnova programs. The CFSP joint action which grants aid to Bosnia was decided upon in 1998, and was only an exceptional measure to help achieve stability. For Russia, the Commission was responsible for initiating the Partnership and Cooperation Agreement of 1994. The only CFSP decision on Russia is the Common Strategy of 1999, which was a general statement on the importance of cooperation between the EU and Russia, and led to no concrete policies.

The Commission can rely on the European Court of Justice to defend its prerogatives against states which favour a CFSP rather than an EC procedure in order to reach a foreign policy decision. It took the Council of the European Union to the European Court of Justice in 2005. The Commission had disagreed with a Council decision taken in the CFSP field on the financing of the Economic Community of West African States (ECOWAS).[62] An important judgment by the Court confirmed the Commission's prerogatives. According to the Commission, the decision should have been made in the first pillar framework, as it was relative to development aid. The Council argued that it was relative to the promotion of security. In the first place, the Court's Advocate General dismissed the Commission's action, arguing that the CFSP decision was strictly related to security, and that even if a CFSP decision might contribute 'indirectly to the social and economic development of developing countries, any encroachment on the Community's competences [was] precluded' (Opinion of Advocate General Mengozzi, 19/09/07, paragraph 175). If his opinion had been followed, CFSP decisions could have been taken in the future on issues considered to relate to security, even if they had indirect consequences for development matters. However, in May 2008, the European Court of Justice decided against the Advocate General's position. The Court argued that the Council decision in the CFSP field was illegal, as this decision could have been adopted on the basis of the EC Treaty in the first pillar. As a result, the European Court of Justice annulled the Council decision. Decision-making in the first pillar clearly takes precedence.

According to Spence (2006, 356), if this case had gone the way of the Advocate General, it would have had 'implications in several policy areas: development, security sector reform, disarmament, demobilisation, reintegration of former combatants and other arms related issues such as landmines and explosive remnants of war.' Instead, the Commission is now confirmed as the exclusive actor in aid and trade issues, and CFSP decisions cannot be made on security issues which have such components. In this respect – a contingency not foreseen by intergovernmentalist theory – CFSP decision-making is constrained. In this part of the CFSP field at least, states cannot take any position they wish.

Finally, the Commission can deliberately use the first pillar framework to make a highly sensitive policy proposal which should really be made and discussed under the second pillar. For this, the Commission uses article 308 of the Treaty of the European Community, in which it is stated:

> If action by the Community should prove necessary to attain, in the course of the operation of the common market, and one of the objectives of the Community ·and this Treaty has not provided the necessary powers, the Council shall, acting unanimously on a proposal from the Commission and after consulting the European Parliament, take the appropriate measures.

Once such a policy is adopted under the first pillar, states have to take every future policy decision related to that topic under the first pillar. In this way, the Commission short-circuits any attempts by member states to discuss sensitive issues under the second pillar.

In spring 1999, for instance, the Commission drafted two regulations on 'the implementation of EC operations in development cooperation *and any other field*' (my emphasis), that is, on all actions to support conflict prevention, such as assistance to Bosnia. On the basis of article 308, it proposed both regulations to the Council of Development in the first pillar, instead of proposing them to the CFSP counsellors group and the GAC in the second pillar.[63] This proposal was accepted by the Council of Development. One official commented to me that this was very cunning on the part of the Commission, and rather embarrassing for the states. National representatives working for the Council of Development did not realize that the issue they had decided on in the first pillar was really, in substance, a CFSP matter. Later, representatives within the CFSP framework were compelled to abandon their own discussions on the issue, as legally a decision had already been taken under the first pillar framework. There are coordination problems among different services within EU states that the Commission can, and does, exploit. The Commission succeeded in making member states adopt these regulations because of its expert knowledge of both EC and CFSP rules, because of the lack of communication between different services within the same states, and because ministers have overlapping responsibilities.

The fact that the Commission can exploit problems of intrastate coordination has already been observed by Nuttall (1988, 108), who has stated: 'The structure of many Foreign Ministries, divided into separate political and economic sections, means that information often does not circulate freely enough within a Ministry to ensure perfect consistency and coordination in European policy at national level.'

Another attempt by the Commission to dupe the Council of the European Union, but one which failed, is the following. In February 2000, the Commission was due to propose a regulation to the Council on the control of the funding of OHR and UNMIK (the Office of the High Representative in Bosnia and Herzegovina, and the United Nations Interim Administration Mission in Kosovo).[64] It insisted on the fact that this was a first pillar issue, and suggested that it was doing member states a favour by discussing it within the CFSP pillar. It then made a proposal, on the basis of article 308, whereby it declared itself responsible for controlling all present and future funding by the European Union of all peacekeeping agencies in the world. The proposal was ultimately rejected; member states refused to agree that it had any legal basis, and expressed strong opposition to the Commission holding so much power.

Article 308 is therefore a powerful weapon for the Commission in the CFSP field. If national representatives do not realize the importance of a Commission proposal for future foreign policy decisions, and this apparently does happen, the Commission can trick the states, and force them into unintended positions. Interestingly, the Treaty of Lisbon introduces a new clause to article 308, which states: 'This Article cannot serve as a basis for attaining objectives pertaining to the common foreign and security policy.' It seems as though the Commission can no longer use article 308 directly to create legislation relating to CFSP. However, it can still propose aid- and trade-related measures that would have indirect effects on CFSP decisions.

Acting as the Voice of the European Union

In the second pillar, the Commission has the right to take part in all CFSP discussions, as it is present at Council meetings. It puts forward informal ideas, which are floated among officials at the level of working groups or of political directors.

According to a Commission official, 'the Commission initiates the majority of the CFSP decisions. It circulated many informal ideas, and they do not necessarily go against the member states' positions; they can simply contribute to the general debate on an issue.' With the Treaty of Lisbon, the Commission loses its right of initiative officially, but not in practice, as the High Representative, who is a vice-president of the Commission, has a right of initiative for CFSP issues.

From the analyses offered by the people I interviewed, it appears that the Commission is also increasingly involved in the decision-making process for exclusively CFSP issues. It has progressively acquired visibility. It is significant that the Commission reorganized the external relations directorate general, DG1, after the Maastricht Treaty. It created a DG1A, with a primarily political focus, to link in with CFSP and its working groups, and also to liaise on political issues with EC representations in third countries.

It is extremely difficult to evaluate which Commission's proposals in the second pillar, if any at all, have had an impact on CFSP common policies with political and diplomatic implications. The Commission participates in CFSP debates, but its positions are not necessarily taken into consideration. For instance, it had no impact on the EU's foreign policy on China's human rights record.

But, in general, the Commission is the external representative in all areas of European Community business, and has the right to express its opinion in foreign policy issues pertaining to these areas; and this can have consequences for CFSP diplomatic initiatives. Before the ratification of the Lisbon Treaty, the Commission acted as if it were responsible for all EU policies, including foreign and defence policies. For instance, speeches made in 2001 by the Head of the European Commission Delegation to the United States, Ambassador Guenter Burghardt, gave the impression that the Commission was responsible for EU foreign policy. State representatives were surprised by some of the actions of the Commission, which took on 'new roles that were not foreseen at the time of [its] creation' (Pollack 1997, 107). A state official remarked that 'it is just crazy that the Commission has all the means to act.' Under the Lisbon Treaty, the Commission now has an official voice in CFSP matters through the High Representative.

To conclude, institutionalist theory explains accurately the role of the Commission. The Commission clearly enjoys prerogatives which work counter to the perceived intergovernmental character of CFSP. The Commission makes good use of its role as an entrepreneur (Peters 1994) in the first pillar in order to have an impact on CFSP outcomes. It has asymmetrical information knowledge of foreign affairs and of EU rules, and is careful not to divulge all its information to states. It constantly and scrupulously defends its own prerogatives. It can blatantly take measures to contradict CFSP decisions, encourage the making of EC foreign policy to the detriment of CFSP decisions, exploit the lack of communication between ministers dealing with different aspects of foreign policy, and give the impression to third states that it is the most important voice in EU foreign affairs.

The reaction of state officials to the actions of the Commission confirms the relevance of the institutionalist theory. State representatives are often surprised by the unintended consequences of treaty rules, and by the extent of the first pillar's decisions, which take precedence over their own operations in the CFSP field. Many representatives resent the Commission using its prerogatives to extend its own responsibilities and those of the European Union.

The Treaty of Lisbon attempts to prevent the Commission from having an impact on CFSP decisions. This confirms the idea that intergovernmentalist theory offers a correct analysis here; states, through the treaty, try to limit the Commission's role. However, with the Treaty of Lisbon, the powers of the Commission are unlikely to be constrained by those of the High Representative, and of the European Council, and by treaty rules. In meetings of Foreign Affairs Ministers, the High Representative takes the place of both the rotating presidency and the Commission. According to Avery (2008, quoted in the House of Commons Document 20/01/08), 'some supporters of the Commission and the "Community method" see the arrival of the new High Representative in the Commission as likely to extend the influence of intergovernmentalism.' Before the treaty was ratified, for example, as the case study on the Balkans shows, presidencies cooperated with the Commission in order to pre-empt EU decisions on sanctions. With the Treaty of Lisbon, the High Representative could decide to work towards decisions on sanctions issues that would satisfy all member states, instead of cooperating with the Commission in order to override the position of the minority. This is not, however, a foregone conclusion: as vice-president of the Commission, the High Representative could equally well decide to support the Commission's approach to sanctions, and to European foreign policy in general, and make proposals that could go against the interests of some member states.

The role of the Commission could also be limited by that of the European Council in foreign affairs. The European Council is responsible for identifying and deciding on the strategic interests and objectives of the Union, both in the CFSP field and in the other areas of the external action of the Union (article 10b of the Treaty of Lisbon). However, these interests and objectives are likely to remain very general. Given that the power of the Commission resides in its implementation role and expertise, its power should not change. The treaty also makes it clear that the Commission cannot use article 308 for legislating on CFSP objectives. But the Commission is still able to use this article for legislation on aid and trade affairs, which may have an indirect effect on CFSP issues. In sum, even with the Treaty of Lisbon, the Commission seems far from 'heeding the bugle call to retreat' (Spence 2006, 394).

Conclusion:
'Constrained Intergovernmentalism':
A More Complete Theorization of the
CFSP System

Researchers such as Puchala (1972, 276–7) have warned that 'attempts to juxtapose or combine conventional frameworks for analytical purposes by and large yield no more than artificial and untidy results.' I would prefer to argue that theory-building is about enhancing existing theories to understand political processes and outcomes. It is through a synthesis of clearly defined theoretical hypotheses that we can best reach a proper understanding of the function of policy-making.

This chapter seeks to realize this synthesis, and to answer the concerns of authors who have regretted the absence of any convincing theory in relation to the study of the European foreign policy system. Weiler and Wessels (1988, 229) deplore what they call the failure of academics to relate European political cooperation to any existing system theory, integration theory, or theory of international relations, let alone create a new general theory to describe it. They themselves use four theories, without nominating any one as better than the others. Holland (1991, 2) writes that EPC has been poorly served by theory, but many authors have sought to explain the functioning of both EPC and CFSP systems. Tonra and Christiansen (2004) give an overview of various theories of international relations, foreign policy, and European integration, but there is no attempt to combine these various approaches to understand the CFSP system. Researchers writing in the March 2006 issue of the *Journal of European Public Policy* (Sjursen 2006) try to assess European foreign policy, its identity, and its importance. They raise both conceptual and empirical questions about what drives foreign policy and what direction current foreign policy is taking. But here, too, there is no attempt to link theory and the study of European foreign policy.

The present book offers for this purpose a theory of 'constrained intergovernmentalism.' This theory takes an important new look at key relationships between actors and processes outside and within the European Union in the foreign policy field. I have chosen the term 'constrained intergovernmentalism' to highlight the fact that in a CFSP outcome state preferences are not protected and promoted by the operations of the system; instead, the process of choosing and implementing policy is determined by a number of constraining factors.

The theory is built upon my findings in the case studies, and upon my study of the role of both the Commission and the United States in the CFSP decision-making process. The hypotheses put forward in this chapter should be valid to explain all future CFSP outcomes.

Constrained intergovernmentalism combines intergovernmentalist theory with some key concepts proposed by realism and institutionalism, that is, the perceived advantages of partial bandwagoning, the impact of Commission entrepreneurship, and the imperative of compliance with the *acquis* of the European Union.

Intergovernmentalism certainly seems the most appropriate theory to explain the functioning of the CFSP system, and the making of CFSP outcomes. The requirement for unanimity makes it difficult for member states to reach a CFSP decision. Whenever states do reach a common decision, it is generally an LCD outcome, since that is the only one with which all states can be satisfied. States follow their national interest when defining their preferences, and they generally assess their national interest in terms of economic and geopolitical factors. There is little evidence of socialization changing those preferences. State representatives socialize among themselves, but this does not seem to have an impact on declared state preferences and CFSP outcomes.

Intergovernmentalism, however, needs to be qualified. Constrained intergovernmentalism points to three forms of constraint which act on state preferences before, during, and after the negotiation process, and in consequence on EU foreign policy-making. There is an external constraint on CFSP, which is the power of the United States. The United States is able to block EU decisions, regardless of the declared preferences of EU states. The European Commission exercises an internal constraint. Whenever the first pillar is directly or indirectly involved in the CFSP system, the Commission is able to transform the outcome of CFSP decisions to fit its own preferences. Finally, there is a legal constraint which comes from the *acquis* of the European Union (that is, past decisions from both the first pillar and the second pillar, with which any new policies must be harmonized), and the rules of the EU.

Power Politics, Peer Group Pressure, and Reputation

As intergovernmentalists have noted, the main actors in the CFSP decision-making process are states, and in particular big states. The most important decisions are constrained by power politics. Whether in cooperation with the United States, or among themselves, the Big Three have a history of intensive cooperation which goes back to the 1970s, when there was talk of a *directoire* among the 'trilateral axis' (Gegout 2002). European states have also developed privileged bilateral relations, such as the Franco-German motor, the UK-Italian relationship, or other ad hoc partnerships. The Big Three are especially active in trying to encourage their fellow-EU states to reach a common position on highly sensitive issues. The case study on the FRY and the examination of the operations of the Quad/Quint show the influence the three big EU states have within the EU structure. In the case study on NATO, the United Kingdom and France set the pace (Germany did not have strong preferences in those negotiations).

In the 2000s this cooperation is continuing, becoming more visible, and extending to topics beyond foreign policy.[65] At the Ghent summit in October 2001, only the British, French, and German leaders Tony Blair, Jacques Chirac, and Gerhard Schroeder met to discuss the military operation in Afghanistan. Italian Prime Minister Silvio Berlusconi was not invited. In November 2001, the United Kingdom tried to organize a dinner in London with France and Germany, in order to raise issues relating to the Israeli-Palestinian conflict, humanitarian aid to Afghanistan, and the post-Taliban order in Afghanistan. The small EU states complained about their exclusion, with Austrian Chancellor Wolfgang Schuessel saying that the smaller EU nations would never accept rule by a select inner circle.

These same Big Three have been responsible since 2003 both for debating ESDP issues such as planning capabilities and weapons procurement, and for negotiating with Iran on the long-term future of its nuclear program. They are using EU economic incentives, but not the EU framework, to negotiate with Iranian authorities. According to Youngs (2006, 79), the Big Three wanted to include the High Representative in their initial negotiations, but they decided against it, as they would have had to include Italy, which was holding the presidency at the time. An interviewee confirmed to me that Italy was not included in these meetings. The Big Three framework was again criticized by other EU states, especially Italy, Spain, Greece, and the Netherlands (Crowe 2005, 15; Kutchesfahani 2006, 18; Sauer 2007, 14). In 2004, the leaders of the Big Three were joined by cabinet ministers, and discussions were widened beyond foreign and defence issues to trade, economics, social, and welfare policies. In February 2008, the EU did not succeed in reaching a common position on recognizing the independence of Kosovo, but the Big Three, together with the United States and Italy, that is, not unsurprisingly, all the Quint members, agreed on recognition. In July 2008, the U.S. presidential candidate Barack Obama focused his European tour on Berlin, Paris, and London.

Some academics (Ash, Mertes, and Moisi 2003) believe that Germany, Britain, and France are Europe's three indispensable actors. They have called for the creation of a 'club of three,' routinely extended to include a serious player in the White House. However, this club already exists, as leaders and political directors from these three states are in constant contact with one another. Experts (Everts and Missiroli 2004) have even claimed that the EU should have its own security council, in which the Big Three would be permanent members, as this 'would give them the status and visibility they deserve.'

The advantage of a group of big powers deciding on CFSP issues is that it makes the EU a more effective actor on the world stage. Helen Wallace (1985, 30) noted some time ago that, 'to be effective, the exercise of West European influence on the world outside requires determined and coherent efforts by weightier European governments.' Representatives of the Big Three states still have to defend themselves from criticism of the fact that they meet within a restricted framework. For German Foreign Affairs Minister Joschka Fischer, speaking at the European University Institute on 17 January 2002, the fact that big states negotiate together independently of the other EU states 'is not a question of *directoire*; it is a question of leadership.' For William Wallace (personal communication), 'an avant-garde of small groups of states is very much part of how European integration develops.' Small groups of states are likely to take the lead in the creation of EU common policies in the CFSP field (see Keukeleire 2001). For some independent observers, the EU security doctrine of December 2003 'can acquire muscle over time, provided the big three of Britain, France and Germany work together' (*Financial Times*, 05/12/03). In 2008, the leaders of Germany and France were the first to react to the crisis in Georgia. When British Minister for Foreign Affairs David Miliband travelled to Tbilisi, he received the backing of France, Germany, and the United States. According to Alexandr Vondra, the Czech deputy prime minister for European affairs, France, Germany, and Britain 'occasionally consult others,' but they still dominate the European Union and want to continue to do so (*New York Times*, 14/02/09).

Hasenclever, Mayer, and Rittberger (1996, 197) along with Krasner (1991, 340) argue that actors who hold a preponderance of power resources set the rules. This can be seen in the CFSP field. Big states determine who plays the real CFSP game when highly sensitive issues are at stake, that is, themselves, with or without the United States, operating outside the legitimate CFSP framework. This informal CFSP decision-making process is similar to the concept of a concert of nations; such a concert is open only to major powers and 'does not entail codified and automatic commitments to collective action' (Kupchan and Kupchan 1991, 140).

In the negotiation process, as intergovernmentalists point out, each state's preferences are generally fixed, and all states try to act according to a rational strategy, which is mainly concerned with securing their own national gains. States are concerned with the geopolitical implications of EU policies. My case studies revealed that geopolitical implications have to be understood as being not only the reaction of the third state concerned by the EU policy, but also as the reaction of the United States to this EU policy. Furthermore, when no geopolitical implications are at stake, states only act at EU level when an EU policy is likely to have a positive impact on national economies.

The negotiation process is one of hard interstate bargaining, and in that process, power counts. As one interviewee told me, 'The EU interest is the result of the one who hits the hardest.' Another interviewee commented that the CFSP decision-making process was a kind of 'haggling.' In that process, issue linkages can take place between issues in the same or different areas. For instance, in the FRY case study, the flight ban was lifted in exchange for the reinforcement of the financial sanctions. In the NATO case study, the agreement on the role of NATO in the EU was linked to the policy on the BSE crisis. Contrary to the assertions of Smith (in Ginsberg 1999, 444) on European political cooperation, that 'EPC outcomes have rarely if ever involved bargaining, side-payments, issue linkages, or any other mechanisms associated with the mere reduction of transaction costs,' the CFSP system is based on cost-benefit analyses and bargaining processes which are generally to the advantage of the biggest states.

At another level, peer pressure comes into play to constrain the choices reached by states. Sociological institutionalism does not provide any simple answers when it comes to understanding the CFSP system. Among the working groups, or the political directors, socialization is possible, but its impact is either nil or negligible. Some interviewees from the working groups certainly believed that it was sometimes harder to negotiate with their own governments than with their colleagues at the Council, and they said that some officials did go beyond their states' instructions. At the political directors' level, where officials also meet on a regular basis, this facilitates negotiations but does not necessarily entail any changes of position. Following the creation of the Political and Security Committee in 2000, the ambassadors meet two to three times a week, and have extremely long agendas, as all foreign policy issues go through this committee. This highly pressured working situation could well bring about a strong esprit de corps among the representatives, but they are still instructed by government officials who are not subject to that socialization process.

At the level of the foreign affairs ministers, the effects of socialization on a state's change in preference are difficult to ascertain. Two events in the China case study deserve attention. In 2000, French representatives agreed to change position in order to accommodate the other representatives' positions. One could argue that French officials were convinced by the arguments of other states as a result of a socialization process, and that following this change in position, France adopted this position as its own new preference in the negotiations of 2001. A change in preference could thus be a long-term consequence of a change in position. However, the change in policy between 2000 and 2001 can be explained by intergovernmentalist theory. There was, in fact, no change in preference, only a change in position. Intergovernmentalism would interpret this change in position as a strategic rational change, which could easily take place because the cost for France was nil. The second event concerns the agreement reached between Denmark and the Netherlands with Italy. These countries changed position but not preference, and this had nothing to do with any socialization process. Each of these states made a clear cost-benefit analysis, and favoured economic interest and European solidarity over the defence of human rights.

A similar case is that of a small state, Greece, which abstained from vetoing sanctions against Serbia in May 1999. As a result, sanctions were implemented. Greek leaders succeeded in giving the impression to their people, who were pro-Serbia, that they had no other choice but to agree with the sanctioning. An interviewee stated, 'I am sure that when Greece had difficulties, it was influenced by the rest of us: we suggested it adopt a different position, and it did.' The change in preference seems to have occurred following a logic of appropriateness, which means that Greek officials, convinced by other EU officials, genuinely felt that their initial position was not appropriate. It could, however, be argued equally well that the Greek minister for foreign affairs deeply believed himself that Serbia should be sanctioned, and that the position of all the other states just strengthened him in his position. At the level of prime ministers and heads of states, socialization might have an impact, but this is extremely difficult to measure.

A long-term socialization process could be taking place within the CFSP field. As a specific example, one can look at EU policy towards the Democratic Republic of the Congo. In the 1990s, troops from several African countries were deployed in the DRC: pro-governmental troops, supported by Zimbabwe and Namibia, fought the rebels in the East, who were supported by Uganda, Rwanda, and Burundi. EU states had different analyses of the reasons why these foreign states invaded the DRC. A common action in relation to the DRC, concerning a mandate for a special envoy, was made in 1996. An interviewee told me in 2000:

> Member states' positions are starting to get closer. This is due to the evolution in Congo, but also to the discussions in Brussels. If France and Belgium hear the same arguments for two or three years, they are likely to be convinced in the end. The discussion in Brussels at least helps in understanding the situation. There is always progress but it is very slow.

This progress eventually led to the Artemis mission in 2003 and the EUFOR RD Congo mission in 2006. (It should be noted, however, that when the UN Secretary General asked the European Union to intervene in the DRC in 2004 in Bukavu, and in 2008 in the Kivus, the EU gave no reply.)

EU policy towards Zimbabwe changed in December 2008, when French President Nicolas Sarkozy declared that Mugabe should resign. However, this change appears to result less from any socialization process within the European Union and more from France's change of mind in the face of the opinion of a growing number of African and international leaders, such as South African Nobel Peace Prize Laureate Archbishop Desmond Tutu, Kenyan Prime Minister Raila Odinga, and former UN General Secretary Kofi Annan.

One other phenomenon identified by intergovernmentalists for the understanding of CFSP outcomes is especially relevant here, namely, maintaining one's reputation. Hasenclever, Mayer, and Rittberger (1996, 186) write that actors with 'good' reputations are likely to be taken as partners for future projects. Intergovernmentalism would consider reputation as a factor that could motivate a representative to change position, once he or she has made a cost-benefit analysis of the situation. The factor of reputation is more likely to occur at the highest level of the negotiation process, namely at the GAC/FAC level, rather than at a lower level. For one interviewee:

> When the instructions are strict, for instance on the Western Balkans and Chechnya, one can block for months and months. However, politically, the discussion then reaches the GAC level. At that level, it is hard to resist. If you want to be credible, you have to agree to give in.

Before the Treaty of Lisbon, the question of reputation was also more likely to influence a state holding the presidency. If a state holding the presidency, or about to hold it, was reluctant to reach an agreement on one issue, it would risk being isolated for six months on all the issues discussed during its presidency, as the other states would have the impression it was promoting or defending its own interest rather than the European interest. It was very important for a state to establish a trustworthy reputation when it was about to hold the presidency. William Wallace (quoted in Ohrgaard 1997, 22) argued that 'reputations are strengthened or damaged by the conduct of each Presidency.' State officials believed it was important to start a presidency with a positive reputation, and they were ready to change their positions to avoid damaging it. The change in position of France, which accepted the establishment of relations between the EU and NATO in the NATO case study, shows the relevance of reputation; France took its forthcoming EU presidency into account.

The concept of reputation seems to have an impact on a state's position when few economic or security interests are at stake, and when a state leader wants to show solidarity with European colleagues. This can come about when he or she is under peer group pressure and when he or she is threatened by other states.

Reputation is unlikely to influence a state's decision if economic or security interests are at stake. For instance, at the time of the recognition of Slovenia and Croatia by Germany, but not by the other EU states, Germany acted without taking into account its reputation. Interviewees, including one who was very close to Genscher at the time, thought that 'the price of disagreement with the other EU states, and the United States, was too high to pay,' that 'Germany's reputation was damaged,' and that 'it had been a mistake for Germany to take a unilateral decision.' By contrast, if an EU foreign policy decision has no or little impact on state economies, representatives seem willing to act against their preferences (this would be expected by intergovernmentalism, as the issue would not consequently be highly sensitive).

The reputation of a state is an important factor when the state is under peer group pressure. Such pressure is mostly effective if exercised over a long period of time on the same official. Telegrams can be sent two to three times a day to this state, because everyone is against it, and over a long period of time. According to one representative, 'There is great pressure on states to find agreement. It is never pleasant to be constantly put into a minority when negotiating.' Pressure works at all levels, from the working groups to the ministers for foreign affairs. In the FRY case study, one interviewee believed that 'Cook accepted the deal on the lifting of the flight ban because of the pressure of his colleagues. After six months, pressure clearly has an impact.' It seems that the British position was changed under the pressure of other representatives; but the change was also helped by the fact that the United Kingdom eventually succeeded in creating an issue linkage to its own advantage.

Another example of the result of pressure was Austria's agreement in December 1999 to abstain on the decision to launch a CFSP joint action on non-proliferation and disarmament in the Russian Federation. The aim of this policy was to help Russia dismantle its weapons of mass destruction in a safe and environmentally friendly way. A further aim was to provide a framework for an enhanced EU role in project-related cooperation with Russia on risk-reduction activities. Initially, Austria had been totally opposed to the wording of the joint action. Austria did not want the EU's program to contribute to 'experimental studies on plutonium transport, storage and disposition.' Austria wanted to add a declaration to the joint action to show its disagreement, but finally withdrew the declaration and abstained. According to interviewees directly involved in the decision-making process, the change was clearly due to the pressure of other states. One interviewee told me that 'there was a long debate within Austria's own administration. It did not publish its declaration because there was pressure put on Austria by the other member states.' However, another interviewee thought that 'Austria finally only accepted the EU joint action, because it realized it had already accepted cooperation with Russia for plutonium related issues through the TACIS [Technical Aid to the Commonwealth of Independent States] program.' Even if Austria realized it could not go against an EU position it had accepted through TACIS, this case still shows that EU states can influence another state's change in position, with the help of the treaty rules. An isolated state that undergoes constant pressure and badgering seems to react in order to protect its reputation.

Finally, a state might change position if it is threatened by other states. In the CFSP field, interviewees who were working on CFSP issues were concerned about not blocking an ongoing negotiation, for fear of retaliation. According to the Secretary General of the Council, Pierre de Boissieu (*Le Figaro*, 07/07/00), 'it is easy to push a German or a British official into a corner, but you know that in three months time, they will pay you back.' In 1982, Ireland was threatened by its peers with a possible reduction of its Community benefits if it did not agree with the sanctions against Argentina. When these sanctions were in place, Martin (1992, 145) wrote that 'Ireland did not lift the sanctions unilaterally, because of solidarity and the consequences for its Community benefits – farm subsidies and access to EC markets.' More recently, according to an interviewee, big member states had to threaten Greece with stopping the creation of the cohesion fund for Greece, as Greece was against the recognition of Macedonia. After two years of negotiations and threats from other member states, Greece eventually changed position in 2003.

The phenomenon of states changing position for fear of retaliation is called 'coerced strategic diffuse reciprocity.' 'Diffuse reciprocity' is a concept developed by constructivists. It occurs when state representatives feel that an agreement accepted today could be 'rewarded' tomorrow (see Wendt 1994, 386; Ruggie 1992, 583). It involves conforming to generally accepted standards of behaviour. Participants make mutual concessions within the context of shared commitments and values (Keohane 1986, 4). The advantage of diffuse reciprocity is that it promotes long-term cooperation much more than simultaneous exchange does, and it increases confidence among members of a social system (Keohane 1986, 22). Representatives make concessions to one another to build credit for the future. According to Lewis (2000, 268), one Coreper ambassador stated that, 'if you help someone, they will remember.' 'Package deals' include issue linkage between two issues, both discussed at the same time, and over a time period, that is, the idea of giving something in order to obtain something else in return in the future. However, these calculations are not always for gains, they are also to avoid losses in future negotiations: this is when the concept of coerced strategic diffuse reciprocity is useful.

Partial Bandwagoning, Commission Manipulation, and the Influence of the *Acquis*

To the effect of internal power struggles between member states described in the previous section, all of which work to reduce or constrain the options open for decision-making, must be added the intervention of actors technically external to the CSFP system. In this respect, intergovernmentalism, as a theory, needs to be modified.

The EU is not as impermeable as intergovernmentalists believe. It seems to be open to U.S. influence. Nothing in intergovernmentalist theory accounts for the power of veto on EU policies that is exercised by this hegemon outside the EU. I have shown how the role of the United States in CFSP is facilitated by the networks of official and unofficial relations between the United States and the EU, including the Quint structure, through which the United States appears to be aware of all EU negotiations on issues of major importance.

In practice, the EU only engages in partial bandwagoning with the United States. Bandwagoning implies two processes: the EU's foreign policy has to support most U.S. policies, and the EU accepts to shape its own foreign policy according to U.S. demands. This would mean that the United States succeeds in exercising total hegemonic power. Howorth (2001, 783) has spoken of 'hegemony through the back door.' However, we cannot speak of complete hegemony. It is plainly not the case that the EU supports most U.S. policies. The EU does not agree to shape most of its own foreign policy decisions according to U.S. demands, but it does make sure the United States agrees with its foreign policy towards third states before it carries them out. It seems from my case studies that CFSP decisions are constrained by the

United States, and are blocked when the United States, at the highest level, opposes the reaching of these decisions. They also appear to be conditioned by the United States when they address other states which consider the United States to be the major actor in their own political context. This was highlighted in the message sent by Javier Solana (*Financial Times*, 20/01/09) to the President of the United States, Barack Obama: 'The EU has been most successful when it has worked with others: with the UN in Lebanon; with the Association of South East Asian Nations in Aceh/Indonesia; with the U.S. everywhere.'

In the FRY and NATO case studies, EU states were permanently aware and informed of the United States' own foreign policy and its opinion of their own positions, and they agreed not to take decisions against U.S. interests. There are not necessarily rewards to be had from the U.S. for such compliance. For instance, in the context of the crisis in Kosovo, big EU states 'first improvised, at Germany's insistence, NATO's ... conditions [that is, U.S. conditions] for an end to the war: an offer which was immediately rejected by the White House' (*The Observer*, 18/07/99). The idea of the EU binding the United States is not valid. This idea that binding takes place is supported by authors such as Ikenberry (2002, 295), who believes that both economic and security institutions, such as the G8 or NATO, bind the United States to other states, and 'reduce – at least to a certain extent – Washington's ability to engage in the arbitrary and indiscriminate use of power. The price for the United States is a reduction in Washington's policy autonomy.' However, Ikenberry is himself ambiguous about this binding power. He does not show that states can reduce U.S. autonomy, but only that they wish to influence U.S. policy. When discussing British foreign policy, he states that 'by binding itself to the superpower, Britain gained a stake in the struggle [against terrorism] but also – *it hopes* – a voice in the policy' (Ikenberry 2002, 294–5; my emphasis). Partial bandwagoning of the United States by the EU is likely to continue, whether the United States is under a Republican or a Democratic presidency.

The EU is not as rigid in its institutional and decision-making process structure as the language of the Treaty of Lisbon would lead us to expect. Contrary to intergovernmentalist expectations, the Commission does not always act as an obedient servant, and the member states cannot always control it. As rational institutionalist theory would argue, it is the Commission that constrains states' positions, and the Commission has communautarised CFSP issues. All CFSP common policies, except ESDP policies, can be shaped by the Commission. The Commission manages to pursue its own interest, that is, its own powers and the protection of EU treaties.

In order to influence CFSP outcomes, the Commission can use the first pillar framework directly, when CFSP common policies require a first pillar implementation, especially, that is, where financing or sanctions are required. The Treaty of Lisbon allows states to put some restrictions on the Commission's budgetary power. The Commission can also use the first pillar framework indirectly, to initiate common policies which properly belong to the second pillar. In these two cases, the Commission can eventually have a policy adopted which is contrary to the initial positions of some big member states. It can make a proposal which is different from that expected by states, delay a policy, or even not act at all and effectively veto a CFSP position.

The Commission chiefly exercises its impact on CFSP outcomes because of its exclusive right of initiative and its particular expertise in the first pillar. In addition, through its strict implementation of EC law, especially its grey zones, and an astute use of the *acquis communautaire*, the Commission can succeed in creating situations of path-dependency in the CFSP field. Its role as a policy implementer of an EU decision may lead to its playing an enhanced role at a later moment in the process, when the EU is called upon to deal with the same or related issues. This could be regarded as a form of spillover. A past action of the Commission in relation to CFSP, when an earlier CFSP decision needed implementing, could have influence on a future decision which otherwise would be the sole responsibility of CFSP. I qualify this a time-contingent form of spillover.

Finally, the Commission is an important actor in CFSP because it can manipulate the lack of consultation between various Council formations. The Commission can initiate a decision in one field and have it accepted, while ministers working in a different field remain unaware of what is happening.

These conditions under which the Commission has an impact on CFSP outcomes – that is, the use to its own advantage of its exclusive right of initiative and its expertise of foreign affairs in the first pillar, the permanent scrutinizing of state actions with respect to the application of EC law, the use of the grey zones within the treaty, and the exploitation of the lack of consultation between various Council formations – complement existing conditions offered by institutionalists in their studies on the role of the Commission in the EC framework.

These conditions should be valid for the analysis of future CFSP out-comes, and they could perhaps also be used more generally by researchers, in order to explain all EU policy outcomes where the Commission plays a role, that is, in the pillars relative to EC and justice and home affairs.

Intergovernmentalist theory is wrong to assume that past decisions are unlikely to constrain states' positions. Moravcsik has been criti-cized by Wallace, Caporaso, and Scharpf (1999, 155–79) for not acknowledging the importance of path-dependency. Past decisions, as historical institutionalism argues, can have consequences for member states, which may be compelled by them to reach a common policy they initially disagreed with. States and institutions remind each other of past EU decisions they are supposed to respect.

In the CFSP field, two types of past decisions, or norms, must be respected by EU states, and can be invoked by EU institutions, espe-cially the Commission, and member states to reach an EU common policy. One norm is respect of the treaty rules, and its grey zones, which must be observed in the first stages of any negotiations within the EU. Another norm is respect of the CFSP *acquis*, which comes into play when a negotiation on a CFSP decision stems directly from another previous CFSP decision; and respect of the *acquis communau-taire*, which is required when new CFSP common policies are being made. These norms are always fully adhered to by states, even when they go against their own preferences. A few instances will show ways in which states have complied with these two types of norms.

As regards the respect of treaty rules and grey zones, states consis-tently abide by the interpretation of the treaty given by the Council's legal service. For instance, in May 1999, Greece accepted the Council's interpretation of the Treaty of Amsterdam concerning the decision on the imposition of sanctions towards the FRY. When Greece was block-ing the sanctioning of the FRY, the Greek minister for foreign affairs decided to make use of the Treaty of Amsterdam in order to satisfy his EU Council colleagues, and tell his people that he had no other option but to agree with the EU position. He had visited the Council's legal service, which found for him the following get-out clause: the Treaty of Amsterdam forced him to agree with an EU decision taking sanc-tions against the FRY, as qualified majority voting was the rule, and he could not oppose it. The Treaty of Amsterdam indeed stipulated that any decision based on an existing common position had to be taken by qualified majority. The treaty's grey zone was that it did not say which common positions it has to be applied to. On this occasion, the Council affirmed that all common positions, not just the ones taken after the Amsterdam Treaty came into effect, but also the ones taken before the Treaty of Amsterdam, could be adopted by qualified majority. This was a watershed rereading of treaty rules. One interviewee said, 'Many of us could not believe what was being done.' As a result of Greece's action, the assets freeze and investment ban, and the flight ban and visa ban towards the FRY of May 1999 were the first CFSP decisions adopted by qualified majority.

The CFSP *acquis*, unlike the *acquis communautaire*, carries no legal obligation. However, once member states have signed a common policy which has instructions for future action, there is no way back. They are forced, as in the EC field, to create other common policies in order to implement this one. EU state officials remind one another about the decision already taken, especially when a state is reluctant to act in order to implement it. For instance, during the negotiations on the Helsinki declaration and on EU–NATO relations in the first half of 2000, state representatives kept reminding one another of the exact wording of the Helsinki conclusions, so that no state could question what the states had signed up to. This has also happened in the more distant past. After sanctions were imposed on Argentina in 1982, according to Martin (1992, 144), 'some members became quite adverse to continuing with sanctions when military action broke out, and maintained them only because the EC as a whole could not agree to their withdrawal.'

When deciding on CFSP common policies, states also have to respect the *acquis communautaire*. If a decision has been taken on an issue under the first pillar framework, for instance by the Development Council, the ministers for foreign affairs cannot take a decision regarding the same issue in the CFSP field. EU states and institutions can thus remind the others that no CFSP decision is possible on this issue.

These rules have unintended consequences. A phenomenon of auto-entrapment can occur, in which a state can feel trapped by its own past decision. Historical institutionalism offers useful insights here: negotiation outcomes cannot be understood without looking at the historical processes. This phenomenon is also known as incrementalism, whereby each decision shapes the next one. There are gaps in states' control of the future, because when a decision is taken, there can be consequences that are undesired and unintended, in the sense that states do not realize the full implications of what they are signing. In the CFSP field, a high degree of uncertainty in the decision-making process is possible. A state can unexpectedly be forced to act differently from what it had originally planned, because of past decisions it has taken. A state can even be constrained by past decisions it was not aware of, because of poor communication among its services.

Acknowledging Constrained Intergovernmentalism: The Way Forward for the EU

Table C.1 shows the relevance and shortcomings of existing theories of international relations, and the hypotheses I have drawn together from different theories to create the constrained intergovernmentalist approach. The hypotheses answer the question, Which actors and factors contribute to, or constrain, a CFSP outcome? Constrained intergovernmentalism, I would argue, which brings together the sharpest insights of existing theory, has the potential to explain satisfactorily all current and future CFSP outcomes, and to predict how future decisions could be made on sensitive foreign policy issues.

The CFSP system is unique in the EU structure, and its functioning is different from that of the EC system. The findings of my study cannot be extended to other EU decision-making areas, except for my analyses relating to the role of the Commission. But in the CFSP context, constrained intergovernmentalism passes the test of what Rosenau (1980, quoted in Viotti and Kauppi 1998, 35) defines as a 'good theory'; that is, one that 'ought never be embarrassed by surprises, by unanticipated events that have major consequences for the system on which the theory focuses.' Despite the changes resulting from two major structural events in the life of the EU, the enlargement process and the ratification of the Treaty of Lisbon, the hypotheses I shall now derive from constrained intergovernmentalism will remain valid for the CFSP system.

Even with the enlargement process, big member states will continue to be the decisive element in the determination of CFSP common policies, when the issue discussed is of major importance for at least one big state. The current reality of the CFSP is that big states are responsible for taking decisions. This is unlikely to change: even with twenty-seven states or more, three states, namely France, the United Kingdom, and Germany, are likely to remain the main CFSP actors, in close contact with the United States. The present High Representative does not have the political legitimacy to influence, let alone alter, the policies of the three big EU states.

Table C.1
The Theory of Constrained Intergovernmentalism

Intergovernmentalism validated, and sociological institutionalism refuted:

Big member states are the main actors. They agree on a CFSP outcome when:

– there are geopolitical and economic gains
– the reputation of a state is at stake:

A common policy can be reached to enhance or prevent damage to a state's reputation. The factor of reputation is more likely to occur at the highest level of the negotiation process, namely at the level of foreign affairs ministers, than at a lower level, and is also more likely to influence the state holding the presidency than another state.

The concept of reputation has an impact on a state's position when few economic or security interests are at stake, and when a state leader wants to show solidarity with European colleagues. She or he decides to do so when she or he is:

- under peer group pressure. This refers to the pressure put on one or a few state officials, who are then completely isolated by the majority who wish to reach a common position. It is mostly effective if exercised over a long period of time on the same official
- threatened by other states. I call this 'coerced strategic diffuse reciprocity'

States act rationally. In order to reach a CFSP outcome, a cost-benefit analysis is made, and there is no socialization process:

– A CFSP decision is unlikely to be reached, at least in the short term, as a result of a change in ideas and preferences of state representatives
– At a low level of EU negotiations, representatives may change preferences, but this is rare, as they are under close and permanent instructions from unsocialized government officials back home

Insight from realism validated: Partial bandwagoning with the United States

A CFSP outcome is unlikely to be reached if it goes against U.S. interests expressed at the highest level, that is, by the U.S. President

A CFSP outcome, which addresses states which consider the United States as a major actor, is reached only if it does not go against U.S. interests

Table C.1 (*continued*)

Rational institutionalism validated: Commission control

A CFSP outcome can be influenced by the Commission when:

- its first pillar agenda-setting powers are involved in the CFSP decision-making process
- it has more expertise in a CFSP issue than member states
- it interprets EC law and its grey zones to its own advantage. It uses the *acquis communautaire* to establish a time-contingent form of spillover
- it manipulates the lack of consultation between various council formations

Historical institutionalism validated: Constraint of EU law and *acquis*

A CFSP outcome can be constrained by past decisions. A path-dependency effect is created, whereby state representatives not only accept past formal and informal institutions but also perpetuate them even if they go against their preferences

This is only possible when state representatives feel they would be breaching the two following norms:

- respect of treaty rules and its grey zones
- respect of the EU *acquis*; namely, of CFSP *acquis* when an EU common policy is based on the implementation of past CFSP common policies; and of the *acquis communautaire*

Within an enlarged EU, the influence of the United States on EU foreign policy should not change, as the United States already has an impact on the foreign policy of new member states. The Czech Republic, Slovakia, Hungary, Poland, Estonia, Latvia, Lithuania, Bulgaria, and Romania all supported the American invasion of Iraq. At the European Convention, which discussed the possible creation of a treaty establishing a constitution for Europe, the Danish representative of the European convention remarked that 'the real problem is that representatives of big EU states should not rush to phone Mr Kissinger [meaning the United States]' (*Le Monde*, 12/07/02). The United States' authority within the CFSP system is now publicly acknowledged by EU states' representatives. Partial bandwagoning with the United States by the EU is likely to continue.

The Commission, and past decisions, should also still constrain states' positions in the CFSP system (with the exception of ESDP military issues), especially as, increasingly, economic relations with third countries are taking up a large part of the foreign affairs agenda. The Treaty of Lisbon seems to limit the creeping power of the Commission in CFSP issues. This phenomenon is expected by the intergovernmentalists: Taylor (1984, 87) emphasized that the authority of European institutions is limited, conditional, dependent, and reversible, meaning that the role of institutions is completely dependent on the goodwill of states, which can modify this role at any time. However, within the framework of this treaty, the Commission can still implement CFSP decisions according to its own initiative, propose measures which have indirect consequences for CFSP matters, and exercise influence in CFSP matters, through the High Representative.

In the 1950s, Jean Monnet launched the idea of European integration, by compromising with states on the issue of unanimous voting as opposed to voting by qualified majority. At the time, he had hoped that blockage of the system would entice his colleagues to revert to qualified majority (Bossuat 1996, 73). This has not happened, and is unlikely to occur in the CFSP field. EU states retain their right to veto foreign policy decisions in political and military affairs, and big EU states are key to creating an EU foreign policy on highly sensitive matters. However, actors within and outside EU institutions have a constraining power on all EU states, and they indirectly contribute to shaping EU foreign policy.

When the EU adopts a foreign policy on highly sensitive issues, it is, in effect, the foreign policy of the Big Three, influenced by U.S. foreign policy. However, European divisions are still rife. Not only did EU leaders disagree on the war on Iraq in 2003, but they neither took action at the beginning of the Darfur crisis in 2003 nor responded to a United Nations request to support the UN in the Democratic Republic of the Congo in 2008. In addition, despite a call in 2009 by the European Parliament for all EU member states to recognize the independence of Kosovo, Spain, Cyprus, Greece, Romania, and Slovakia still do not agree with all other EU states on this recognition. This state of affairs is damaging to both EU and national foreign policies.

The EU foreign policy system is likely to remain intergovernmental with the Lisbon Treaty. French and British cooperation is key to an independent, vocal, and effective EU foreign policy, which would also make the EU credible vis-à-vis the United States. In September 1956, French Prime Minister Guy Mollet asked his British counterpart Anthony Eden either to create a union between France and the United Kingdom or to allow France to enter the Commonwealth (BBC News, 15/01/07). Today, without going this far, consistent, systematic, and unitary Franco-British foreign policy positions are crucial in a world where China, Russia, and all the developing countries have a legitimate and rising voice in foreign policy affairs.

Appendix: Situating 'Constrained Intergovernmentalism' in the Literature on European Foreign Policy

Topics	Authors
General and specific aspects of EU foreign policy	
General overview of CFSP and ESDP	Hazel Smith (2002), Karen Smith (2003), Carlsnaes et al. (2004), Michael E. Smith (2004), Holland (2004), Hill and Smith (2005), Ginsberg (2007), Casarini and Musu (2007), Howorth (2007), Merlingen and Ostrauskaite (2007), and Keukeleire and McNaughtan (2008)
Specific policies and concepts – on a geographical area or towards another international actor	Holland (1995), Dannreuther (2003), Karen Smith and Laatikainen (2006), and Bicchi (2007) – relations with South Africa, with the EU's Neighbourhood, with the United Nations, and with the Mediterranean
– concepts	Hill (1993) – 'capability-expectation gap' Jorgensen (1998) – EC / EU's successes and failures Karen Smith (1999), Hill (2001), Whitman (2002), and Manners (2002) – influence on the world stage Lucarelli and Manners (2006) – values and principles
Impact of CFSP decisions on the external world	
Negative	Neuhold (1997), Zielonka (1998b), Rosecrance (1998), and Hill and Smith (2000)
Positive	Duchêne (1972), Sjoestedt (1977), Taylor (1983), Allen and Smith (1990), Hill (1996), Caporaso and Jupille (1998), Rhodes (1998), Bretherton and Vogler (1999), and Young (2000)
Conditions for a positive impact	Stavridis and Hutchence (2000), and Ginsberg (2001)

Topics	Authors
Interaction between national and European structures	
Europeanization	Larsen (1999), Morisse Schilbach (1999), Gillespie (2000), Tonra (2001), Wong (2006), and Dover (2007)
Interplay between national and European level	Hill (1983, 1996), Manners and Whitman (2000), Mérand (2008)
National governments benefit from the EU	Allen, Rummel, and Wessels (1982), Pijpers et al. (1988), Regelsberger et al. (1997), and Zielonka (1998a)
Theoretical insights	
Unique foreign policy system	Hill and Wallace (1996)
Realism	Ifestos (1987), Pijpers (1991), Pijpers et al. (1988), Keens-Soper (1999), Posen (2004, 2006), and Hyde-Price (2006)
Intergovernmentalism	Hoffmann (1966), Wallace and Allen (1977), Taylor (1982), Wallace (1983), Ifestos (1987), Pijpers et al. (1988), Rummel (1992), Carlsnaes and Smith (1994), Regelsberger and Wessels (1996), Peterson (1997), Gordon (1997–8), Rosecrance (1998), Rummel and Wiedemann (1998), Zielonka (1998a, 2000), White (1999), Stavridis and Hutchence (2000), Hoffmann (2000), Moravcsik (2002), Holland (2004), and Ginsberg (2007)
Constrained intergovernmentalism	Gegout (2009)
Rational and sociological institutionalism, and institutionalization	Von der Gablentz (1979), Nuttall (1992, 2000), Michael E. Smith (1996, 1998, 2000), Jorgensen (1997), Tonra (1997), De Wilde d'Estmael (1998), Glarbo (1999), Egeberg (1999), Peterson and Bomberg (1999), Lewis (2000), Sjursen (2001), White (2001), and Meyer (2006)

Notes

1 Under the Treaty of Lisbon, the pillar framework disappears. But the conduct of EU foreign policy is still an issue for discussion in two different arenas. The Lisbon Treaty has two distinct components: the Treaty on the Functioning of the European Union (TFEU) and the Treaty on European Union (TEU). Provisions on previous EC issues are in the TFEU, and those on previous CFSP issues are in the TEU. In effect, the CFSP pillar remains distinctive from the EC pillar, even though legally the EC term disappears. In this book, the distinction between first and second pillars is still used to distinguish issues that are strictly Community issues from CFSP issues.

2 In the 1950s, three treaties were created: the European Coal and Steel Community (ECSC), the European Economic Community (EEC), and the European Atomic Energy Community, Euratom. They were known from 1967 onwards as the European Communities. In 1992, with the Treaty of Maastricht, the EEC changed its name to the European Community (EC). The EC, the ECSC, and Euratom are part of the first pillar of the EU system. In 2002, the ECSC Treaty expired, and some of its provisions were incorporated in the EC framework. Euratom has not merged with the European Union, and it retains a separate legal personality.

3 All translations from French, unless otherwise stated, are my own.

4 Hoffmann (1966) makes a distinction between low and high politics. Low politics involves technocratic and uncontroversial issues: material benefits, trade, and economics. High politics involves non-material issues of *grandeur* (a state's concept of its own greatness), prestige, rank and security, and domination and dependence, where the autonomy and sovereignty of governments, or aspects of national identity, are at stake. In high politics, there is little or no solidarity among the contenders. In a

later text, Hoffmann (1982) does not consider that foreign policy and defence are always and exclusively high, and economic and social policies are low. As early as 1983, Webb argued that the autonomy of high politics was doubtful as EPC issues developed into the foreign policy sphere of the EC. For Light (1994, 100), economic instruments of foreign policy have become at least as important as diplomacy and force. The definition of high politics can therefore change over time, and include different policies.

5 A CFSP issue is not necessarily one of major importance. For example, states easily agreed on the following policies: cooperation with the Western European Union (WEU) for demining in Croatia (1998), support for East Timor independence (1999), support for and cooperation with the International Criminal Court (2001), the creation of the EU Border Assistance Mission at Rafah crossing point (2005), and the establishment of the EU Police Mission in Afghanistan (2007).

6 See the appendix for a list of authors who are sceptical of the possibility of EU actors reaching foreign policy decisions in highly sensitive issues which would go against the initial preferences of all states. The appendix situates this book in the literature on European foreign policy.

7 For a useful overview of intergovernmentalist assumptions, see Moravcsik (1991, 1993, 1997, 1998), Hoffmann (1966), Webb (1983), Taylor (1983), Milward (1992), Keohane and Hoffmann (1990), Garrett (1992), Garrett and Weingast (1993), Garrett and Tsebelis (1996), and Falkner (2002).

8 ESDP and CESDP are the same policy. The term CESDP was used in 1999 and 2000 in European Council conclusions. At the Nice European Council of December 2000, the term ESDP instead of CESDP was preferred, and has been ever since.

9 See, for example, the debates in the 1990s on realist-liberal syntheses, and the subsequent emergence of new approaches – Ruggie (1983), Baldwin (1993), Kegley (1993), Powell (1994), and Wendt (1999).

10 Historically, the two main theories, intergovernmentalism and neofunctionalism, have been challenged by other theories. Neofunctionalism is a theory of regional integration, which places emphasis on the role of states and of non-state actors, especially European institutions, in the integration process. In the early 1950s, federalism, functionalism, and transactionalism were also used to explain the development of European integration, but none of the three could do so. In the 1970s, interdependence theory (Keohane and Nye 1977) appeared to be a middle ground theory between neofunctionalism and intergovernmentalism. It recognized states as major actors, but also acknowledged the existence and influence

of other actors. Currently, liberal intergovernmentalism and two-level games approach descend from intergovernmentalism, whereas new institutionalism, multi-level governance and policy networks have features common to neofunctionalism (Rosamond 2000; Wallace and Wallace 2000; Pollack 2005; and Nugent 2006). The theories of multi-level governance and policy networks are not used in this book, as they emphasize the interdependence between governmental and non-governmental actors.

11 The literature using a sociological institutionalist approach to focus on first and second pillar negotiations is extensive. It studies the existence of norms among decision-makers, which create a 'groupthink' phenomenon (recent work includes Checkel and Moravcsik 2001; Checkel 2003; Hooghe 2005.) The *Journal of European Public Policy* (1999) and *International Organization* (2005) both deal with sociological institutionalist approaches to European issues. Sociological institutionalists use concepts such as socialization (Risse, Ropp, and Sikkink 1999), learning and emulation (Deutsch 1988, 173; Finnemore 1996; Keck and Sikkink 1998), argumentative persuasion (Lewis 2000; Johnston 2001; Price 1998; Checkel 2000), or deliberation and argumentation (Joerges and Neyer 1997; Risse 2000).

12 See Pollack (2001, 223) and Collard-Wexler (2006) for an analysis of the realist prediction on European integration.

13 For Hoffmann (1966), cooperation would be unlikely, and qualified as a 'fiasco' in the high politics sphere of strategy and diplomacy. Morgenthau (1973) argues that, as states fear being exploited by others, they prefer being autonomous to cooperating with others. Grieco (1997, 168) also asserts that 'states seek to have an independent capacity for diplomacy, for the gathering of intelligence, and ultimately for the credible threat or actual employment of force.' Waltz (1979, 70–1), however, explains European integration by arguing that, as European states' security is guaranteed by the United States, they can concentrate on developing economic relations with one another. For him, cooperation is possible, when security is guaranteed by an external actor.

14 Balancing is a concept supported by Carr (1946), Morgenthau (1973), Waltz (1979), and Mearsheimer (2003).

15 See, for example, Waltz (1979, 126), Walt (1987, 21–2), Jervis and Snyder (1991), Van Evera (1990–1, 20), and Mearsheimer (2003, 162).

16 According to Schroeder (1994, 117), states can also use other strategies: hiding and ignoring difficult issues, withdrawing into isolation, or transcending problems by creating rules and institutions to solve them. Basing their thinking on Waltz's concept of 'balancing,' Christensen and

Snyder (1990, 138) have developed the notions of 'chain-ganging' and 'buck-passing.' Chain-ganging is when states 'commit themselves uncon- ditionally to reckless allies,' and buck-passing is '[reliance on] third parties to bear the costs of stopping a rising hegemon.'

17 The following authors apply historical-institutionalism to the study of the EU: Pierson (1996, 2000), Ross (1995), Sandholtz (1992), Bulmer (1993), and Armstrong and Bulmer (1998).

18 All the titles and articles referred to in this book are numbered according to the Treaty of Lisbon, unless reference needs to be made to the articles as they existed in previous treaties.

19 Some CFSP decisions, such as the implementation of sanctions or the financing of policies, need to be passed over to the EC pillar in order to be put into effect. This kind of bridging (*passerelle*) should not be con- fused with the '*passerelle* clause' in the Lisbon Treaty. (The latter states that a unanimous decision of the European Council can require CFSP issues with no military or defence implications to be taken by qualified majority instead of by unanimity.)

20 Title V, Chapter Two in the Lisbon Treaty.

21 See for instance Brecher, Steinberg, and Stein (1969, 79), and Light (1994, 94).

22 The Council of the European Union is composed of several Councils operating in various fields (for instance, Council of Agriculture, Council of Transport, Council of Development, General Affairs Council) and at various levels (the lowest level is the working group level, made up of states' experts; the highest level is the GAC). In the 1990s (Gomez and Peterson 2001, 61), the GAC dealt 80 per cent of the time with external issues, and 20 per cent with other EU policies. In September 2002, the GAC was split in two to relieve its workload. The council dealing specifi- cally with foreign policy was named the Council on External Affairs. With the Treaty of Lisbon, this council is known as the Foreign Affairs Council. In this book, references are mainly made to the GAC, and not the FAC, as the period studied starts in the early 1990s.

23 In 2001, the PSC replaced the former Interim political committee, which was created by the Feira European Council in June 2000, and the political committee (Poco), which has existed since the beginning of EPC in 1970. The political committee was perceived by Nuttall (1992, 16) as 'the hub of Political Cooperation ... frequently taking decisions on its own responsi- bility.' At the Poco, a state's delegation was represented by the political director, the European correspondent, the CFSP counsellor and the CFSP deputy counsellor.

24 The COREU network (*Correspondence Européenne*) is a system that enables states and EU institutions to exchange telegrams. There is also an ESDP–Net communications network for issues relative to ESDP.

25 The working groups are named after the issues they deal with. For instance, in 2008, working groups are named as follows: Eastern Europe and Central Asia, Western Balkans, Latin America, atomic questions, international environment issues, Asia Oceania, Middle East/Gulf, Global disarmament and arms control, Dual use goods, Transatlantic relations, Africa Carribean Pacific (ACP) states, Human rights, Euromediterranean, Energy, Outermost regions, Trade questions, Africa, Joint EU-Africa strategy, Organization for Security and Co-operation in Europe (OSCE) and the Council of Europe, Law of the Sea, Middle East Peace Process, Conventional arms exports, and Public international law. Most of the working groups cover both first and second pillar issues. The fusion of first and second pillar groups was decided under the Finnish presidency in July 1999.

26 The Petersberg tasks were set out in the Petersberg Declaration adopted at the Ministerial Council of the WEU in June 1992. They were included in the Treaty on European Union in 1997. They cover various tasks; humanitarian and rescue, peacekeeping, and combat forces in crisis management, including peacemaking.

27 The Council Secretariat is composed of the following Directorate Generals: DG A (personnel and administration), DG B (agriculture and fisheries), DG C (internal market, competitiveness, industry, research, energy, transport, information, society), DG E (external economic relations, CFSP), DG F (press-communication, protocol), DG G (economic and social affairs), DG H (justice and home affairs), DG I (protection of the environment and consumers, civil protection, health foodstuffs, education, youth, culture, audiovisual). There is no DG D.

28 DGE is divided into the following sections: Coordination; Enlargement; Development and the ACP; Multilateral Economic Affairs and non-EU Western Europe; Americas; UN and Counter-terrorism; Middle/East/Mediterranean Region/Gulf; Africa; Asia and Oceania; Western Balkans, Eastern Europe, and Central Asia; ESDP; Defence Issues; Civilian Crisis Management; Office of the Personal Representative of the Sec. Gen/H.R. for Non-proliferation; Human Rights; Geneva Liaison Office to the UN and to the WTO; and New York Liaison Office to the UN (EU Document, Structure of the General Secretariat, 2009).

29 The description of the High Representative's post in the Treaty of Amsterdam is vague. The initial Intergovernmental Conference proposal for

the creation of a 'Mr or Ms CFSP' post recommended a candidate from ministerial level. The United Kingdom wished to appoint a civil servant, while France preferred a senior politician (Sjursen 2001b, 194). After the shock of the Kosovo crisis in 1999, EU state representatives decided that they needed to appoint someone with more visibility.

30 The Brussels Treaty, signed by Belgium, France, Luxembourg, the Netherlands, and the United Kingdom on 17 March 1948, created the Western European Union in response to Soviet moves to impose control upon the countries of Central Europe. Since then, other European states have joined the WEU. Its members have a commitment to mutual defence, should any of the signatories be the victim of an armed attack in Europe. The WEU was dormant for over thirty years as its functions were taken over by NATO. It was reactivated in the mid-1980s. Its crisis management functions were incorporated into the EU framework with the Treaty of Amsterdam in 1997.

31 SitCen is divided into three units: the Civilian Intelligence Cell, with civilian intelligence analysts working on political and counter-terrorism assessment; the General Operations Unit, providing twenty-four-hour operational support, research, and non-intelligence analysis; and the Communications Unit, dealing with communications security issues and running the Council's Communications Centre.

32 EU mediation is not a new phenomenon. In 1981, the then President in office, Lord Carrington, visited Moscow, where he presented the Ten's proposal for a neutral and non-aligned Afghanistan. Several missions to the Middle East were organized. Fact-finding missions to South Africa were made by a ministerial troika in 1985 and 1992, and by Sir Geoffrey Howe on behalf of the twelve EC states in 1986 (Regelsberger, quoting Keukeleire 1994, 175). The EU has developed a European Neighbourhood Policy since 2004 with the following countries: Algeria, Armenia, Azerbaijan, Belarus, Egypt, Georgia, Israel, Jordan, Lebanon, Libya, Moldova, Morocco, Occupied Palestinian Territory, Syria, Tunisia, and Ukraine. Its main aim is to set out an agenda of political and economic reforms with short and medium-term priorities.

33 For literature on policy-making in the European Union, see Peterson (1995), Richardson (1996), Peterson and Bomberg (1999), Wallace and Wallace (2000), Andersen and Eliassen (2001), Hix (2005), and Nugent (2006).

34 See Spaak (1980, 283), Keukeleire (1994, 145), Peters (1997), Héritier (1999, 9), Regelsberger (1997, 67–83), Zielonka (1998a, 188), Moravcsik (2002, 606), and Poos (2004).

35 The fifty-three member-countries in the CHR were elected for a term of three years by the Economic and Social Council of the United Nations. Fifteen members were from Africa, twelve from Asia, five from Eastern Europe, eleven from Latin American and Caribbean States, and ten from Western Europe and other States. Not all EU states served on this commission. During its sessions, testimonies from NGOs, such as Amnesty International and the International Federation for Human Rights, were given. The aim of the Human Rights Council is to be more effective than its predecessor.

36 For an overview of the evolution of the French position towards China, see Wong (2006).

37 Because of the changes in the Commission's composition, with many EU countries members of the CHR in 2000, China stood less chance than usual of preventing the U.S. resolution from coming to a vote. However, in April 2000, the motion of non-action was adopted by twenty-two out of fifty-three votes.

38 IMF, Direction of Trade Statistics, ESDS International, MIMAS, University of Manchester, July 2008. The figures shown here cover the period 1989–2006, from Tiananmen until the reform of the UN Commission on Human Rights. From 1989 until 1997, and from 1998 until 2006, trade relations between the EU and China showed a constant rise.

39 In 1997, there was a double-standard EU policy, which depended on the importance of trade relations between EU states and other states. EU states did not reach a common policy on China, but they agreed to condemn Cuba and other states. This double standard policy is evoked by K. Smith (1998, 76) who argued that 'the Community has suspended development cooperation aid with weak states, such as Sudan and Haiti. With respect to more important countries outside the EU, such as Algeria and Indonesia, the EU relies on persuasion or *démarches* and declarations.' In general, the condemnation of human rights abuses in Burma or Guinea-Bissau is easily accepted by EU states, but the confronting of China and Russia is more problematic.

40 The 1998 decision was slightly different, as the EU did not wish to express any opinion against China. But this 1998 decision was apparently taken in full cooperation between the EU presidency, at the time held by the United Kingdom, and the United States.

41 Common Position No. 98/326/CFSP, OJ L 143, 15/05/98. Common Position No. 98/374/CFSP, OJ L 165, 10/06/98. Common Position No. 98/426/CFSP, OJ L 190, 04/07/98. Common Position No. 99/604/CFSP,

OJ L 236, 07/09/99. Common Position No. 99/273/CFSP, OJ L 108, 27/04/99. Common Position No. 99/357/CFSP, OJ L 140, 03/06/99.

42 A management committee is one of the three types of EU committees, the other two being advisory and regulatory committees. These committees take decisions according to the comitology procedure, and they adopt and implement EC law. The Treaty on European Union provides for the comitology procedure which specifies the scope of the implementing powers conferred on the Commission by the Council of the European Union.

43 'A' points are ones that have already been agreed on by representatives of ministers at an earlier stage; 'B' points are ones on which no agreement could be reached.

44 For an overview of European policy towards the Balkans, when Germany in 1991, followed by the EC states in 1992, recognized the independence of Slovenia and Croatia, see Brenner (1993), Edwards (1992, 1997), Nuttall (1994), Gow and Smith (1992), Simic (1992), Lucarelli (1995), Gow (1997). For an overview of the international community's action in the Balkans, see Bildt (1998), Boyd (1998), Hutchings (1997), Neville-Jones (1996–7), Renwick (1999), Holbrooke (1999), Woodward (1995), Owen (1995), Clark (2001), Danchev and Halverson (1996).

45 In this case, the role of the United States is similar to the one the United States played in 1982 during the Falkland crisis. According to Martin (1992, 146 and 150), 'officials noted that U.S. negotiations had been an important factor in convincing the EC to impose sanctions' and Italy received 'a personal visit from the U.S. Secretary of State Haig, urging him to support a renewal.'

46 It is important to emphasize here that the creation of the sanctions committee for the FRY did not signify that a sanctions committee would be created every time a sanctions policy was decided upon. For instance, despite the wish of the Commission to have a sanctions committee for the sanctions against the Taliban, EU states refused it. However, it did set a precedent, and it did widen the Commission's prerogatives in CFSP matters.

47 The first meeting was held on 30 November 1999, and the third one on 10 April 2000. The intention of the Commission was to have a monthly meeting, in order to establish more effective sanctions against the FRY.

48 Sweden, Finland, and the United Kingdom sat effectively behind the other member states, because there was a lack of physical space in the room to have all states at the same level. Twenty-seven states are now present in Council and management committee meetings with the 2004 and 2007 enlargement process.

49 On Delors and the EMU, Moravcsik (1998, 460) states: 'Delors acted essentially in a technical secretariat function, as coordinator, rapporteur and drafter; he drafted some compromise texts but he did not influence their content … Ross's own source, on closer inspection, speaks of Delors "correcting" the texts.'

50 According to Sipri (Web document, 2007), in 2006, the United States spent $528.7 billion on defence expenditures, the United Kingdom $59.2 billion, France $53.1 billion, China $49.5 billion, Japan $43.7 billion, Germany $37 billion, Russia $34.7 billion, and Italy $29.9 billion.

51 This section is adapted from my article written for *Politique Européenne* (September 2002) under the title 'The French and British Change in Position vis-à-vis NATO in the Elaboration of the CESDP.'

52 An exception to this was when President Jacques Chirac negotiated with the United States in 1996, in order to reintegrate NATO's military command structure, which de Gaulle had left in 1966.

53 Another reason often given as a reason for a change in attitude of the United Kingdom towards the EU is the change from a Conservative to a Labour government. However, a change might have also occurred under a Conservative government. According to an interviewee, the Conservatives could have adopted the same position as the Labour government, as the Conservatives had had arguments with the U.S. government during the Balkan crisis. In addition, they could have also learnt from the failures in the Balkans, and they also could have felt isolated within EU decision-making.

54 In addition to this letter, 'through the various U.S. embassies, Deputy Assistant Secretary of State for European Affairs James Dobbins made it plain that while the United States would welcome a stronger European voice in NATO, it was most uneasy about the development of a WEU which was not closely connected to NATO' (Lundestad 1998, 115).

55 Negotiations on the future of Europe in the defence field had already taken place within NATO and in Western European circles in the past, in 1973–4 when the United Kingdom entered into the European Communities, and in 1991 when the Maastricht Treaty was discussed.

56 Books on ESDP to date have focused chiefly on relations with NATO, and especially on the duplication of capabilities, the importance of NATO for ESDP, and the impact of ESDP on NATO. See Hunter (2002), Sloan (2002), Howorth and Keeler (2004), Howorth (2007), and Mérand (2008).

57 The original *Directoire* was the body of five and then three *directeurs* (leaders) that governed France from 1795 to 1799.

58 This section is adapted from my article in the *Journal of Common Market Studies* (June 2002) under the title 'The Quint: Acknowledging the Existence of a Big-Four – U.S. *Directoire* at the Heart of the European Union's Foreign Policy Decision-Making Process.'

59 The first G8 summit took place in 1975, in Rambouillet, with France, Italy, Germany, the United Kingdom, Japan, and the United States. The Commission has participated in the G7 since 1977. The range of issues now covered is extremely wide. The agendas include discussions on counterterrorism, global energy security, global economy, arms control, education, the fight against infectious diseases, and developments in regions and countries such as Afghanistan, India/Pakistan, the Middle East, the Western Balkans, and Africa.

60 The personality of the official responsible for foreign policy is also an important factor to take into account. Chris Patten took several unilateral decisions, which gave visibility and legitimacy to the Commission in the field of political foreign policy. For instance, in the Balkans, he was the first Western politician to visit Montenegro after the Kosovo conflict. He underlined his support by pledging a multi-million-pound package of European funds for Montenegro. He also decided to try to visit at least one of the six countries every six weeks or so, in order to increase the EU's visibility. As regards the defence of Human Rights, he made statements on the human rights situations in Chechnya and East Timor. After 11 September 2001, he gave the Commission's position on the U.S. attitude in the world; he warned that unilateralism would be self-defeating, and that cooperation was necessary because of the interconnectedness of the modern world.

61 The Court of Justice has repeatedly ruled that, while the individual security interests of member states in this field must be catered to, trade measures, including export controls, are a matter of exclusive Community competence under article 133 (ex-113) of the TEC, irrespective of the objective of the measures or of the military applications of these items. See Werner Case C-70/94 and Leifer Case C-83/94.

62 CFSP Joint Action 2002/589/CFSP and Council decision 2004/833/CFSP.

63 The two regulations were the following: (1) Council Regulation (EC) No. 975/1999 of 29 April 1999 laid down 'the requirements for the implementation of development cooperation operations, which contribute to the general objective of developing and consolidating democracy and the rule of law and to that of respecting human rights and fundamental freedoms.' (2) Council Regulation (EC) No. 976/1999 of 29 April 1999 laid down 'the requirements for the implementation of Community opera-

tions, other than those of development cooperation, which, within the framework of Community cooperation policy, contribute to the general objective of developing and consolidating democracy and the rule of law and to that of respecting human rights and fundamental freedoms in third countries.'

64 OHR, the lead international civilian agency in Bosnia and Herzegovina, was set up by the Dayton Peace Agreement in 1995. UNMIK was set up in June 1999 by the UN. The EU is responsible for the reconstruction and economic development within UNMIK, and contributes around 53 per cent of the OHR budget.

65 Articles have been written about the role of big states within the EU framework (Magnette and Nicolaidis 2004; Hill 2004; Janning 2005). Academics have focused on relations between two of the Big Three states (van Ham 1999; Charillon 2001; Grabbe and Muenchau 2002; Heisbourg 2004). However, the role of the Big Three member states in the CFSP field is seldom mentioned (Keukeleire 2001; Stark 2002; Gegout 2002; Crowe 2005).

Bibliography

Secondary Sources

Adler, Emmanuel, and Michael Barnett, eds. *Security Communities*. Cambridge: Cambridge University Press, 1998.

Akçakoca, Amanda, Thomas Vanhauwaert, Richard Whitman, and Stefan Wolff. *After Georgia: Conflict Resolution in the EU's Eastern Neighbourhood*. EPC Issue Paper No. 57, April 2009.

Allen, David. 'Foreign Policy at the European Level: Beyond the Nation-State?' In William Wallace and William Paterson, eds., *Foreign Policy-Making in Western Europe*, 135–53. Farnborough: Saxon House, 1978.

Allen, David, Reinhardt Rummel, and Wolfgang Wessels. *European Political Cooperation: Towards a Foreign Policy for Western Europe*. London: Butterworth Scientific, 1982.

Andersen, Svein S., and Kjell A. Eliassen, eds. *Making Policy in Europe*. 2nd ed. London: Sage, 2001.

Andreani, Gilles. 'La France et l'OTAN après la Guerre Froide.' *Politique Etrangère* 1 (1998): 77–92.

Andreani, Gilles, Christoph Bertram, and Charles Grant. *Europe's Military Revolution*. London: Centre for European Reform, 2001.

Armstrong, Kenneth, and Simon Bulmer. *The Governance of the Single European Market*. Manchester: Manchester University Press, 1998.

Aron, Raymond. *Paix et Guerre entre les Nations*. Paris: Calmann-Levy, 1975.

Art, Robert J. 'Why Western Europe Needs the United States and NATO.' *Political Science Quarterly* 111 (Spring 1996): 1–39.

Aspinwall, Mark D., and Gerald Schneider. 'Same Menu, Separate Tables: The Institutionalist Turn in Political Science and the Study of European Integration.' *European Journal of Political Research* 38, no. 1 (August 2000): 1–36.

Bailes, Alyson J.K. 'European Defence and Security.' *Security Dialogue* 27, no. 1 (1996): 55–64.

Baldwin, David A., ed. *Neorealism and Neoliberalism: The Contemporary Debate.* New York: Columbia University Press, 1993.

Bermann, George, Matthias Herdegen, and Peter Linseth. *Transatlantic Regulatory Cooperation: Legal Problems and Political Prospects.* Oxford: Oxford University Press, 2000.

Bicchi, Federica. *European Foreign Policy-Making towards the Mediterranean.* Palgrave: Macmillan, 2007.

Biden, Joseph R. 'Unholy Symbiosis: Isolationism and Anti-Americanism.' *The Washington Quarterly* 23, no. 4 (Autumn 2000): 7–14.

Bildt, Carl. *Peace Journey: The Struggle for Peace in Bosnia.* London: Weidenfeld and Nicholson, 1998.

Bossuat, Gérard. 'Jean Monnet, La Mesure d'une Influence.' *Vingtième Siècle, Revue d'Histoire* 51 (1996): 68–84.

Bourne, Angela, and Michelle Cini. 'Exporting the Third Way in Foreign Policy: New Labour, the European Union and Human Rights Policy.' In Richard Little and Mark Wickham-Jones, eds., *New Labour's Foreign Policy,* 168–85. Manchester: Manchester University Press, 2000.

Boyd, Charles G. 'Making Bosnia Work.' *Foreign Affairs* 77, no. 1 (January–February 1998): 42–55.

Brecher, Michael, Blema Steinburg, and Janice Stein. 'A Framework for Research on Foreign Policy Behavior.' *Journal of Conflict Resolution* 13, no. 1 (March 1969): 75–101.

Brenner, Michael. 'EC: Confidence Lost.' *Foreign Policy* 91 (Summer 1993): 24–44.

Bretherton, Charlotte, and John Vogler. *The European Union as a Global Actor.* London: Routledge, 1999.

Brooks, Steven, and William Wohlforth. 'American Primacy in Perspective.' *Foreign Affairs* 81, no. 4 (2002): 20–33.

Bull, Hedley. *The Anarchical Society: A Study of Order in World Politics.* London: Macmillan, 1977.

Bulmer, Simon. 'The Governance of the European Union: A New Institutionalist Approach.' *Journal of Public Policy* 13, no. 4 (1993): 351–80.

– 'New Institutionalism and the Governance of the Single European Market.' *Journal of European Public Policy* 5 (1998): 365–86.

Bulmer, Simon, and Martin Burch. 'The Europeanization of British Central Government.' In R.A.W. Rhodes, ed., *Transforming British Government.* Vol. 1, *Changing Institutions,* 46–62. London: Macmillan, 2000.

Burdett, Elizabeth Jane. 'The Effectiveness of European Political Cooperation as a System of Collective Diplomacy. A Study of the CSCE Process, 1972–1992.' PhD dissertation, London School of Economics, 1997.

Cabestan, Jean-Pierre. 'Paris-Pékin: Un Dialogue sans Complexes?' *Politique Internationale* 75 (Spring 1997): 335–52.

Cameron, Fraser. 'Building a Common Foreign Policy.' In John Peterson and Helene Sjursen, eds., *A Common Foreign Policy for Europe? Competing Visions of the CFSP*, 59–76. London: Routledge, 1998.

– 'Review of *Foreign and Security Policy in the European Union* by Kjell A. Eliassen, ed.' *European Foreign Affairs Review* 4, no. 1 (Spring 1999): 147–9.

Caporaso, James. 'The European Union and Forms of State: Westphalian, Regulatory or Post-Modern?' *Journal of Common Market Studies* 34 (1996): 29–52.

Caporaso, James, and Joseph Jupille. 'States, Agency, and Rules: The European Union in Global Environmental Politics.' In Carolyn Rhodes, ed., *The European Union in the World Community*, 213–29. Boulder, CO: Lynne Rienner, 1998.

Carlsnaes, Walter, and Steve Smith. *EC and Changing Perspectives in Europe.* London: Sage, 1994.

Carlsnaes, Walter, Helene Sjursen, and Brian White, eds. *Contemporary European Foreign Policy.* London: Sage, 2004.

Carr, Edward Hallet. *The Twenty Years' Crisis, 1919–39: An Introduction to the Study of International Theories.* London: Macmillan, 1946.

Charillon, Frédéric. 'De Suez à Skopje: Un Nouveau Partenariat Franco-britannique pour le XXIe siècle?' *Politique Etrangère* 4 (2001): 953–71.

Checkel, Jeffrey T. 'Bridging the Rational-Choice/Constructivist Gap? Theorizing Social Interaction in European Institutions.' Arena Working Paper No. 11. Oslo: University of Oslo, 2000.

– 'Going Native in Europe, Theorizing Social Interaction in European Institutions.' *Comparative Political Studies* 36, nos. 1/2 (February–March 2003): 209–31.

Checkel, Jeffrey T., and Andrew Moravcsik. 'A Constructivist Research Program in EU Studies?' *European Union Politics* 2, no. 2 (2001): 219–49.

Chilton, Patricia. 'A European Security Regime: Integration and Cooperation in the Search for Common Foreign Security Policy.' Paper presented at the international seminar organized by the Université Libre de Bruxelles, 'EU's CFSP and World Responsibilities.' Brussels, 3–5 October 1997.

Christiansen, Thomas J., and Jack Snyder. 'Chain Gangs and Passed Bucks: Predicting Alliance Patterns in Multipolarity.' *International Organization* 44 (1990): 137–68.

Christiansen, Thomas, Erik Knud Jorgensen, and Antje Wiener. 'The Social

Construction of Europe.' *Journal of European Public Policy on the Social Construction of Europe* 6, no. 4 (1999): 528–44.

– *The Social Construction of Europe*. London: Sage, 2001.

Chubin, Shahram. *Iran's Nuclear Ambitions*. Washington, DC: Carnegie Endowment for International Peace, 2006.

Clark, Wesley. *Waging Modern War: Bosnia, Kosovo, and the Future of Combat*. Oxford: Public Affairs, 2001.

Clarke, Michael, and Brian White, eds. *Understanding Foreign Policy*. Cheltenham: Edward Elgar, 1989.

Clarke, Michael. 'Foreign Policy Analysis: A Theoretical Guide.' In Stelios Stavridis and Christopher Hill, eds., *Domestic Sources of Foreign Policy, West European Reactions to the Falklands Conflict*, 19–39. Oxford: Berg, 1996.

Collard-Wexler, Simon. 'Integration Under Anarchy: Neorealism and the European Union.' *European Journal of International Relations* 12, no. 3 (2006): 397–432.

Cook, Robin. 'Foreign Policy and National Interest.' Speech by the Foreign Secretary, Chatham House, 28 January 2001.

Cooper, Neil. 'The Pariah Agenda and New Labour's Ethical Arms Sales Policy.' In Richard Little and Mark Wickham-Jones, eds., *New Labour's Foreign Policy*, 147–67. Manchester: Manchester University Press, 2000.

Crawford, Beverley. 'Explaining Defection from International Cooperation: Germany's Unilateral Recognition of Croatia.' *World Politics* 48, no. 4 (1996): 482–521.

Croci, Osvaldo, and Amy Verdun, eds. *The Transatlantic Divide: Foreign and Security Policies in the Atlantic Alliance from Kosovo to Iraq*. Manchester: Manchester University Press, 2006.

Crowe, Brian. 'A Common European Foreign Policy after Iraq?' *International Affairs* 79, no. 3 (May 2003): 533–46.

– *Foreign Minister of Europe*. London: The Foreign Policy Centre, February 2005.

Curtin, Deirdre, and Ramses A. Wessel. *Good Governance and the European Union*. Antwerp: Intersentia, 2005.

Danchev, Alex, and Thomas Halverson, eds. *International Perspectives on the Yugoslav Conflict*. Oxford: Palgrave Macmillan, 1996.

Dannreuther, Roland. *European Union Foreign and Security Policy: Towards a Neighbourhood Strategy*. New York: Routledge, 2003.

De Gaulle, Charles. *Mémoires d'Espoir*. Vol. 1, *Le Renouveau (1958–1962)*. Paris: Plon, 1970.

De Wilde, D'Estmael Tanguy. *La Dimension Politique des Relations Economiques*

Extérieures de la Communauté Européenne. Brussels: Editions Bruylant, 1998.

Dehousse, Franklin. 'After Amsterdam: A Report on the CFSP of the EU.' *European Journal of International Law* 9, no. 3 (1998): 525–39.

Deighton, Anne. 'The European Security and Defence Policy.' *Journal of Common Market Studies* 40, no. 4 (November 2002): 719–41.

Deutsch, Karl A. *The Analysis of International Relations*. Englewood Cliffs, NJ: Prentice Hall, 1988.

Deutsch, Karl, et al., eds. *Political Community and the North Atlantic area: International Organization in the Light of Historical Experience*. New York: Greenwood Press, 1957.

Dinan, Desmond. *Ever Closer Union? An Introduction to European Union Integration*. 2nd ed. London: Macmillan, 1999.

Donnelly, Jack. *Realism and International Relations*. Cambridge: Cambridge University Press, 2000.

Dover, Robert. *Europeanization of British Defence Policy*. Aldershot, UK: Ashgate, 2007.

Dowding, Keith. 'Institutionalist Research on the European Union: A Critical Review.' *European Union Politics* 1 (2000): 125–44.

Doyle, Michael W. *Ways of War and Peace*. New York: W.W. Norton, 1997.

Duchêne, François. 'Europe's Role in World Peace.' In R. Mayner, ed., *Europe Tomorrow: Sixteen Europeans Look Ahead*, 32–47. London: Fontana/Collins for Chatham House, PEP, 1972.

– *Monnet*. New York: W.W. Norton, 1994.

Duke, Simon. *The Elusive Quest for European Security*. St Anthony's Series. London: Macmillan, 1999.

Edwards, Geoffrey. 'European Responses to the Yugoslav Crisis: An Interim Assessment.' In Reihnardt Rummel, ed., *Toward Political Union*, 165–90. Boulder, CO: Westview Press, 1992.

– 'The Potential and Limits of the CFSP: The Yugoslav Example.' In Elfriede Regelsberger et al., eds., *Foreign Policy of the European Union: From EPC to CFSP and Beyond*, 173–96. London: Lynne Rienner, 1997.

Egeberg, Morten. 'The Impact of Bureaucratic Structure on Policy-Making.' *Public Administration* 77 (1999): 155–70.

Elgstroem, Ole, and Joensson Christer. 'Negotiating in the European Union: Bargaining or Problem-Solving?' *Journal of European Public Policy, Special Issue* 7, no. 5 (2000): 684–704.

Elgstroem, Ole, and Michael Smith. 'Introduction: Negotiation and Policy-Making in the EU Processes, System and Order.' *Journal of European Public Policy, Special Issue* 7, no. 5 (2000): 673–83.

Eliassen, Kjell A. *Foreign and Security Policy in the European Union.* London: Sage, 1998.

Falke, Andreas. 'The EU-US Conflict over Sanctions Policy: Confronting the Hegemon.' *European Foreign Affairs Review* 5, no. 2 (2001): 139–63.

Falkner, Gerda. 'How Intergovernmental Are Intergovernmental Conferences? An Example from the Maastricht Treaty Reform.' *Journal of European Public Policy* 9, no. 1 (2002): 98–119.

Featherstone, Kevin, and Roy Ginsberg. *The United States and the European Community.* London: Macmillan, 1996.

Finnemore, Martha. *National Interests in International Society.* Ithaca, NY: Cornell University Press, 1996.

Forster, Anthony. 'Britain.' In Ian Manners and Richard G. Whitman, eds., *The Foreign Policies of European Union Member States*, 44–63. Manchester: Manchester University Press, 2000.

Friis, Lykke, and Anna Murphy. 'Negotiating in a Time of Crisis: The EU's Response to the Military Conflict in Kosovo.' EUI Working Papers, RSC no. 2000/20. Florence: European University Institute, 2000.

Gaddis, John Lewis. 'International Relations Theory and the End of the Cold War.' *International Security* 17, no. 3 (Winter 1992/1993): 5–58.

Gardner, Hall, and Radoslava Stefanova, eds. *The New Transatlantic Agenda: Facing the Challenges of Global Governance.* Burlington, VT: Ashgate, 2001.

Garrett, Geoffrey. 'International Cooperation and Institutional Choice: The European Community's Internal Market.' *International Organization* 46, no. 2 (1992): 533–60.

Garrett, Geoffrey, and Barry R. Weingast. 'Ideas, Interests, and Institutions: Constructing the European Community's Internal Market.' In Judith Goldstein and Robert Keohane, eds., *Ideas and Foreign Policy*, 173–206. Ithaca, NY: Cornell University Press, 1993.

Garrett, Geoffrey, and George Tsebelis. 'An Institutional Critique of Intergovernmentalism.' *International Organization* 50, no. 2 (1996): 269–99.

Gegout, Catherine. 'The Quint: Acknowledging the Existence of a Big-Four – US *Directoire* at the Heart of the European Union's Foreign Policy Decision-Making Process.' *Journal of Common Market Studies* 40, no. 2 (June 2002): 331–44.

– 'The French and British Change in Position vis-à-vis NATO in the Elaboration of the CESDP.' *Politique Européenne*, Special Issue, 'L'Europe de la défense: Institutionnalisation, européanisation,' no. 8 (September 2002): 62–87.

– 'Causes and Consequences of the EU's Military Intervention in the Democratic Republic of Congo (DRC): A Realist Explanation.' *European Foreign Affairs Review* 10, no. 3 (2005): 427–43.

– 'The EU and Security in the Democratic Republic of Congo in 2006: An Unfinished Business.' *FORNET CFSP Forum* 5, no. 1 (January 2007): 5–9.

Gerbet, Pierre. Interview by Étienne Deschamps, 28:48. Editing, Original Sound Track. Paris: CVCE [Prod.], 23 January 2004. Retrieved from www.cvce.lu, 30 July 2008.

Gillespie, Richard. *Spain and the Mediterranean: Developing a European Policy towards the South*. London: Macmillan, 2000.

Gilpin, Robert. *War and Change in World Politics*. Cambridge: Cambridge University Press, 1981.

Ginsberg, Roy. *Foreign Policy Actions of the European Community*. Boulder, CO: Lynne Rienner Publishers, 1989.

– 'Conceptualizing the European Union as an International Actor: Narrowing the Theoretical Capability-Expectation Gap.' *Journal of Common Market Studies* 37, no. 3 (1999): 429–54.

– *The European Union in International Politics: Baptism by Fire*. Lanham, MD: Rowman and Littlefield, 2001.

– *Demystifying the European Union*. Lanham, MD: Rowman and Littlefield, 2007.

Glarbo, Kenneth. 'Wide-Awake Diplomacy: Reconstructing the CFSP of the EU.' *Journal of European Public Policy Special Issue* 6, no. 4 (1999): 634–51.

– 'Reconstructing a Common European Foreign Policy.' In Thomas Christiansen, Knud Erik Jorgensen, and Antje Wiener, eds., *The Social Construction of Europe*, 140–57. London: Sage, 2001.

Gomez, Ricardo, and John Peterson. 'The EU's Impossibly Busy Foreign Ministers: "No One Is in Control."' *European Foreign Affairs Review* 6, no. 1 (Spring 2001): 53–74.

Gordon, Philip H. 'Europe's Uncommon Foreign Policy.' *International Security* 22, no. 3 (Winter 1997/1998): 74–100.

– *NATO's Transformation: The Changing Shape of the Atlantic Alliance*. Lanham: Rowman and Littlefield, 1997.

Gordon, Philip H., and Jeremy Shapiro. *Allies at War: America, Europe, and the Crisis over Iraq*. Washington, DC: Brookings Institution, 2004.

Gourlay, Catriona, and Eric Remacle. 'The 1996 IGC.' In Kjell A. Eliassen, ed., *Foreign and Security Policy in the European Union*, 58–93. London: Sage, 1998.

Gow, James. *Triumph of the Lack of Will: International Diplomacy and the Yugoslav War*. New York: Columbia University Press, 1997.

Gow, James, and G.D.D. Smith. *Peace-Making, Peace-Keeping: European Security and the Yugoslav Wars*. London: Brassey's for the Centre for Defence Studies, 1992.

Gowa, Joanne. 'Anarchy, Egoism, and Third Image: The Evolution of Cooperation and International Relations.' *International Organization* 40 (Winter 1986): 167–86.

Grabbe H., and W. Muenchau. *Germany and Britain: An Alliance of Necessity*. London: Centre for European Reform, 2002.

Gray, Colin. 'World Politics as Usual after September 11: Realism Vindicated.' In Ken Booth and Tim Dunne, eds., *Worlds in Collision*, 226–34. London: Palgrave, 2006.

Grieco, Joseph. 'Realist International Theory and the Study of World Politics.' In Michael W. Doyle and G. John Ikenberry, eds., *New Thinking in International Relations Theory*, 163–201. Boulder, CO: Westview Press, 1997.

Grosser, Alfred. *The Western Alliance. New York:* Macmillan, 1980.

Hasenclever, Andreas, Peter Mayer, and Volker Rittberger. 'Interests, Power, Knowledge: The Study of International Regimes.' *Mershon International Studies Review* 40 (1996): 177–228.

Hayes-Renshaw, Fiona, and Helen Wallace. *The Council of Ministers*. New York: St Martin's Press, 1996.

Heisbourg, François. Europe's Strategic Ambitions: The Limits of Ambiguity.' *Survival* 42, no. 2 (Summer 2000): 5–15.

– 'The French-German Duo and the Search for a New European Security Model.' *The International Spectator* 39, no. 3 (2004): 61–72.

Heisbourg, François, et al. 'European Defence: Making It Work.' Chaillot Paper No. 42. Paris: Institute for Security Studies, Western European Union, 2000.

Héritier, Adrienne. *Policy-Making and Diversity in Europe: Escape from Deadlock*. Cambridge: Cambridge University Press, 1999.

Hermann, Charles F. 'Changing Course: When Governments Choose to Redirect Foreign Policy.' *International Studies Quarterly* 34, no. 1 (March 1990): 3–21.

Heurlin, Bertel. 'Constraining and Disposing Structural Forces: The Role of the United States.' In Anders Wivel, ed., *Explaining European Integration*, 190–214. Copenhagen: Core, 1998.

Hiester, Dan. 'The United States as a Power in Europe.' In Robert Jordan, ed., *Europe and the Superpowers, Essays on European International Politics*, 27–47. London: Pinter Publishers, 1991.

Hill, Christopher, ed. *National Foreign Policies and European Political Cooperation*. Winchester, MA: G. Allen and Unwin, 1983.

– 'National Interests: The Insuperable Obstacle?' In Christopher Hill, ed.,

National Foreign Policies and European Political Cooperation, 185–202. Winchester, MA: G. Allen and Unwin, 1983.

– 'European Preoccupations with Terrorism.' In Alfred Pijpers, Elfriede Regelsberger, and Wolfgang Wessels, eds., *European Political Cooperation in the 1980s*, 166–93. Dordrecht: Nijhoff, 1988.

– 'The Capability-Expectations Gap, or Conceptualizing Europe's International Role.' *Journal of Common Market Studies* 31, no. 3 (1993): 305–28.

– *The Actors in Europe's Foreign Policy*. London: Routledge, 1996.

– 'Convergence, Divergence and Dialectics: National Foreign Policies and the CFSP.' EUI Working Paper No. 66. Florence: European University Institute, 1997.

– 'The Geo-Political Implications of Enlargement.' EUI Working Paper No. 30. Florence: European University Institute, 2000.

– 'The EU's Capacity for Conflict Prevention.' *European Foreign Affairs Review* 6 (2001): 315–33.

– *The Changing Politics of Foreign Policy*. New York: Palgrave Macmillan, 2003.

– 'Renationalizing or Regrouping? EU Foreign Policy Since 11 September 2001.' *Journal of Common Market Studies* 42, no. 1 (2004): 143–63.

– 'The European Powers in the Security Council: Differing Interests, Differing Arenas.' In Katie Verlin Laatikainen and Karen Smith, eds., *The European Union at the United Nations: Interesting Multilateralisms*, 49–69. New York: Palgrave, 2006.

Hill, Christopher, and William Wallace. 'Introduction: Actors and Actions.' In Christopher Hill, *The Actors in Europe's Foreign Policy*, 1–16. London, Routledge, 1996.

Hill, Christopher, and Karen Smith, eds. *European Foreign Policy: Key Documents*. New York: Routledge, 2000.

Hill, Chistopher, and Michael Smith. 'The International Relations of the European Union.' Paper presented at an EUI Workshop, Florence, Italy, 17–18 May 2002.

– *The International Relations of the European Union*. Oxford: Oxford University Press, 2005.

Hindley, Brian. 'New Institutions for Transatlantic Trade?' *International Affairs* 75, no. 1 (1999): 45–60.

Hix, Simon. *The Political System of the European Union*. 2nd ed. Basingstoke, UK: Palgrave, 2005.

Hocking, Brian, and Steven McGuire, eds. *Trade Politics*. 2nd ed. London: Routledge, 2004.

Hodder-Williams, Richard. 'Reforging the Special Relationship: Blair, Clinton and Foreign Policy.' In Richard Little and Mark Wickham-Jones, eds., *New*

Labour's Foreign Policy, 234–50. Manchester: Manchester University Press, 2000.

Hoffmann, Stanley. 'Obstinate or Obsolete? The Fate of the Nation-State and the Case of Western Europe.' *Daedalus* 95, no. 3 (1966): 862–915.

– 'Preface.' In Alfred Grosser, *The Western Alliance.* New York: Macmillan, 1980.

– 'The European Community: Past, Present and Future.' *Journal of Common Market Studies* 21, nos. 1–2 (1982): 21–38.

– *The European Sisyphus: Essays on Europe, 1964–1994.* Boulder, CO: Westview Press, 1995.

– 'Towards a Common Foreign and Security Policy.' *Journal of Common Market Studies* 38, no. 2 (2000): 189–98.

Holbrooke, Richard. 'The United States, a European Superpower.' *Foreign Affairs* 74, no. 2 (March/April 1995): 38–51.

– *To End a War.* New York: Modern Library, 1999.

Holland, Martin. *The Future of European Political Cooperation, Essays on Theory and Practice.* London: Macmillan, 1991.

– *European Union Common Foreign Policy: From EPC to CFSP Joint Action and South Africa.* London: St Martin's Press, 1995.

– ed. *Common Foreign and Security Policy: The Record and Reforms.* London: Pinter, 1997.

– ed. *Common Foreign and Security Policy: The First Decade.* 2nd ed. London: Continuum, 2004.

Holsti, Ole R. 'Theories of International Relations and Foreign Policy: Realism and Its Challengers.' In Charles W. Kegley Jr., ed., *Controversies in International Relations: Realism and the Neoliberal Challenge*, 35–65. New York: St Martin's Press, 1995.

Holzman, Marie. 'Chine: Requiem pour les Droits de l'Homme.' *Politique Internationale* (Spring 1997): 369–83.

Hooghe, Liesbet. 'Several Roads Lead to International Norms, but Few via International Socialization: A Case Study of the European Commission.' *International Organization* 59, no. 4 (Fall 2005): 861–98.

Howard, Roger. 'EU3-Iran Nuclear Deal Exposes Underlying International Tensions.' Royal United Services Institute Newsbrief, December 2004.

Howorth, Jolyon. 'Britain, France and the European Defence Initiative.' *Survival* 42, no. 2 (Summer 2000): 33–55.

– 'European Defence and the Changing Politics of the EU: Hanging Together or Hanging Separately?' *Journal of Common Market Studies* 39, no. 4 (November 2001): 765–90.

– *Security and Defence Policy in the European Union.* New York: Palgrave, 2007.

Howorth, Jolyon, and John T.S. Keeler. *Defending Europe: The EU, NATO, and the Quest for European Autonomy.* New York: Palgrave Macmillan, 2004.

Hunter, Robert E. *The European Security and Defence Policy: NATO's Companion or Competitor?* Santa Monica, CA: RAND Corporation, 2002.

Huntington, Samuel P. 'The Lonely Superpower.' *Foreign Affairs* 78, no. 2 (March/April 1999): 35–49.

Hutchings, Robert L. *American Diplomacy and the End of the Cold War.* Washington, DC: Woodrow Wilson Center Press, 1997.

Hyde-Price, Adrian. '"Normative" Power Europe: A Realist Critique.' *Journal of European Public Policy* 13, no. 2 (March 2006): 217–34.

Ifestos, Panayiotis. *European Political Cooperation, Towards a Framework of Supranational Diplomacy?* Aldershot, UK: Avebury, 1987.

Ikenberry, G. John. *After Victory: Institutions, Strategic Restraint and the Rebuilding of Order after Major Wars.* Princeton, NJ: Princeton University Press, 2001.

– *America Unrivalled: The Future of the Balance of Power.* Ithaca, NY: Cornell University Press, 2002.

Janning, Josef. 'Leadership Coalitions and Change: The Role of States in the European Union.' *International Affairs* 81, no. 4 (2005): 821–34.

Jervis, Robert, and Jack Snyder. *Dominoes and Bandwagons: Strategic Beliefs and Great Power Competition in the Eurasian Rimland.* Oxford: Oxford University Press, 1991.

Joerges, Christian, and Jürgen Neyer. 'Transforming Strategic Interaction into Deliberative Problem-Solving: European Comitology in Foodstuffs Sector.' *Journal of European Public Policy* 4, no. 4 (1997a): 609–25.

– 'From Intergovernmental Bargaining to Deliberative Political Process: The Constitutionalization of Comitology.' *European Law Journal* 3 (1997b): 273–99.

Johansson-Nogues, Elizabeth. 'The Fifteen and the Accession States in the UN General Assembly: What Future for European Foreign Policy in the Coming Together of the "Old" and the "New" Europe?' *European Foreign Affairs Review* 9 (2004): 67–92.

Johnston, Alastair Iain. 'Treating International Institutions as Social Environments.' *International Studies Quarterly* 45 (2001): 487–515.

Jones, Erik. 'Debating the Transatlantic Relationship: Rhetoric and Reality.' *International Affairs* 80, no. 4 (October 2004): 595–613.

Jones, Seth. 'The European Union and the Security Dilemma.' *Security Studies* 12, no. 3 (2003): 114–56.

– *The Rise of European Security Cooperation.* Oxford: Oxford University Press, 2007.

Jopp, Mathias. *The Strategic Implications of European Integration*. IISS Adelphi Paper No. 290. London: International Institute for Strategic Studies, 1994.

Jorgensen, Knud Erik. 'PoCo.' In Knud Erik Jorgensen, ed., *Reflective Approaches to European Governance*, 167–80. Basingstoke, UK: Macmillan, 1997a.

– ed. *Reflective Approaches to European Governance*. Basingstoke, UK: Macmillan, 1997b.

– 'The European Union's Performance in World Politics: How Should We Measure Success?' In Jan Zielonka, ed., *Paradoxes of European Foreign Policy*, 87–103. The Hague: Kluwer Law International, 1998.

Jupille, Joseph, and James A. Caporaso. 'Institutionalism and the European Union: Beyond International Relations and Comparative Politics.' *Annual Review of Political Science* 2 (1999): 429–44.

Kagan, Robert. *Of Paradise and Power: America versus Europe in the New World Order*. New York: Alfred A. Knopf, 2003.

Keck, Margaret, and Kathryn Sikkink. *Activists beyond Borders*. Ithaca, NY: Cornell University Press, 1998.

Keens-Soper, Maurice. *Europe in the World: The Persistence of Power Politics*. New York: Palgrave Macmillan, 1999.

Kegley, Charles W. *Controversies in International Relations: Realism and the Neoliberal Challenge*. London: Macmillan, 1995.

Kennan, George. *America Diplomacy*. Chicago: University of Chicago Press, 1984.

Keohane, Robert O. *After Hegemony: Cooperation and Discord in the World Political Economy*. Princeton, NJ: Princeton University Press, 1984.

– 'International Institutions: Two Approaches.' In Robert O. Keohane, *International Institutions and State Power*, 158–82. Boulder, CO: Westview Press, 1989.

Keohane, Robert O., and Stanley Hoffmann. 'Conclusion: Community Politics and Institutional Change.' In William Wallace, ed., *The Dynamics of European Integration*, 276–300. London: Pinter, 1990.

Keohane, Robert O., and Joseph S. Nye. *Power and Interdependence*. Boston: Little, Brown, 1977.

Kerremans, Bart. 'Non-institutionalism, Neo-institutionalism and the Logic of Common Decision-Making in the EU.' *Governance* 9, no. 2 (1996): 217–40.

Keukeleire, Stephan. 'Directorates in the CFSP/CESDP of the European Union: A Plea for a Restricted Crisis-management Group.' *European Foreign Affairs Review* 6, no. 1 (2001): 75–101.

Keukeleire, Stephan, and Jennifer McNaughton. *The Foreign Policy of the European Union*. London: Palgrave, 2008.

King, Gary, Robert O. Keohane, and Sidney Verba. *Designing Social Inquiry: Scientific Inference in Qualitative Research*. Princeton, NJ: Princeton University Press, 1994.

Kingdon, John W. *Agendas, Alternatives and Public Policies*. Boston: Little, Brown, 1984.

Kintis, Andreas G. 'The EU's Foreign Policy and the War in Ex-Yugoslavia.' In Martin Holland, ed., *Common Foreign and Security Policy: The Record and Reforms*, 149–73. London: Pinter/Cassells, 1997.

Kissinger, Henry. *Diplomacy*. New York: Touchstone, 1994.

Kopstein, Jeffrey. 'The Transatlantic Divide over Democracy Promotion.' *The Washington Quarterly* 29, no. 2 (2006): 85–98.

Krasner, Stephen D., ed. *International Regimes*. Ithaca, NY: Cornell University Press, 1983.

– 'Global Communications and National Power: Life on the Pareto Frontier.' *World Politics* 43, no. 3 (April 1991): 336–66.

Krauthammer, Charles. 'The Unipolar Moment.' *Foreign Affairs* 70, no. 1 (1990–1991): 23–33.

Kupchan, Charles A. 'From European Union to Atlantic Union.' In Jan Zielonka, ed., *Paradoxes of European Foreign Policy*, 147–64. The Hague: Kluwer Law International, 1998.

Kupchan, Charles, and Clifford Kupchan. 'Concerts, Collective Security, and the Future of Europe.' *International Security* 16, no. 1 (Summer 1991): 114–61.

Kutchesfahani, Sara Z. 'Iran's Nuclear Challenge and European Diplomacy.' EPC Issue Paper, No. 46. Brussels: European Policy Centre, 2006.

Laatikainen, Katie Verlin, and Karen Smith. *The European Union at the United Nations: Interesting Multilateralisms*. New York: Palgrave, 2006.

Larsen, Henrik. *Foreign Policy and Discourse Analysis: France, Britain, and Europe*. New York: Routledge/LSE, 1997.

– 'British and Danish European Policies in the 1990s: A Discourse Approach.' *European Journal of International Relations* 5, no. 4 (1999): 451–83.

Layne, Christopher. 'Less is More: Minimal Realism in East Asia.' *National Interest* 43 (Spring 1996): 64–77.

– 'The Unipolar Illusion, the Coming End of the United States' Unipolar Moment.' *International Security* 31, no. 2 (Fall 2006): 7–41.

Le Gloannec, Anne-Marie. 'Europe by Other Means.' *International Affairs* 73, no. 1 (1997): 83–98.

Lebow, Richard Ned. 'The Long Peace, the End of the Cold War, and the Failure of Realism.' *International Organization* 48, no. 2 (Spring 1994): 249–77.

Lewis, Jeffrey. 'Constructing Interests: The Committee of Permanent Representatives and Decision-Making in the European Union.' PhD dissertation, Wisconsin-Madison University, 1998a.

– 'Is the Hard Bargaining Image of the Council Misleading? The Committee of Permanent Representatives and the Local Elections Directive.' *Journal of Common Market Studies* 36, no. 4 (December 1998b): 479–504.

– 'The Methods of Community in EU Decision-Making and Administrative Rivalry in the Council's Infrastructure.' *Journal of European Public Policy* 7, no. 2 (2000): 261–89.

Light, Margot. 'Foreign Policy Analysis.' In A.J.R. Groom and Margot Light, eds., *Contemporary International Relations: A Guide to Theory*, 93–108. London: Pinter, 1994.

Lindberg, Leon N., and Stuart A. Sheingold. *Europe's Would-Be Polity: Patterns of Change in the European Community*. Englewood Cliffs, NJ: Prentice Hall, 1970.

Lucarelli, Sonia. 'The International Community and the Yugoslav Crisis: A Chronology of Events.' EUI Working Paper RSC No. 95/8. Florence: European University Institute, 1995.

– 'Western Europe and the Break-Up of Yugoslavia: A Political Failure in Search of a Scholarly Explanation.' PhD dissertation, European University Institute, 1998.

Lucarelli, Sonia, and Ian Manners, eds. *Values and Principles in European Union Foreign Policy*. London: Routledge, 2006.

Luif, Paul. *EU Cohesion in the UN General Assembly*. EU-ISS Occasional Paper No. 49. Paris: Chaillot Papers, Institute for Security Studies, 2003.

Lundestad, Geir. *'Empire' by Integration: The United States and European Integration, 1945–1997*. Oxford: Oxford University Press, 1998.

Macleod, Alex. 'Competing for Leadership in West European Defence: France, Great Britain and the Wars in Kosovo and Iraq.' In Osvaldo Croci and Amy Verdun, eds., *The Transatlantic Divide: Foreign and Security Policies in the Atlantic Alliance from Kosovo to Iraq*, 126–41. Manchester: Manchester University Press, 2006.

Magnette, Paul, and Kalypso Nikolaidis. 'The European Convention: Constitutional Politics or Diplomatic Bargaining?' *West European Politics* 27, no. 3 (2004): 381–404.

Mahncke, Dieter. 'The Role of the USA in Europe: Successful Past but Uncertain Future?' *European Foreign Affairs Review* 4 (1999): 353–69.

Manners, Ian. 'Normative Power Europe: A Contradiction in Terms?' *Journal of Common Market Studies* 40, no. 2 (2002): 235–58.

Manners, Ian, and Richard G. Whitman. *The Foreign Policies of European Union Member States*. Manchester: Manchester University Press, 2000.

March, James G., and Johan P. Olsen. *Rediscovering Institutions: The Organizational Basis of Politics*. New York: The Free Press, 1989.

Marks, Gary, Liesbet Hooghe, and Kermit Blank. 'European Integration from the 1980s.' *Journal of Common Market Studies* 34 (1996): 341–78.

Martin, Lisa. *Coercive Cooperation: Explaining Multilateral Economic Sanctions*. Princeton, NJ: Princeton University Press, 1992.

Mastanduno, Michael. 'Preserving the Unipolar Moment: Realist Theories and U.S. Grand Strategy after the Cold War.' *International Security* 21, no. 4 (Spring 1997): 49–88.

Matlary, Jane H. 'Epilogue: New Bottles for New Wine.' In Knud Erik Jorgensen, ed., *Reflective Approaches to European Governance*, 201–13. Basingstoke, UK: Macmillan, 1997.

Mearsheimer, John J. 'Back to the Future: Instability in Europe after the Cold War.' *International Security* 15, no. 1 (Summer 1990): 5–56.

– 'The False Promise of International Institutions.' *International Security* 19, no. 3 (1994–1995): 5–49.

– *Tragedy of Great Power Politics*. New York: W.W. Norton, 2003.

Meiers, Franz-Joseph. 'La Politique Allemande de Sécurité et de Défense à la Croisée des Chemins.' *Politique Etrangère* (January 2000): 47–65.

Menon, Anand, Anthony Forster, and William Wallace. 'How Common a European Security Policy.' *Survival* 34, no. 3 (Autumn 1992): 98–118.

Mérand, Frédéric. *European Defence Policy: Beyond the Nation State*. Oxford: Oxford University Press, 2008.

Merlingen, Michael, and Rasa Ostrauskaite. *European Security and Defence Policy: An Implementation Perspective*. London: Routledge, 2007.

Meyer, Christoph. *The Quest for a European Strategic Culture: A Comparative Study of Strategic Norms and Ideas in the European Union*. Basingstoke, UK: Palgrave Macmillan, 2006.

Michel, Leo. 'NATO and the EU Stop the Minuet: It's Time to Tango.' *EuroFuture* (Winter 2004). Retrieved from www.ndu.edu/inss/Repository/Outside_Publications/Michel/Michel_EuroFuture_Winter2004.pdf, 6 June 2007.

Milward, Alan S. *The Reconstruction of Western Europe 1945–51*. Berkeley: University of California Press, 1984.

– *The European Rescue of the Nation-State*. London: Routledge, 1992.

Missiroli, Antonio. 'European Security and Defence: The Case for Setting Convergence Criteria.' *European Foreign Affairs Review* 4 (1999): 485–500.

Monar, Joerg. 'The Financial Dimension of the CFSP.' In Martin Holland, ed., *Common Foreign and Security Policy: The Record and Reforms*, 34–51. London: Pinter 1997.

– 'Institutional, Legal and Decision-Making in the Sphere of External Economic Relations.' Paper presented at the European Consortium for Political Research Summer School, Geneva, Switzerland, 28 August–9 September 2000.

Monar, Joerg, and Roger Morgan, eds. *The Third Pillar of the European Union.* Brussels: European Interuniversity Press, 1995.

Monnet, Jean. *J. Monnet and R. Schuman: Correspondence 1947–1953.* Lausanne: Fondation J. Monnet pour l'Europe, 1986.

Moravcsik, Andrew. 'Negotiating the Single European Act: National Interests and Conventional Statecraft in the European Community.' *International Organization* 45, no. 1 (Winter 1991): 19–56.

– 'Preferences and Power in the European Community: A Liberal Intergovernmentalist Approach.' *Journal of Common Market Studies* 31, no. 4 (December 1993): 473–524.

– 'Taking Preferences Seriously: A Liberal Theory of International Politics.' *International Organization* 51, no. 4 (Autumn 1997): 513–53.

– *The Choice for Europe: Social Purpose and State Power from Messina to Maastricht.* Ithaca, NY: Cornell University Press, 1998.

– 'In Defence of the "Democratic Deficit": Reassessing Legitimacy in the European Union.' *Journal of Common Market Studies* 40, no. 4 (November 2002): 603–24.

Moravcsik, Andrew, and Kalypso Nicolaidis. 'Explaining the Treaty of Amsterdam: Interests, Influence, Institutions.' *Journal of Common Market Studies* 37, no. 1 (March 1999): 59–85.

Morgenthau, Hans Joachim. *Politics among Nations: The Struggle for Power and Peace.* 5th ed. New York: Alfred A. Knopf, 1973.

Morisse-Schilbach, Melanie. *L'Europe et la Question Algérienne. Vers une Européanisation de la Politique Algérienne de la France?* Séries Perspectives internationales. Paris: Presses Universitaires de France (PUF), 1999.

Mueller, Harald, and Lars van Dassen. 'From Cacophony to Joint Action: Successes and Shortcomings of the European Nuclear Non-Proliferation Policy.' In Martin Holland, ed., *Common Foreign and Security Policy: The Record and Reforms*, 52–72. London: Pinter, 1997.

Musu, Costanza, and Nicolas Casarini, eds. *EU Foreign Policy in an Evolving International System: The Road to Convergence.* London: Palgrave Macmillan, 2007.

Neuhold, Hanspeter. 'The Common Foreign and Security Policy of the European Union: A Poor Record and Meagre Prospects.' *CFSP Forum* 3 (1997): 3–5.

Neville-Jones, Pauline. 'Dayton, IFOR and Alliance Relations in Bosnia.' *Survival* 4, no. 38 (Winter 1996–1997): 45–65.

Niebuhr, Reinhold. *Nations and Empires: Recurring Patterns in the Political Order.* London: Faber and Faber, 1959.

Nugent, Neill. *The European Commission.* London: Palgrave Macmillan, 2001.

– *The Government and Politics of the EU.* London: Macmillan, 2006.

Nuttall, Simon. 'Where the European Commission Comes.' In Alfred Pijpers, Elfriede Regelsberger, and Wolfgang Wessels, eds., *European Political Cooperation in the 1980s*, 104–17. Dordrecht: Nijhoff, 1988.

– *European Political Cooperation.* New York: Oxford University Press, 1992.

– 'The EC and Yugoslavia: Deus ex Machina or Machina sine Deo?' *Journal of Common Market Studies* 32 (August 1994): 11–25.

– 'The CFSP Provisions of the Amsterdam Treaty: An Exercise in Collusive Ambiguity.' *CFSP Forum* 3 (1997): 1–3.

– 'Two Decades of EPC Performance.' In Elfriede Regelsberger, Philippe de Schoutheete, and Wolfgang Essels, eds., *Foreign Policy of the European Union*, 19–40. Boulder, CO: Westview Press, 1997.

– *European Foreign Policy.* New York: Oxford University Press, 2000.

– 'Consistency and CFSP: A Categorisation and Its Consequences.' Paper presented at an EUI Workshop, Florence, Italy, 17–18 May 2002.

Ohrgaard, Jakob. 'Less than Supranational, More than Intergovernmental: European Political Cooperation and the Dynamics of Intergovernmental Integration.' *Millennium* 26 (1997): 1–29.

Ojanen, Hanna, Gunilla Herolf, and Rutger Lindahl. *Non-alignment and European Security Policy.* Helsinki: The Finnish Institute of International Affairs, 2000.

Owen, David. *Balkan Odyssey.* London: Victor Gollancz, 1995.

Parmentier, Guillaume. 'Redressing NATO's Imbalances.' *Survival* 42, no. 2 (Summer 2000): 96–112.

Patten, Chris. 'A European Foreign Policy: Ambition and Reality.' Speech presented at the Institut Français des Relations Internationales, Paris, France, 15 June 2000.

– *Not Quite the Diplomat.* New York: Penguin Books, 2005.

Paul, T.V. 'Soft Balancing in the Age of U.S. Primacy.' *International Security* 30, no. 1 (Summer 2005): 46–71.

Perret, Philippe. 'La Défense dans le Projet Européen.' *Relations Internationales et Stratégiques* 18 (Summer 1995): 65–83.

Peters, Guy B. 'Agenda-Setting in the European Community.' *Journal of European Public Policy* 1, no. 1 (June 1994): 9–26.

– 'Escaping the Joint Decision Trap: Repetition and Sectoral Policies in the European Union.' *West European Politics* 20, no. 2 (1997): 22–36.

Peters, Joel. 'Europe and the Arab-Israeli Peace Process.' In Sven Behrendt and Christian-Peter Hanlet, eds. *Bound to Cooperate: Europe and the Middle East*, 150–71. Gütersloh, DEU: Bertelsmann Foundation Publishers, 2001.

Peterson, John. 'Decision-Making in the European Union: Towards a Framework for Analysis.' *Journal of European Public Policy* 2, no. 1 (1995): 69–93.

– *Europe and America in the 1990s: Prospects for Partnership*. London: Routledge, 1996.

– 'Assessment of the Current State of EU-US Relations.' In Christoph Bail et al., eds. *EU–U.S. Relations: Balancing the Partnership*, 105–9. Baden Baden: Nomos Verlagsgesellschaft, 1997.

– 'The Santer Era: The European Commission in Normative, Historical and Theoretical Perspective.' *Journal of European Public Policy* 6, no. 1 (March 1999): 46–65.

– 'Get Away From Me Closer, You're Near Me Too Far: Europe and America after the Uruguay Round.' Paper presented at EU External Capability and Influence in International Relations, European Consortium for Political Research Summer School, Geneva, Switzerland, 28 August–9 September 2000.

– 'U.S. and EU in the Balkans, America Fights the Wars, Europe Does the Dishes.' Paper presented at EUI Conference, Florence, Italy, 9 February 2002.

Peterson, John, and Elizabeth Bomberg. *Decision-Making in the European Union*. New York: St Martin's Press, 1999.

Peterson, John, and Maria Green Cowles. 'U.S. Economic Diplomacy: What Makes the EU Different?' *Governance* 11, no. 3 (1998): 251–71.

Peterson, John, and Mark Pollack, eds. *Europe, America, Bush: Transatlantic Relations in the Twenty-First Century*. London: Routledge, 2003.

Peterson, John, and Helène Sjursen, eds. *A Common Foreign Policy for Europe? Competing Visions of the CFSP*. London: Routledge, 1998.

Petit, Yves. 'Le Traité d'Amsterdam et le Financement de la PESC.' *Europe, Editions du Juris-Classeur* (January 1998): 5–8.

Pfetsch, Frank. 'Tensions in Sovereignty: Foreign Policies of EC Members Compared.' In Walter Carlsnaes and Steve Smith, eds., *EC and Changing Perspectives in Europe*, 120–37. London: Sage, 1994.

Philippart, Eric, and Pascaline Winand, eds. *Ever Closer Partnership: Policy-Making in US–EU Relations*. Berne: Peter Lang, 2001.

Pierson, Paul. 'The Path to European Integration: A Historical Institutionalist Analysis.' *Comparative Political Studies* 29, no. 2 (April 1996): 123–63.

– 'Increasing Returns, Path Dependence, and the Study of Politics.' *American Political Science Review* 94 (2000): 251–67.

Pijpers, Alfred. 'European Political Cooperation and the Realist Paradigm.' In

Martin Holland, ed., *The Future of European Political Cooperation*, 8–35. London: Macmillan, 1991.

– *The Vicissitudes of European Political Cooperation: Towards a Realist Interpretation of the EC's Collective Diplomacy*. Proefschrift: Leiden, 1990.

Pijpers, Alfred, Elfriede Regelsberger, and Wolfgang Wessels. 'A Common Foreign Policy for Western Europe?' In Alfred Pijpers, Elfriede Regelsberger, and Wolfgang Wessels, eds., *European Political Cooperation in the 1980s*, 259–76. Dordrecht: Nijhoff, 1988.

Piris, Jean-Claude. 'L'Union européenne a-t-elle une Constitution? Lui en faut-il une?' *Revue Trimestrielle de Droit Européen*, no. 4 (October–December 1999): 599–635.

Poettering, Hans-Gert. 'Perspektiven für Eine Gemeinschaftliche Außen-und Sicherheitspolitik der EG.' *Europa Archiv* 45, no. 11 (1990): 341–50.

Pollack, Mark A. 'The New Institutionalism and EC Governance: The Promise and Limits of Institutional Analysis.' *Governance* 9, no. 4 (October 1996): 429–58.

– 'Delegation, Agency, and Agenda Setting in the European Community.' *International Organization* 51, no. 1 (Winter 1997): 99–134.

– 'International Relations Theory and European Integration.' *Journal of Common Market Studies* 39, no. 2 (June 2001): 221–44.

– *The Engines of European Integration: Delegation, Agency and Agenda Setting in the EU*. Oxford: Oxford University Press, 2003.

– 'The New Institutionalisms and European Integration.' In Antje Wiener and Thomas Diez, eds., *European Integration Theory*, 137–56. New York: Oxford University Press, 2004.

– 'Theorizing the European Union: International Organization, Domestic Polity, or Experiment in New Governance?' *Annual Review of Political Science*, no. 8 (2005): 357–98.

Pollack, Mark, and Gregory Shaffer, eds. *Transatlantic Governance in the Global Economy*. Lanham, MD: Rowman and Littlefield, 2001.

Poos, Jacques F. Interview by Alexandre Germain, Sanem, Centre Virtuel de la Connaissance sur l'Europe, 16 April 2004. Retrieved from http://www.cvce.lu, 14 August 2008.

Posen, Barry. 'ESDP and the Structure of World Power.' *The International Spectator* 39, no. 1 (January–March 2004): 5–17.

– 'European Union Security and Defence Policy: Response to Unipolarity.' *Security Studies* 15, no. 2 (2006): 149–86.

Posen, Barry, and Andrew Ross. 'Competing Visions for U.S. Grand Strategy.' *International Security* 21, no. 3 (Winter 1996–1997): 5–53.

Powell, Robert. 'Anarchy in International Relations Theory: The Neorealist-

Neoliberal Debate, Neorealism and Its Critics, Review Essays.' *International Organization* 48, no. 2 (Spring 1994): 313–44.

Price, Richard. 'Reversing the Gun Sights: Transnational Civil Society Targets Land Mines.' *International Organization* 52, no. 3 (Summer 1998): 613–44.

Puchala, Donald. 'Of Blind Men, Elephants and International Integration.' *Journal of Common Market Studies* 10, no. 4 (1972): 267–84.

Putnam, Robert D. *Making Democracy Work: Civic Traditions in Modern Italy.* Princeton, NJ: Princeton University Press, 1993.

Putnam, Robert D., and Nicholas Bayne. *Cooperation and Conflict in the Seven-power Summits.* London: Sage, 1987.

Quilès, Paul. *L'OTAN, Quel Avenir?* (What Future for NATO?) Rapport d'Information de la Commission de la Défense de l'Assemblée Nationale No. 1495. New York: United Nations, 1999.

Quilès, Paul, and François Lamy. *Kosovo: Une Guerre d'Exceptions.* United Nations Document No. 2022. New York: United Nations, 1999.

Rees, G. Wyn, 'Setting the Parameters for European Defence: The UK and the WEU.' *Studia Diplomatica* 51, nos. 1/2 (1998): 61–70.

Regelsberger, Elfriede. 'EPC in the 1980s: Reaching Another Plateau?' In Alfred Pijpers, Elfriede Regelsberger, and Wolfgang Wessels, eds., *European Political Cooperation in the 1980s,* 3–48. Dordrecht: Nijhoff, 1988.

Regelsberger, Elfriede, Philippe de Schoutheete, and Wolfgang Wessels, eds. *Foreign Policy of the European Union.* Boulder, CO: Westview Press, 1997.

Regelsberger, Elfriede, and Wolfgang Wessels. 'The CFSP Institutions and Procedures: A Third Way for the Second Pillar.' *European Foreign Affairs Review* 1 (1996): 29–54.

Reichard, Martin. *The EU-NATO Relationship: A Legal and Political Perspective.* Aldershot, UK: Ashgate, 2006.

Renwick, Robin. *Fighting with Allies: America and Britain in Peace and at War.* New York: Times Books, 1996.

Rhodes, Carolyn, ed. *The EU in the World Community.* Boulder, CO: Lynne Rienner Publishers, 1998.

Richardson, Jeremy. 'Policy-Making in the EU: Interests, Ideas and Garbage Cans of Primeval Soup.' In Jeremy Richardson, ed., *European Union: Power and Policy-Making,* 3–23. London: Routledge, 1996.

Risse-Kappen, Thomas. *Bringing Transnational Relations Back In.* Cambridge: Cambridge University Press, 1995.

– 'Exploring the Nature of the Beast: International Relations Theory and Comparative Policy Analysis Meet the European Union.' *Journal of Common Market Studies* 34, no. 1 (March 1996): 53–80.

Risse, Thomas. '"Let's Argue!" Communicative Action in World Politics.' *International Organization* 54, no. 1 (2000): 1–39.

– 'U.S. Power in a Liberal Security Community.' In G. John Ikenberry, ed., *American Unrivalled: Unipolarity and the Future of the Balance of Power*, 260–83. Ithaca, NY: Cornell University Press, 2002.

Risse, Thomas, Stephen Ropp, and Kathryn Sikkink, eds. *The Power of Principles: Human Rights Norms, and Domestic Political Change*. Cambridge: Cambridge University Press, 1999.

Rittberger, Volker, ed. *German Foreign Policy since Unification: Theories and Case Studies*. Manchester: Manchester University Press, 2001.

Rosamond, Ben. *Theories of European Integration*. London: Palgrave, 2000.

Rosecrance, Richard. 'The European Union: A New Type of International Actor.' In Jan Zielonka, ed., *Paradoxes of European Foreign Policy*, 15–24. The Hague: Kluwer Law International, 1998.

Rosenthal, Glenda. *The Men behind the Decisions*. Lexington, MA: Lexington Books, 1975.

Ross, George. *Jacques Delors and European Integration*. Oxford: Oxford University Press, 1995.

Roudsari, Sahar Arfazadeh. 'Talking Away the Crisis? The E3/EU-Iran Negotiations on Nuclear Issues.' College of Europe, EU Diplomacy Papers (June 2007). Retrieved from http://www.coleurop.be/file/content /studyprogrammes/ird/research/pdf/EDP%206-2007%20Arfazadeh Roudsari.pdf, 3 April 2008.

Rubin, Jeffrey Z., and Walter C. SWAP. 'Small Group Theory: Forming Consensus through Group Processes.' In I. William Zartman, ed., *International Multilateral Negotiation: Approaches to the Management of Complexity*, 132–47. San Francisco: Jossey-Bass, 1994.

Rudolf, Peter. 'Critical Engagement: The European Union and Iran.' In Richard N. Haass, ed., *Transatlantic Tensions: The United States, Europe and Problem Countries*, 71–101. Washington, DC: Brookings Institution, 1999.

Ruggie, John Gerard. 'Continuity and Transformation in the World Polity: Toward A Neorealist Synthesis.' *World Politics* 35, no. 2 (January 1983): 261–85.

– 'Multilateralism: The Anatomy of an Institution.' *International Organization* 46, no. 3 (Summer 1992): 561–98.

Rummel, Reinhardt, ed. *Toward Political Union: Planning a Common Security and Foreign Policy in the EC*. Baden Baden: Nomos, 1992.

Rummel, Reinhardt, and Joerg Wiedemann. 'Identifying Institutional Paradoxes of CFSP.' In Jan Zielonka, ed., *Paradoxes of European Foreign Policy*, 53–66. The Hague: Kluwer Law International, 1998.

Sandholtz, Wayne. 'Membership Matters: Limits of the Functional Approach to European Institutions.' *Journal of Common Market Studies* 34, no. 3 (1996): 403–29.

– *High Tech Europe: The Politics of International Cooperation.* Berkeley: University of California Press, 1992.

Sauer, Tom. 'Coercive Diplomacy by the EU: The Case of Iran.' Discussion Papers in Diplomacy, No. 106. Glingendael: Netherlands Institute of International Relations, January 2007.

Sbragia, Alberta M., ed. *Euro-Politics. Institutions and Policy-Making in the 'New European Community.'* Washington, DC: Brookings Institution, 1992.

Schake, Kori, Amaya Bloch-Laine, and Charles Grant. 'Building a European Defence Capability.' *Survival* 41, no. 1 (Spring 1999): 20–40.

Scharpf, Fritz W. *Games Real Actors Play.* Boulder, CO: Westview Press, 1997.

Schimmelfennig, Frank. *The EU, NATO and the Integration of Europe: Rules and Rhetoric.* Cambridge: Cambridge University Press, 2003.

Schmitter, Philippe C. 'Examining the Present Euro-Polity with the Help of Past Theories.' In Gary Marks, Fritz W. Scharpf, Philippe C. Schmitter, and Wolfgang Streeck, eds., *Governance in the European Union,* 121–50. London: Sage, 1996.

Schroeder, Paul. 'Historical Reality vs. Neo-Realist Theory.' *International Security* 19, no. 1 (Summer 1994): 108–48.

Schuman, Robert. *Pour l'Europe.* Paris: Editions Nagel, 1963.

Schweller, Randall. 'Bandwagoning for Profit: Bringing the Revisionist State Back In.' *International Security* 19, no. 1 (Summer 1994): 72–107.

Sharp, Jane M.O. *Anglo-American Relations and Crisis in Yugoslavia.* Les Notes de l'IFRI, no. 9, Série transatlantique. Paris: Institut français des relations internationales, 1999.

Simic, Predrag. 'After the Cold War: Europe, the Balkans and Yugoslavia.' *International Spectator* 27, no. 4 (1992): 81–94.

Sjostedt, Gunnar. *The External Role of the European Community.* Westmead, UK: Saxon House, 1977.

Sjursen, Helene. 'New Forms of Security Policy in Europe.' Arena Working Paper 04/01. Oslo: University of Oslo, 2001a.

– 'The Common Foreign and Security Policy: Limits of Intergovernmentalism and the Search for a Global Role.' In Svein S. Andersen and Kjell A. Eliassen, eds., *Making Policy in Europe,* 187–205. London: Sage, 2001b.

– 'What Kind of Power? European Foreign Policy in Perspective.' Special Issue, *Journal of European Public Policy* 13, no. 2 (2006): 167–327.

Sloan, Stanley. *NATO, the European Union and the Atlantic Community: The Transatlantic Bargain Reconsidered.* Boulder, CO: Rowman and Littlefield, 2002.

Smith, Karen. 'The Instruments of European Union Foreign Policy.' In Jan Zielonka, ed., *Paradoxes of European Foreign Policy*, 67–85. The Hague: Kluwer Law International, 1998.

– *The Making of EU Foreign Policy: The Case of Eastern Europe*. London: Macmillan, 1999a.

– 'The End of Civilian Power EU: A Welcome Demise or Cause for Concern?' *International Spectator* 23, no. 2 (1999b): 11–28.

– 'The EU and the Promotion of Human Rights at the United Nations.' Paper presented at International Studies Association Convention, New Orleans, Louisiana, March 2002.

Smith, Michael. 'The "Europeanization" of EPC: Trust, Transgovernmental Relations and the Power of Informal Norms.' Berkeley, CA: Center for German and European Studies, 1996.

– 'Rules, Transgovernmentalism, and European Political Cooperation.' In Wayne Sandholtz and Alec Stone Sweet, eds., *European Integration and Supranational Governance*, 304–33. New York: Oxford University Press, 1998.

– 'Conforming to Europe: The Domestic Impact of EU Foreign Policy Cooperation.' *Journal of European Public Policy* 7, no. 4 (October 2000): 613–31.

– 'The Quest for Coherence: Institutional Dilemmas of External Action from Maastricht to Amsterdam.' In Alec Stone Sweet, Wayne Sandholtz, and Neil Fligstein, eds., *The Institutionalization of Europe*, 171–93. Oxford: Oxford University Press, 2001.

– *Europe's Foreign and Security Policy: The Institutionalization of Cooperation*. Cambridge: Cambridge University Press, 2004.

– 'Between Two Worlds? The European Union, the United States and World Order.' *International Politics* 41, no. 1 (March 2004): 95–117.

Smith, Michael, and Rebecca Steffenson. 'The European Union and the United States.' In Christopher Hill and Michael Smith, eds., *The International Relations of the European Union*, 343–63. New York: Oxford University Press, 2005.

Snyder, Glenn H. 'The Security Dilemma in Alliance Politics.' *World Politics*, no. 36 (1983–1984): 461–95.

Soetendorp, Ben. *Foreign Policy in the European Union: Theory, History and Practice*. New York: Longman, 1999.

Spaak, Paul Henri. 'Document 52.' In Paul-F. Smets, ed., *La Pensée Européenne et Atlantique de Paul-Henri Spaak (1942–1972)*, vol. 1, 280–7. Brussels: Fondation Spaak, 1980.

Spence, David. *The European Commission*. London: John Harper Publishing, 2006.

Stark, Hans. 'Paris, Berlin et Londres vers l'Emergence d'un Directoire Européen?' *Politique Etrangère* 4 (2002): 967–82.

Stavridis, Stelios, and Justin Hutchence. 'Mediterranean Challenges to the EU's Foreign Policy.' *European Foreign Affairs Review* 5 (2000): 35–62.

Stromvik, Maria. 'Fifteen Votes and One Voice? The CFSP and Changing Voter Alignment in the UN.' *Statsvetenskaplig Tidskrift, Argang* 101, no. 2 (1998): 181–97.

Tallberg, Jonas. 'The Anatomy of Autonomy: An Institutional Account of Variation in Supranational Influence.' *Journal of Common Market Studies* 38, no. 5 (2000): 843–64.

Taylor, Paul. 'Intergovernmentalism in the European Communities in the 1970s: Patterns and Perspectives.' *International Organization* 36, no. 4 (Autumn 1982): 741–66.

– *The Limits of European Integration.* London: Croom Helm, 1983.

Thelen, Kathleen. 'Historical Institutionalism in Comparative Politics.' *Annual Review of Political Science* 2 (1999): 369–404.

Tonra, Ben. 'The Impact of Political Cooperation.' In Knud E. Jorgensen, ed., *Reflective Approaches to European Governance*, 181–200. Basingstoke, UK: Macmillan, 1997.

– *The Europeanisation of National Foreign Policy: The Netherlands, Denmark and Ireland.* London: Ashgate, 2001.

Tonra, Ben, and Thomas Christiansen, eds. *Rethinking European Union Foreign Policy.* Manchester: Manchester University Press, 1996.

Tsakaloyannis, Panos. 'Greece, the Limits to Convergence.' In Christopher Hill ed., *The Actors in Europe's Foreign Policy*, 186–207. London: Routledge, 1996.

Tziampiris, Aristotle. 'Greece, European Political Cooperation and the Macedonian Question.' PhD dissertation, London School of Economics, 1999.

Van Cleveland, Harold. *The Atlantic Idea and its European Rivals.* New York: McGraw-Hill Paperbacks, Council on Foreign Relations, 1966.

Van Evera, Stephen. 'Primed for Peace: Europe after the Cold War.' *International Security* 15, no. 3 (Winter 1990–1991): 7–57.

Van Ham, Peter. 'EU, NATO, OSCE: Interaction, Cooperation and Confrontation.' In Gunther Hauser and Franz Kernic, eds., *European Security in Transition*, 23–38. London: Ashgate, 2006.

– 'Europe's Precarious Centre: Franco-German Co-operation and the CFSP.' *European Security* 8, Issue 4 (Winter 1999): 1–26.

Vasquez, John. A. 'The Realist Paradigm and Degenerative versus Progressive Research Programs: An Appraisal of Neotraditional Research on Watz's Balancing Proposition.' *American Political Science Review* 91, no. 4 (December 1997): 899–912.

- *The Power of Power Politics, from Classical Realism to Neotraditionalism.* Cambridge: Cambridge University Press, 1998.

Védrine, Hubert. *Les Mondes de François Mitterrand: À l'Elysée, 1981–1995.* Paris: Fayard, 1996.

Verbeke, Johan. 'A New Security Concept for a New Europe.' *Studia Diplomatica* 51, nos. 3/4 (1998): 125–39.

Viotti, Paul R., and Mark V. Kauppi. *International Relations Theory.* New York: Allyn and Bacon, 1999.

Von der Gablentz, Otto. 'Luxembourg Revisited, or the Importance of European Political Cooperation.' *Common Market Law Review* 16, no. 6 (November 1979): 685–99.

Von Geusau, Alting. *The External Relations of the European Community.* Farnborough, Hants, UK: Saxon House, Lexington Books, 1974.

Wallace, Helen. *Europe, the Challenge of Diversity.* Boston: Routledge and Kegan Paul, 1985.

- 'Bilateral, Trilateral and Multilateral Negotiations in the European Community.' In Roger Morgan and Caroline Bray, eds., *Partners and Rivals in Western Europe: Britain, France and Germany,* 156–74. Aldershot, UK: Gower, 1986.

Wallace, Helen, William Wallace, and Carole Webb. *Policy-Making in the European Community.* 2nd ed. London: John Wiley and Sons, 1983.

Wallace, Helen, James A. Caporaso, Fritz Scharpf, and Andrew Moravcik. 'Review Section Symposium: The Choice for Europe: Social Purpose and State Power from Messina to Maastricht.' *Journal of European Public Policy* 6, no. 1 (March 1999): 155–79.

Wallace, Helen, and William Wallace. *Policy-Making in the European Union.* New York: Oxford University Press, 2000.

Wallace, William. *Foreign Policy and the Political Process.* New York: Macmillan, 1971.

- 'Issue Linkage among Atlantic Governments.' *International Affairs* 52, no. 2 (April 1976): 163–79.

- 'Political Cooperation: Integration through Intergovernmentalism.' In Helen Wallace, William Wallace, and Carole Webb, eds., *Policy-Making in the European Community,* 2nd ed., 373–401. London: John Wiley and Sons, 1983.

- 'Living with the Hegemon: European Dilemmas.' Social Science Research Council, New York (2001). Retrieved from http://www.sscr.org/sept11/essays/wallace.htm, 4 May 2003.

- 'The Euro-Atlantic Relations.' London Goodenough Trust Port Talk, Goodenough College, London, 10 May 2001.

Wallace, William, and David Allen. 'Political Cooperation: Procedure as a Substitute for Policy.' In Helen Wallace, William Wallace, and Carole Webb, eds., *Policy-Making in the European Communities*, 1st ed., 227–48. London: John Wiley and Sons, 1977.

Walt, Stephen M. *The Origins of Alliances*. Ithaca, NY: Cornell University Press, 1987.

– 'Alliances in Theory and Practice: What Lies Ahead?' *Journal of International Affairs* 43, no.1 (Summer/Fall 1989): 1–17.

– 'Alliance Formation in Southwest Asia: Balancing and Bandwagoning in Cold War Competition.' In Robert Jervis and Jack Snyder, eds., *Dominoes and Bandwagons: Strategic Beliefs and Great Power Politics in the Eurasian Rimland*, 51–84. Oxford: Oxford University Press, 1991.

– 'The Ties that Fray: Why Europe and America Are Drifting Apart.' *National Interest*, no. 54 (Winter 1998–1999): 3–11.

Waltz, Kenneth. *Theory of International Relations*. Reading, MA: Addison-Wesley, 1979.

– 'The Emerging Structure of International Politics.' *International Security* 18, no. 2 (Fall 1993): 44–79.

Watson, Adam. *The Evolution of International Society*. London: Routledge, 1992.

Webb, Carole. 'Theoretical Perspectives and Problems.' In Helen Wallace, William Wallace, and Carole Webb, eds., *Policy-Making in the European Community*, 2nd ed., 1–42. London: John Wiley and Sons, 1983.

Weiler, Joseph. 'The Evolution of a European Foreign Policy: Mechanisms and Institutions.' In I. Greilsammer et al., eds., *Europe and Israel: Troubled Neighbours*, 233–54. New York: Walter de Gruyter, 1988.

– ed. *The EU, the WTO and the NAFTA: Towards a Common Law of International Trade*. Oxford: Oxford University Press, 2000.

Weiler, Joseph, and Wolfgang Wessels. 'EPC and the Challenge of Theory.' In Alfred Pijpers, Elfriede Regelsberger, and Wolfgang Wessels, eds., *European Political Cooperation in the 1980s*, 229–58. Dordrecht: Nijhoff, 1988.

Wendt, Alexander. 'Collective Identity Formation and the International State.' *American Political Science Review* 88, no. 2 (June 1994): 384–96.

– *Social Theory of International Politics*. New York: Cambridge University Press, 1999.

Wessels, Wolfgang. 'The EC Council: The Community's Decision-Making Centre.' In Robert O. Keohane and Stanley Hoffmann, eds., *The New European Community: Decision-Making and Institutional Change*, 133–54. Boulder, CO: Westview Press, 1991.

– 'The Third Pillar: Plea for a Single Theoretical Research Agenda.' In Joerg

Monar and Roger Morgan, eds. *The Third Pillar of the European Union*. Brussels: European Interuniversity Press, 1995.

Wessels, Wolfgang, and Juergen Withtag. 'Theoretical Perspectives on Administrative Interaction in the European Union.' In Thomas Christiansen and Emil Kirchner, eds., *Committee Governance in the European Union*, 23–44. Manchester: Manchester University Press 2000.

White, Brian. 'The European Challenge to Foreign Policy Analysis.' *European Journal of International Relations* 5, no. 1 (1999): 37–66.

– *Understanding European Foreign Policy*. New York: Palgrave, 2001.

White, Brian, and Michael Clarke. *Understanding Foreign Policy: The Foreign Policy Systems Approach*. Aldershot, UK: Gower, 1989.

Whitman, Richard. 'The Fall, and Rise of Civilian Power Europe?' Technical Report NEC Paper No. 16, National Europe Centre, ANU (2002). Retrieved from http://www.anu.edu.au/NEC/whitman.pdf, 15 May 2004.

– 'NATO, the EU and ESDP: An Emerging Division of Labour?' *Contemporary Security Policy* 25, no. 3 (December 2004): 430–51.

Wickham-Jones, Mark. 'Labour's Trajectory in Foreign Affairs: The Moral Crusade of a Pivotal Power?' In Richard Little and Mark Wickham-Jones, eds., *New Labour's Foreign Policy*, 3–32. Manchester: Manchester University Press, 2000.

Wind, Marlene. 'Rediscovering Institutions: A Reflectivist Critique of Rational Institutionalism.' In Knud Erik Jorgensen, ed., *Reflective Approaches to European Governance*, 15–38. Basingstoke, UK: Macmillan, 1997.

Wohlforth, William C. 'The Stability in a Unipolar World.' *International Security* 24, no. 1 (1999): 5–41.

Wong, Y. Reuben. *The Europeanization of French Foreign Policy: France and the EU in East Asia*. New York: Palgrave Macmillan, 2006.

Woodward, Susan. *Balkan Tragedy: Chaos and Dissolution after the Cold War*. Washington, DC: Brookings Institution, 1995.

Yee, Herbert S., and Ian Storey. *The China Threat: Perceptions, Myths and Reality*. New York: Routledge, 2002.

Young, Alasdair. 'Extending European Cooperation: The EU and the "New" International Trade Agenda.' EUI Working Paper, RSC WP 2001/12. Florence: European University Institute, 2001.

Young, Oran R. 'Political Leadership and Regime Formation: On the Development of Institutions in International Society.' *International Organization* 45, no. 3 (1991): 281–308.

Youngs, Richard. *Europe and the Middle East: In the Shadow of September 11*. Boulder, CO: Lynne Rienner Publishers, 2006.

Zartman, I. William. *International Multilateral Negotiation: Approaches to the*

Management of Complexity. San Francisco: Jossey-Bass, 1994.

Zielonka, Jan. *Explaining Euro-Paralysis: Why Europe is Unable to Act in International Politics*. London: Macmillan, 1998a.

– *Paradoxes of European Foreign Policy*. The Hague: Kluwer Law International, 1998b.

– 'Transatlantic Relations Beyond the CFSP.' *The International Spectator* 35, no. 4 (October–December 2000): 27–40.

– *Europe as Empire: The Nature of the Enlarged European Union*. Oxford: Oxford University Press, 2006.

Press Articles and European Union Documents by Chapter

Introduction

ARTICLES

Agence Europe No. 7593, 18/11/99.

Draft Treaty, Fouchet Plan I, 2 November 1961, http://www.ena.lu/.

Letter from Robert Silvercruys, Belgian Ambassador to the United States, to Paul van Zeeland, Belgian Foreign Minister, on U.S. concerns over the delay in ratifying the EDC Treaty in Europe (24 June 1953), http://www.ena.lu/, accessed on 30/07/08.

NATO Document, 'NATO-Russia Compendium of Financial and Economic Data Relating to Defence,' http://www.nato.int/docu/pr/2007 /p07-141.pdf, accessed on 21/12/07.

Pleven Plan, Statement by René Pleven on the establishment of a European army, 24/10/50, www.cvce.lu, accessed on 30/07/08.

'EU to go ahead with satellite system.' *Financial Times*, 27/03/02.

'Lost in space: Europe's ambitions to launch a satellite navigation system to compete with the United States's monopoly risk being thwarted by a dispute over funding.' *Financial Times*, 22/12/01.

EU DOCUMENTS

EU Document, Declaration of 9 May 1950, http://europa.eu/abc/symbols/9-may/decl_en.htm, accessed on 11/11/09.

EU Document, Treaty of Lisbon, OJ C306 of 17.12.2007, http://www.consilium .europa.eu/showPage.aspx?id=1296&lang=en, accessed on 11/11/09.

EU Document, Treaty of Maastricht, OJ C 191 of 29.7.1992, http://eur-lex.europa.eu/en/treaties/dat/11992M/htm/11992M.html, accessed on 11/11/09.

EU Document, Treaty of Amsterdam, OJ C 340 of 10.11.1997,
   www.europarl.europa.eu/topics/treaty/pdf/amst-en.pdf, accessed on
   11/11/09.
EU Document, Treaty of Nice, OJ C 80 of 10.3.2001, eur-lex.europa.eu/en
   /treaties/dat/12001C/pdf/12001C_EN.pdf, accessed on 11/11/09.

Chapter 1

ARTICLES
'Déjà vu in Kosovo, Personal view Carl Bildt.' *Financial Times*, 09/06/98.
'L'Europe s'exaspère du cavalier seul de Silvio Berlusconi.' *Le Monde*,
   10/12/01.

Chapter 2

ARTICLES
'A Balkan success story.' *Financial Times*, 14/03/02.
'Assault on islet exposes EU rifts.' *Financial Times*, 19/07/02.
'Communiqué du ministère des affaires étrangères sur les essais nucléaires
   au Pakistan.' *Paris*, 31/05/98.
'Deuxième véto américain à l'ONU.' *Le Monde*, 16–17/12/01.
'Etats-Unis et Europe, le grand écart de budget de défense.' *Le Monde*,
   06/02/02.
'EU and NATO clash over Macedonian operations.' *Financial Times*,
   05/03/02.
'EU toots its own horn in Belgrade, but locals don't want to hear it.' *Wall
   Street Journal*, 06/04/01.
'EU tries to boost presence.' *Ha'aretz*, 10/06/01.
'Europe signs up.' *Financial Times*, 15/10/01.
'Europeans embargo sale of defence supplies to Israel.' *Ha'aretz*, 22/05/02.
'Faire contre mauvaise fortune bonne figure.' *Le Monde*, 21/10/00.
'Former MI6 officer represents EU.' *Washington Times*, 02/09/02.
'France forces fudge on Mugabe sanctions.' *The Guardian*, 13/02/03.
'Ignoring critics, Bonn to decide support for Croatia, Slovenia.' Reuters,
   16/12/91.
'Informations économiques.'
   http://www.1stmaroc.com/affaires/infoeco/economique10.html, accessed
   on 31/10/02.
'Key Mid-East role for British envoy.' *The Daily Telegraph, 28/03/98.*
'L'Eufor se déploiera à la mi-février dans l'est du Tchad.' Reuters, 11/01/08.

'L'heure de l'Europe a sonné en Macédoine.' *La Libre Belgique*, 03/04/01.

'Les bombardements contre Bagdad mettent les Européens mal à l'aise.' *Le Monde*, 21/02/01.

'Major lays into nuclear idiocy.' *The Guardian*, 11/11/95.

'Nuclear test fly in the face of EU.' *The Irish Times*, 10/07/95.

'Peres meets Palestinians in tentative move to resume talks.' *Financial Times*, 05/04/01.

'Secret UK ban on weapons for Israel: Embargo blocking of sales mirrors German action.' *The Guardian*, 13/04/02.

'Solana Javier: The biggest test of the EU capabilities for preventive diplomacy.' *International Herald Tribune*, 09/07/01.

'Solana asks EU to weigh Iran sanctions.' *International Herald Tribune*, 11/04/06.

'U.S. boosts Gulf strength.' CNN, 17/12/98, http://www.cnn.com/US/9812/17/iraq.us.forces.01/, accessed on 9/12/03.

'U.S. brokers peace talks on dispute Armenian enclave.' *Financial Times*, 04/04/01.

'U.S. in talks to cement Middle East ceasefire.' *The Guardian*, 08/06/01.

'While Britain is making peace with pariahs Robin Cook's "inclusive" foreign policy is widening a diplomatic rift between Europe and America.' *The Daily Telegraph*, 09/07/99.

'Yougoslavie: l'éventuelle reconnaissance internationale de la Slovénie et de la Croatie. La France essaie de résister aux pressions allemandes.' *Le Monde*, 17/12/91.

'Words of war: Europe's first security doctrine backs away from a commitment to U.S.-style pre-emption.' *Financial Times*, 05/12/03.

Agence Europe No. 7518, 30/07/99.

Agence Europe No. 7543, 03/09/99.

De Schoutheete, Philippe. Former Belgian Ambassador to the EU, interview with author, 25/03/01.

Déclaration du porte-parole du Quai d'Orsay, Human Rights Commission, 16/04/02.

Diplomatie-actualités, web document, 18/07/02.

European Security Review, No. 4, March 2001.

House of Commons Document, 'Foreign Policy Aspects of the Lisbon Treaty.' Third Report of Session 2007–8, Foreign Affairs Committee, 20/01/08.

International Herald Tribune, 20/02/01.

La Libre Belgique, 25/04/01.

Mitchell Committee report, 30/04/01, http://www.state.gov/p/nea/rls
/rpt/3060.htm, accessed on 16/05/03.

NATO document, 'NATO Russia Compendium of financial and economic
data relating to defence.' http://www.nato.int/docu/pr/2007
/p07-141.pdf, accessed on 23/01/08.

NATO Document, 'Fourth Stage Internet Communication System for Turk-
menistan's NREN.' 02/05/07,
http://www.nato.int/science/studies_and_projects/nato_funded/nigs
/nig_982532/nig_982532.htm, accessed on 16/11/08.

NATO Document, 'Exercise on CBRN Defence at NATO HQ.' 15/04/08,
http://www.nato.int/docu/update/2008/04-april/e0415a.html, accessed
on 16/11/08.

The New York Times. 'Impairing the European Union, Gibe by Gibe.'
http://www.nytimes.com/2009/02/14/world/europe/14union.html?hp,
accessed on 14/02/09.

OECD 2006 statistics, http://www.oecd.org/dataoecd/61/24/39829897.jpg,
accessed on 21/12/07.

OECD 2007 statistics,
http://www.oecd.org/document/9/0,3343,en_2649_33721_1893129_1_1_1
_1,00.html, accessed on 21/12/07.

Solana, Javier. 'Europe's place in the World.' EU Document, Speech at the
Danish Institute of International Affairs, Copenhagen, S0101/02,
23/05/02.

– 'Common strategies for third countries: suggestions and criticism from
Javier Solana.' Agence Europe Documents, n. 2228, 31/01/01, pp. 2–3.

– Speech addressed to the External Action Working Group of the Convention, 15/10/02.

Wallace, William. 'Europe's impossible foreign policy brief.' *Financial Times*,
11/11/03.

Woodrow Wilson International Centre for Scholars. 'European Mediators and
Ukraine's Orange Revolution,'15/10/07,
http://www.wilsoncenter.org/index.cfm?fuseaction=events.event&event_i
d=279607, accessed on 12/11/08.

EU DOCUMENTS

'Improving the Coherence and Effectiveness of European Union Action in the
Field of Conflict Prevention.' Report from the Commission and the Secre-
tary General / High Representative (SG/HR) Solana, Nice European
Council, December 2000.

Cologne European Council, 04/06/99, Press 0, No. 150/99.

Council Document. 'Coordination of implementation of the plan of action to combat terrorism.' 12800/01, 16/10/01.

Council document. 'Javier Solana, Haut Représentant de l'Union européenne pour la PESC, appelle le Président Laurent Gbagbo à arrêter toute opération militaire en Côte d'Ivoire.' S0298/04, 06/11/04, http://ue.eu.int/uedocs/cms_Data/docs/pressdata/fr/declarations/82559.pdf.

Declaration of Intent, 17/09/04, http://www.eurogendfor.org/DECLARATION%20OF%20INTENT.htm, accessed on 24/11/06.

European Parliament Briefing Paper. October 2007, http://www.europarl.europa.eu/meetdocs/2004_2009/documents/dv/st udybattlegrouppe381401_/s tudybattlegrouppe381401_en.pdf), accessed on 29/07/08.

European Union Document 2006. 2006 General Budget, http://europa.eu/eur-lex/budget/data/D2006_VOL4/EN/nmc-titleN188CA/nmc-chapterN19003/index.html#N19003, accessed on 15/12/07.

EU Council Document. 16/05/02.

EU Document. 'EU demarches on the issue of the death penalty.' GAC Declaration Luxembourg, 29/06/98, Press 227, No. 9730/98.

EU Document, Structure of the General Secretariat, 2009, http://www.consilium.europa.eu/uedocs/cmsUpload/2009_STRUCTURE_GENERAL_SECRETARIAT_EN.pdf, accessed on 12/11/09.

EU Factsheet, European security and defence policy: the civilian aspects of crisis management. June 2008, http://www.consilium.europa.eu/uedocs/cmsUpload/BackgroundJPO2008-Civilian_aspects_compressed.pdf, accessed on 04/09/08.

GAC conclusions, Luxembourg, 26/04/99, Press 118, No. 7561/99.

Göteborg European Council, 15/06/01, no. 200/1/01.

Patten, Chris. Cyril Foster Lecture, Balliol College, Oxford, 30/01/03.

Solana, Javier. Speech pronounced by the High Representative at the inaugural session of the 2002 Conference of Ambassadors, S0141/02, 24/07/02.

Statement by an extraordinary EPC Ministerial Meeting concerning Yugoslavia, Brussels, The Hague, 91/465, 16/12/91.

Chapter 3

ARTICLES

'America retreats from human rights motion against China.' *The Times*, 16/03/98.

'Asian economic crisis: Blair hails new dawn in co-operation with China;

Economic woes dominated an agenda that included human rights.' *The Guardian*, 03/04/98.

'Britain drops China rights protest at UN.' *Telegraph*, 17/03/00.

'China brings its critics to heel with mixture of threats and promises.' *The Daily Telegraph*, 15/04/97.

'China hints at an accord on rights.' *The New York Times*, 28/02/97.

'China outflanks U.S. to avoid scrutiny of its human rights.' *The New York Times*, 24/04/96.

'China gives Airbus lift with order for 150 jets.' *International Herald Tribune*, 26/10/06.

'China ready to sign UN pledge on human rights.' *The Times*, 13/03/98.

'China selects the Blair that's fit to share.' *The Independent*, 11/10/98.

'China uses prostitutes to bring shame on Tibetan monks.' *Sunday Telegraph*, 28/03/99.

'China warns Denmark on resolution.' *The New York Times*, 08/04/97, http://www.nytimes.com/1997/04/08/world/china-warns-denmark-on-resolution.html, accessed on 25/02/02.

'China warns West to shun dissidents.' *The Times*, 16/03/99.

'Cuba cited by UN on human rights.' *The Washington Times*, 19/04/02.

'Danes court China's fury and shame the EU by speaking out on rights.' *The Independent*, 08/04/97.

'Danes take on China over rights.' *The European*, 10/04/97.

'Dissent on China "damages EU."' *The Daily Telegraph*, 04/04/97.

'Dissident Chinese poet sentenced to five years for "literary subversion."' *The Independent*, 15/03/00.

'Duped by China.' *The Daily Telegraph*, 23/12/98.

'Espoirs de contrats.' *L'Humanité*, 15/05/97. http://www.humanite.presse.fr/journal/1997/1997-05/1997-05-15/1997-05-15-034.html, accessed on 03/10/01.

'EU split over rights draft against Beijing.' *World Tibet Network News and South China Morning Post*, 20/03/00.

'France may block move to censure Beijing.' *The Daily Telegraph*, 11/03/97.

'Greedy and myopic.' *The Daily Telegraph*, 16/03/98.

'It's time Mr Cook applied his ethics to China; an angry dissident brings a message for us all: defend human rights, whatever it costs.' *The Independent*, 06/03/98.

'La Chine échappe à la condamnation de l'Europe sur les droits de l'homme.' *Le Monde*, 28/02/98.

'La session de la Commission des droits de l'homme de l'ONU s'ouvre dans un climat tendu.' *Le Monde*, 19/03/01.

'La défense des droits de l'homme en Chine divise les Quinze; La France,
soutenue par l'Allemagne, l'Italie et l'Espagne, souhaite que les pays de
l'Union européenne mettent une sourdine aux protestations contre le
régime de Pékin.' *Le Monde*, 09/04/97.

'La France adopte un profil bas sur les droits de l'homme en Chine; Paris
veut ménager Pékin avant la visite du premier ministre.' *Le Monde*,
19/03/96.

'Le texte de l'entretien télévisé du Président de la République.' *Le Monde*,
14/12/96.

'Les Quinze décident de s'exprimer à l'unisson sur la Chine à l'ONU.' *Le
Monde*, 25/02/98.

'L'Europe veut exercer une influence durable en Asie; Le second forum
Asie-Europe (ASEM) s'est achevé, samedi, à Londres.' *Le Monde*,
06/04/98.

'Li Peng arrive à Paris avec une brassée de contrats: Airbus, Gaz de France,
Alcatel Alsthom.' *Le télégramme*, 10/04/96,
http://archives.letelegramme.com/data/1996/19960410/article/594953
.htm, accessed on 06/11/01.

'L'Union européenne adresse une protestation à la Chine.' *Le Monde*,
24/05/97.

'Plusieurs chefs d'Etat se sont rendus à la Commission des droits de l'homme
de l'ONU.' *Le Monde*, 31/03/01.

'Rifkind takes orphans case up with China.' *The Herald*, 11/01/96.

'Rights and wrongs; Chinese visit leaves a sour aftertaste.' *The Guardian*,
06/03/00.

'Time to confront Beijing.' *The Daily Telegraph*, 22/03/99.

Birmingham Evening Mail, 13/03/98.

France Diplomatie, http://www.diplomatie.gouv.fr/fr/pays-zones-
geo_833/chine_567/france-chine_1123/relations-
economiques_4428/index.html, accessed on 26/01/08.

Human Rights Watch Document. 'UN rights body in serious decline,'
25/04/03, http://hrw.org/english/docs/2003/04/25/global5796.htm,
accessed on 27/01/08.

IMF, Direction of Trade Statistics. ESDS International, (MIMAS) University of
Manchester, July 2008.

Rubin, James. Daily Press Briefing, U.S. Department of State, 26/03/99,
http://secretary.state.gov/www/briefings/9903/990326db.html, accessed
on 27/02/02.

– Daily Press Briefing, U.S. Department of State, 20/04/00,
http://secretary.state.gov/www/briefings/0004/000420db.html, accessed
on 27/02/02.

UK-China Trade 1996–2001. China Britain Business Council,
http://www.cbbc.org/ezine/statistics.html#2, accessed on 04/11/02.

U.S. State Department, UN Commission on Human Rights China Resolution,
22/03/04, http://www.state.gov/r/pa/prs/ps/2004/30650.htm, accessed
on 02/11/02.

Web document, 'La France dans le commerce mondial.'
http://www4.finances.gouv.fr/spi_cgi-bin/nph-
dblist.exe?SpiHtmlFile=rech_ini.htm, accessed on 01/11/02.

World Tibet Network News, 20/03/00, http://www.tibet.ca/wtnar-
chive/2000/03/20_3.html, accessed on 04/11/02.

Wye, Rod. 'UK: China relations: The UK government dimension.' ETI
Seminar Report, May 2000, http://www.eti.org.uk/pub/publica-
tions/2000/05-sem5-chirel/index.shtml, accessed on 04/11/02.

EU DOCUMENTS

Commission web document, 'The EU's relations with Iran,'
http://www.europa.eu.int/comm/external_relations/iran/intro/,
accessed on 06/06/02.

EU Document, Speech by The Rt Hon Chris Patten, speech/00/99, Geneva,
27/03/00,
http://www.europa.eu.int/comm/external_relations/news/patten/
speech_00_99.htm, accessed on 17/05/05.

EU Document, Statement by H.E. Ambassador Alphonse Berns, Permanent
Representative of the Grand Duchy of Luxembourg on behalf of the European Union, Geneva, 7524/05, Presse 66, 24/03/05.

European Parliament Document, European Parliament resolution on the
EU's priorities and recommendations for the 61st session of the UN Commission on Human Rights in Geneva, 24/02/05,
http://www.europarl.europa.eu/sides/getDoc.do?pubRef=-
//EP//TEXT+TA+P6-TA-2005-0051+0+DOC+XML+V0//EN, accessed on
07/05/06.

GAC conclusions, Brussels, 23/02/98, Press 44, no. 6060/98.

GAC conclusions, Brussels, 20/03/00, Press 73, no. 6810/00.

GAC conclusions, Brussels, 19/03/01, Press 110, no. 6933/01.

GAC conclusions, Brussels, 11/03/02, Press 48, no. 6596/02.

GAC conclusions, Brussels, 18/03/03, Press 63, no. 6941/03.

GAC conclusions, Brussels, 22/03/04, Press 80, no. 7383/04.

GAC conclusions, Brussels, 16/03/05, Press 44, no. 6969/05.

'Declaration by the Presidency on behalf of the European Union on Iran,'
10/04/97, no. 19/97, http://www.eurunion.org/news/press/1997-
2/pr19-97.htm, accessed on 06/05/01.

Chapter 4

ARTICLES

'Betrayal in the Balkans.' *The Observer*, 04/11/01.

'Clinton orders trade, financial sanctions on Serbia lifted.' Relief Web, US Department of State, 12/10/00, http://wwww.reliefweb.int/w/rwb.nsf/9ca65951ee22658ec1256633004085 99/6680081770161085 85256976006c6505?OpenDocument, accessed on 23/10/01.

'EU edges nearer to lifting ban on flights to Serbia.' *Financial Times*, 08/02/00.

'L'UE suspend l'embargo aérien.' *Le Figaro*, 15/02/00.

'Posible reunion del grupo de contacto.' *El Mundo*, 18/03/00.

'Serbia sanctions seek to separate good from bad.' *Financial Times*, 16/06/00.

'Yougoslavie: l'embargo aérien pourrait être suspendu.' *Le Monde*, 11/02/00, 5.

Agence Europe No. 7755, 10–11/07/00, 7.

EU DOCUMENTS

Council Regulation (EC) No. 1294/1999 of 15 June 1999 concerning a freeze of funds and a ban on investment in relation to the Federal Republic of Yugoslavia (FRY) and repealing Regulations (EC) No. 1295/1998 and (EC) No. 1607/1998 8, Official Journal L 153, 19/06/199, 65–82.

GAC conclusions, Brussels, 19/07/99, Press 227, no. 10135/99.

GAC conclusions, Brussels, 24/01/00, Press 10, no. 5046/00.

GAC conclusions, Brussels, 14/02/00, Press 32, no. 6108/00.

GAC conclusions, Brussels, 20/03/00, Press 73, no. 6810/00.

Presidency handbook, 'Council Guide: I. Presidency Handbook,' Council Secretariat, Luxembourg, Office for Official Publications of the European Communities, 1996.

Chapter 5

ARTICLES

'Annan tells EU, NATO more help needed in Sudan.' Reuters, 13/02/05, http://www.sabcnews.com/africa/north_africa/0,2172,97836,00.html, accessed on 20/05/08.

'Army dreamers, the European Commission should stay out of defence policy.' *The Times*, 10/02/00.

'Blair "frustrated" over Clinton's war strategy.' *Sunday Times*, 16/05/99.

'Blair says isolation cost UK influence in Europe.' *Financial Times*, 24/02/00.

Blair, Tony. Speech, Prime Minister Opens University's European Research Institute, Birmingham, 23/11/01, http://www.independent.co.uk/news/uk/politics/blair-the-argument-is-simple-we-are-part-of-europe-617916.html, accessed on 05/11/09.

'Bush would stop US peacekeeping in Balkan fights.' *The New York Times*, 21/10/00.

Chirac, Jacques. Speech, Président de la République devant l'Assemblée générale de l'Association du Traité de l'Atlantique, Strasbourg, 19/10/99, http://www/elysee.fr, accessed on 16/02/03.

'Commissioner Chris Patten sets out guidelines and goals for European Union external relations.' Europe Documents No. 2194, 21/06/00.

'Défense européenne.' *Le Monde*, 27/03/01.

'EU ponders using troops to help quell Darfur strife.' *Financial Times*, 22/04/05.

'European Union: Europe's army.' Oxford Analytica Brief, 28/11/00.

'Euro-force still cause of division.' *Telegraph*, 09/12/00, http://www.telegraph.co.uk/news/main.jhtml?xml=/news/2000/12/09/wnice109.xml, accessed on 29/09/08.

'L'OTAN décide de confier à l'Eurocorps le commandement de la force de paix au Kosovo.' *Le Monde*, 31/01/00.

'La politique étrangère de la France en matière de sécurité et de désarmement, mai 2000,' http://www.diplomatie.gouv.fr/frmonde/desarm/index.html, accessed on 13/02/03.

'Les petits pas de l'Europe militaire.' *Le Figaro*, 29/02/00.

'M. Védrine s'interroge sur l'aptitude americaine au partenariat.' *Le Monde*, 04/11/99.

'Meet your new European army.' *The Economist*, 23/11/00.

'Nato chief scorns Europe forces.' *The Guardian*, 09/11/02, http://www.guardian.co.uk/eu/story/0,7369,836722,00.html, accessed on 13/02/03.

'Nato on alert to provide help in Darfur.' *The Guardian*, 19/05/05, http://www.guardian.co.uk/sudan/story/0,14658,1487084,00.html, accessed on20/05/08.

'Paris fury as Solana boosts NATO role.' *The Daily Telegraph*, 06/03/00.

'Sarkozy fears defensive Brown will resist push for EU military.' *Financial Times*, 12/11/07.

'The European way of defence.' *The Economist*, 24/06/00.

'US and EU in dispute on control of Bosnia force.' *Financial Times*, 09/03/04.

'US seems increasingly uncomfortable with EU Defence plan.' *International Herald Tribune*, 06/03/00.

AFP/Reuters, *Le Monde*, 21/03/01, 3.

'Warning shot on EU army by White House.' *Telegraph*, 05/02/2001, http://www.telegraph.co.uk/news/main.jhtml;$sessionid$HBUFH3HHD 4EYBQFIQMFCFFOAV CBQYIV0?xml=/news/2001/02/05/wnat05.xml, accessed on 14/02/03.

Agence Europe No. 7665, 28-29/02/00.

Agence Europe No. 7743, 23/06/00.

Albright, Madeleine. Press Conference at NATO Headquarters Brussels, Belgium, 08/12/98, http://secretary.state.gov/www/statements/1998/981208b.html, accessed on 27/03/03.

Birmingham declaration, 07/05/96, http://www.weu.int/documents/960507en.pdf, accessed on 27/03/03.

Blair, Tony. The Labour Party's Manifesto 1997, http://www.bbc.co.uk/election97/background/parties/manlab/2labmanprog.html, accessed on 27/03/03.

– Speech at RUSI (Royal United Services Institute), 06/03/99.

Bono, Giovanna. 'Operation Concordia: The first step towards a new strategic EU-NATO relationship.' Weltpolitik net 14/03/04, http://www.weltpolitik.net/Sachgebiete/Internationale%20Sicherheitspolitik/GASP/Analysen/Operation%20Concordia:%20The%20first%20step%20towards%20a %20new%20strategic%20EU-NATO%20relationship%3F.html, accessed on 20/05/05.

Bush, George W., and Tony Blair. Joint Press Conference at Camp David. The White House, Office of the Press Secretary, 23 February 2001, http://www.fas.org/news/usa/2001/usa-010223zwb.htm, accessed on 19/03/03.

Cook, Robin. *Jonathan Dimbleby Program*, ITV, 1 April 2001.

Department of State, Briefing by Senior U.S. Official on U.S.-EU Summit Dec. 17 (Clinton, Ahtisaari, Prodi, Lipponen, Barshefsky meet at White House), 17/12/99, http://64.0.91.34/scripts/cqcgi.exe/@pdqtest1.env?CQ _SESSION_KEY=UFPGJQBMTHCD&C Q_QUERY_HANDLE=125371&CQ _CUR_DOCUMENT=6&CQ_PDQ_DOCUMENT_VIEW= 1&CQSUB-MIT=View&CQRETURN=&CQPAGE=1, accessed on 22/02/02.

Department of State, Clinton Statement on Results of NATO Foreign Ministers Meeting (Reaffirmed commitments, advanced goals of NATO-EU cooperation), 19/12/00, http://64.0.91.34/scripts/cqcgi.exe/@pdqtest1 .env?CQ_SESSION_KEY=WHSBLVDNTHCD&C Q_QUERY _HANDLE=125408&CQ_CUR_DOCUMENT=1&CQ_PDQ_DOCUMENT

_VIEW= 1&CQSUBMIT=View&CQRETURN=&CQPAGE=1, accessed on 22/02/02.

Department of State, Clinton Welcomes EU Progress on Security and Defence Policy (Statement issued by White House June 20), 20/06/00, http://64.0.91.34/scripts/cqcgi.exe/@pdqtest1.env?CQ_SESSION_KEY=AKWDISBMTHCD&C Q_QUERY_HANDLE=125372&CQ_CUR_DOCUMENT=1&CQ_PDQ_DOCUMENT_VIEW= 1 &CQSUBMIT=View&CQRETURN=&CQPAGE=1, accessed on 23/02/02.

Department of State, Transcript: Powell Briefing with British Foreign Secretary (He and Cook discuss Libya, ESDI, Iraq, Middle East, NMD, Balkans), 06/02/01.

Discours de Jacques Chirac, Président de la République devant l'Assemblée générale de l'Association du Traité de l'Atlantique, Strasbourg, http://www/elysee.fr, 19/10/99.

Document of the French Government, 'Nicolas Sarkozy confirme le retour de la France dans l'Otan,' 13/03/09, http://www.premier-ministre.gouv.fr /chantiers/defense_853/nicolas_sarkozy_confirme_retour_62920.html.

Eighth Report on European Security and Defence of the Defence Committee of the House of Commons, 1999–2000, accessed on 20/02/02.

Fischer, Joschka. Speech at the European University Institute, 17/01/02.

Heisbourg, François. 'Europe de la défense: la dimension industrielle,' *Le Monde*, 21/12/99.

House of Commons (1997–1998), 138-III, Q 1630.

House of Commons Document, 28/10/92, http://www.publications.parliament.uk/pa/cm199293/cmhansrd/1992-10-28/Orals-1.html, accessed on 19/02/02.

Il Sole-24 Ore, 28/02/01.

Maples, John. http://pubs1.tso.parliament.uk/pa/cm199899/cmhansrd /vo990610/debtext/90610-14.htm, accessed on 24/11/03.

Ministry of defence, 'UK-French Bilateral Defence Cooperation,' 09/02/01, http://www.mod.uk/issues/cooperation/uk_french.htm, accessed on 22/12/03.

Ministry of Defence, 'European Defence,' Paper n. 3, London, 2001, http://www.mod.uk/NR/rdonlyres/817B556A-0AA0-4761-804B-211D52F375EF/0/polpaper3_european_def.pdf, accessed on 25/11/03.

Morningstar, Richard. 'A Comprehensive Review of US/EU Relations.' Salzburg seminar, session 385, 23/03/01.

– 'Remarks to the EU committee of the American Chamber of Commerce Plenary Session,' 23/01/01, http://useu.usmission.gov/Article.asp?ID=707BBDED-7486-474D-9832-5FADB350DE60, accessed on 16/11/09.

NATO Notes, 2001, Vol. 3, n. 2, p. 2.

Sipri web document, 'The 15 major spender countries in 2006,' 2007, http://www.sipri.org/contents/milap/milex/mex_trends.html, accessed on 27/05/08.

Speech by the Minister of Foreign Affairs on foreign and security policy, 20/01/00, http://www.odin.dep.no/ud/taler/2000/000120e.htm, accessed on 22/11/03.

The Military Balance 2000–2001. The International Institute for Strategic Studies, Oxford University Press, 2000, p. 38.

EU DOCUMENTS

'Presidency Report on the ESDP,' Annex VI of the Presidency Conclusions of the Nice European Council (07-09/12/00).

The Declaration on Western European Union, http://eur-lex.europa.eu/en/treaties/dat/11992M/htm/11992M.html#0105000050, accessed on 16/11/03.

St Malo Declaration, 04/12/98, http://www.atlanticcommunity.org/Saint-Malo%20Declaration%20Text.html, accessed on 11/11/09.

Helsinki European Council, Presidency conclusions, 10-11/12/99, Press Release no. 00300/1/99.

Chapter 6

ARTICLES

'Anger over secret Blair war talks.' *The Guardian*, 19/10/01, http://politics.guardian.co.uk/attacks/story/0,1320,576843,00.html, accessed on 10/10/03.

'Blair's EU war council.' Radio Netherlands, 12/11/01, http://www.rnw.nl/hotspots/html/eu011105.html, accessed on 10/10/03.

'EU caves in to Washington over International Criminal Court.' *The Guardian*, 30/09/02.

'EU nations agree to consider recognition of Palestinian state.' *Washington Post Foreign Service*, 27/03/99.

'EU to go ahead with satellite system.' *Financial Times*, 27/03/02.

'Europeans reject Bush 'axis of evil' line on Iran.' *Financial Times*, 05/02/02.

'Fanfare for despatch of marines matched by silence in Washington.' *Financial Times*, 21/03/02.

'France: Gears Up for Elections, Nation seeks new direction and world role.' *EUROPE Magazine*, Issue no. 406 (June 2001), http://www.eurunion.org/magazine/0106/p6.htm, accessed on 05/10/03.

'French anger at US policy on Israel.' *The Guardian*, 07/02/02.

'Javier Solana, l'homme pressé de Bruxelles.' *Le Figaro*, 26/01/00.

'Joint Quint/Kosovar talks take place at U.S. office.' U.S. Office in Pristina, 12/01/02, http://www.usofficepristina.usia.co.at/pressr/prl13.htm, accessed on 03/10/03.

'Kosovo: The untold story; How the war was won.' *The Observer*, 18/07/99.

'La Convention à la recherche d'une politique extérieure de l'UE.' *Le Monde*, 12/07/02, http://www.lemonde.fr/article/0,5987,3214—284588-,00.html, accessed on 18/12/03.

'Lost in space: Europe's ambitions to launch a satellite navigation system to compete with the US's monopoly risk being thwarted by a dispute over funding.' *Financial Times*, 22/12/01.

'Saddam's capture improves US-EU ties.' *Washington Times*, 17/02/03, http://washingtontimes.com/upi-breaking/20031217-025139-6297r.htm, accessed on 22/12/03.

'SAS is preparing Macedonia for Nato to intervene.' *Telegraph*, 15/06/01.

'Summit reveals complexities of EU's shifting allegiances: the new entente cordiale between Tony Blair and Jacques Chirac.' *Financial Times*, 01/12/01.

'The Middle East's tangled web.' *Financial Times*, 01/02/02.

'The phantom body which runs NATO.' *The Guardian*, 28/07/99.

'US, EU moving closer on Iran.' ABC News online, 23/11/03, http://www.abc.net.au/news/newsitems/s995282.htm, accessed on 21/12/03.

'U.S. and Germany to recognize Kosovo independence, diplomats say.' *International Herald Tribune*, 10/01/08, http://www.iht.com/articles/2008/01/10/europe/kosovo.php, accessed on 05/04/08.

Agence Europe No. 7389, 23/01/99.

Albright, Madeleine K., and Lamberto Dini. Rome, Italy, 28/07/99, http://secretary.state.gov/www/statements/1999/990728.htm, accessed on 14/07/03.

Albright, Madeleine K., and Klaus Kinkel. Bonn, Germany, 17/02/97, http://secretary.state.gov/www/statements/970217.htm, accessed on14/07/03.

Albright, Madeleine. Agence Europe No. 7645, 01/02/00.

Beta News Agency, No. 2496, 22/09/06.

Davis, D. Commons Written Answers (13 Feb. 1995). House of Commons Hansard Debates, Foreign and Commonwealth Affairs.

Déclaration du porte-parole du Quai d'Orsay, 19/02/02.

Diplomatie-actualités, 02/04/03.

Diplomatie-actualités, 03/04/02.

Diplomatie-actualités, 06/02/03.

Fischer, Joschka. 'Les Etats-Unis dilapident le capital de sympathie qu'ils avaient recueilli lors des attentats du 11 septembre.' *Le Monde*, 16/02/02.

Grossman, Marc. 'American foreign policy and the International Criminal Court.' Under Secretary for Political Affairs, Remarks to the Center for Strategic and International Studies, Washington, DC, 06/05/02, http://www.state.gov/p/9949.htm, accessed on 22/12/03.

Hannay, David. Speech at the seminar 'Europe in the Global Community: Economics, Diplomacy, and Security,' Schloss Leopoldskron, Salzburg, 23/03/01.

House of Commons, Foreign Affairs Committee. 'Developments in the European Union,' Lord Owen, 05/12/07, http://www.publications.parliament.uk/pa/cm200708/cmselect/cmfaff/c120-ii/c12002.htm, accessed on 08/08/08.

IAEA Resolution on 'Implementation of the Non-Proliferation Treaty Safeguards Agreement in the Islamic Republic of Iran,' 26/11/03, http://www.iaea.org/Publications/Documents/Board/2003/gov2003-81.pdf, accessed 01/10/06.

Libération, 04/04/02.

Lockwood, C. 'The Quint emerges as seat of West's political power.' *London Daily Telegraph*, 25/11/99.

Luzi, G. 'How we managed to convince the Russians.' *La Repubblica*, 19/11/99.

SIPRI Mini Yearbook. 'Armaments, Disarmament and International Security,' 2007.

Solana, Javier. 'The situation in and around Kosovo.' Statement Issued at the Extraordinary Ministerial Meeting of the North Atlantic Council held at NATO Headquarters, Brussels, 12/04/99, http://www.nato.int/docu/pr/1999/p99-051e.htm, accessed on 02/12/03.

Point de presse, ministère des affaires étrangéres, 29/03/02.

Statement by the Secretary General following the meeting of the North Atlantic Council, 12/04/99, http://www.nato.int/docu/pr/1999/p99-058e.htm, accessed on 03/12/03.

Strauss, J., and M. Smith. 'SAS is preparing Macedonia for Nato to intervene.' *The Daily Telegraph*, 15/06/01.

UNMIK-UNHCR-OSCE-EU Press Briefing, 19/01/01, http://www.unmikonline.org/press/2001/trans/tr190101.html, accessed on02/12/03.

Védrine, Hubert. Interview of the French Foreign Affairs Minister. *Le Nouvel Observateur*, 24/06/99.

EU DOCUMENTS

Berlin European Council. Presidency Conclusions, 24-25/03/99, Press Release 0, n. 100/1/99 rev.

Conclusions adopted by the Council (Justice and Home Affairs), Brussels, SN 3926/6/01, Rev 6, 20/09/01.

European Defence Agency. 'European–United States Defence Expenditure in 2007,' December 2008, accessed 20/01/09, http://www.eda.europa.eu/, accessed on 27/04/09.

Eurostat Document, DG Trade Statistics, 15/09/06.

GAC Press Release, 28/01/02.

House of Commons Document. 'Foreign Policy Aspects of the Lisbon Treaty,' Third Report of Session 2007–08, Foreign Affairs Committee, 20/01/08.

Patten, Chris. 'Commissioner Chris Patten sets out guidelines and goals for European Union external relations.' Europe Documents No. 2194, 21/06/00.

– 'Devotion or Divorce? The Future of Transatlantic Relations.' *European Foreign Affairs Review* 6 (2001): 287–90.

– 'Why does America fear this court?' *Washington Post*, 09/07/02, http://www.washingtonpost.com/wp-, accessed 18/11/02.

Solana, Javier. 'Le développement de la politique européenne commune de sécurité et de défense de l'Union Européenne.' Revue du Marché Commun et de l'Union Européenne, No. 442 (October/November 2000): 589.

– Statement by the EU High Representative for the Common Foreign and Security Policy (CFSP), on the UN Security Council Resolution on Iraq, Brussels, 08/11/02, S0206/02.

Chapter 7

ARTICLES

'Assault on islet exposes EU rifts.' *Financial Times*, 19/07/02.

'Chris Patten: Jaw-jaw, not war-war, Military success in Afghanistan has encouraged the US to ignore European doubts about confronting the "axis of evil."' *Financial Times*, 14/02/02.

'Serb jets buzz Patten convoy as it crosses into Montenegro.' *The Independent*, 11/03/00.

Agence Europe No. 7637, 20/01/00.

Agence Europe No. 7638, 21/01/00.

Diplomatie-actualités, 14/03/03.

House of Commons Document. 'Foreign Policy Aspects of the Lisbon Treaty,' Third Report of Session 2007–08, Foreign Affairs Committee, 20/01/08.

OHR general information, http://www.ohr.int/ohr-info/gen-info/#5, accessed on 22/11/02.

EU DOCUMENTS

Commission communication. 'Proposal for a Council Regulation on support to bodies set up by the International Community after conflicts either to take charge of the interim civilian administration of certain regions or to implement peace agreements,' 24/02/00, COM (2000) 95 final, CNS 2000/42, in Official Journal C 177 E, 27/06/2000, p. 0091–0092.

Commission document. 'Dual-Use Export Controls,' October 2002, http://europa.eu.int/comm/trade/goods/dualuse/index_en.htm, accessed on 05/03/03.

Commission webpage, http://ec.europa.eu/comm/external_relations/cfsp/intro/index.htm, accessed 10/08/06.

Council Regulation (EC) No 975/1999 of 29 April 1999, Official Journal L 120, 08/05/1999, P. 0001–0007.

Council Regulation (EC) No 976/1999 of 29 April 1999, Official Journal L 120, 08/05/1999, P. 0008–0014.

Council Regulation (EC) No. 2454/1999 amending Regulation (EC) No. 1628/96 relating to aid for Bosnia and Herzegovina, Croatia, the Federal Republic of Yugoslavia and the former Yugoslav Republic of Macedonia (the 'Obnova regulation') and setting up the European Agency for Reconstruction, Bulletin EU 11-1999, Relations with the western Balkans (8/12), http://europa.eu.int/abc/doc/off/bull/en/9911/p105060.htm, accessed on 18/02/02.

ECJ Case C-91/05, Commission v. Council (small arms and light weapons) [2008] 3 CMLR 5, http://eur-lex.europa.eu/LexUriServ/LexUriServ.do ?uri=CELEX:62005J0091:EN:HTML, accessed on 19/08/08.

GAC conclusions, Brussels, 06/12/99, Press 390, no. 13687/99.

GAC conclusions, Brussels, 14/02/00, Press 32, no. 6108/00.

GAC conclusions, Brussels, 15/11/99, Press 344, no. 12642/99.

GAC conclusions, Brussels, 20/03/00, Press 73, no. 6810/00.

GAC conclusions, Brussels, 22/05/00, Press 160, no. 8575/00.

GAC conclusions, Brussels, 24/01/00, Press 10, no. 5046/00.

GAC conclusions, Luxembourg, 10/04/00, Press 101, no. 7533/00.

Helsinki European Council, Presidency conclusions, 10-11/12/99, Press Release n. 00300/1/99.

Lisbon European Council, Presidency conclusions, 24/03/00, Press Release n. 100/1/00.

Opinion of Advocate General Mengozzi, Case C-91/05, Commission of the
European Communities v. Council of the European Union,
19/09/07PRODI Romano, Commission web document,
http://europa.eu.int/comm/external_relations/morocco/intro/ip02_1064.
htm, consulted 23/11/02.
CFSP joint action 2002/589/CFSP.
Council decision 2004/833/CFSP.

Conclusion

ARTICLES
'La Convention à la recherche d'une politique extérieure de l'UE.' *Le Monde*,
12/07/02, http://www.lemonde.fr/article/0,5987,3214—284588-,00.html,
accessed on 18/06/04.
'Impairing the European Union, Gibe by Gibe.' *The New York Times*,
14/02/09,
http://www.nytimes.com/2009/02/14/world/europe/14union.html?hp,
accessed on 26/05/09.
BBC News. 'When Britain and France nearly married,' 15/01/07,
http://newsvote.bbc.co.uk/1/hi/uk/6261885.stm?dynamic_vote=ON#
vote_Britain_France, accessed on 25/05/09.
Agence Europe No. 6964, 28/04/97.
Albright, Madeleine. Agence Europe No. 7645, 01/02/00.
Ash, T.G., M. Mertes, and D. Moisi. 'Only a club of three can bring European
unity.' *Financial Times*, 11/07/03.
Chirac, Jacques. Discours, 06/03/02,
http://www.chiracaveclafrance.net/PDFArticle/Strasbourg.pdf, accessed
on 05/07/03.
De Boissieu, Pierre. 'Les bâtisseurs secrets de l'Union.' *Le Figaro*, 07/07/00.
Déclaration du porte-parole du Quai d'Orsay, 19/02/02.
Everts, Steven, and Antonio Missiroli. 'Beyond the "Big Three": To claim a
global role, the EU needs its own security council.' *International Herald
Tribune*, 10/03/04.
Fischer, Joschka. Speech at the European University Institute, 17/01/02.
White House news, 25/03/03.

EU DOCUMENTS
Council Joint Action of 17/12/99 establishing a European Union Cooperation
Program for Non-Proliferation and Disarmament in the Russian Federa-
tion, Official Journal, 23/12/99.

Solana, Javier. 'Five lessons in global diplomacy.' *Financial Times*, 20/01/09, http://www.consilium.europa.eu/ueDocs/cms_Data/docs/pressdata/en /articles/105395.pd, accessed on 25/05/09.

Index